Behavioral Approaches for Children and Adolescents

Challenges for the Next Century

Behavioral Approaches for Children and Adolescents

Challenges for the Next Century

Edited by

Henck P. J. G. van Bilsen
Pedologisch Instituut
Rotterdam, The Netherlands

Philip C. Kendall
Temple University
Philadelphia, Pennsylvania

and

Jan H. Slavenburg
Pedologisch Instituut
Rotterdam, The Netherlands

Plenum Press • New York and London

1995

Library of Congress Cataloging-in-Publication Data

On file

Proceedings of an International Conference on Cognitive Behavior Therapies and Applied Behavior
Analysis with Children and Adults: Challenges for the Next Century,
held July 3–5, 1995, in Rotterdam, The Netherlands

ISBN 0-306-45122-0

© 1995 Plenum Press, New York
A Division of Plenum Publishing Corporation
233 Spring Street, New York, N. Y. 10013

PREFACE

Challenges for the next decade as the subtitle of a book is a statement of ambition.

In the present time we have to be ambitious as scientists, clinicians, and teachers. Without ambition we would not be able to confront the problems of young people in an effective way.

In this decade, we can see an abundance of problems of young people: football hooliganism, school drop out, vandalism, delinquency, lack of social skills, aggression, and depression.

The problem seems to grow. Governments, parents, and concerned citizens call for action now. Unfortunately, the action that is taken is often impulsive and not based on scientifically proven methods: longer jail sentences for young first offenders, putting young offenders in military look-alike training camps, etc.

For some reason, the usage of effective interventions is limited. In this, book the reader will find an extensive overview of what we know to be effective as a "cure" or prevention for the above-mentioned problems. The first four chapters will give the reader a clear insight of what the "state of the art" is today.

An integrative overview of cognitive behavioural therapies with children and adolescents is given by Kendall, Panichelli-Mindel, and Gerow. Russo and Navalta provide some new dimensions of behavior analysis and therapy. What behavioral approaches can offer to education is described by Slavenburg and van Bilsen in two chapters.

In Part II authors from Australia, the United States, and the Netherlands describe programs for specific clinical populations: attention deficit disorder, anti-social youth, learning problems, social skills problems, depression, and aggression.

In Part III the problem of unwilling and unmotivated clients is discussed. What to do when they don't want?

Henck P. J. G. van Bilsen
Philip C. Kendall
Jan H. Slavenburg

CONTENTS

1. Cognitive-Behavioral Therapies with Children and Adolescents: An Integrative Overview 1
   Philip C. Kendall, Susan M. Panichelli-Mindel, and Michael A. Gerow

2. Some New Dimensions of Behaviour Analysis and Therapy 19
   Dennis C. Russo and Carryl P. Navalta

3. Behaviour Therapy and Educational Reform: A Review of Study Findings 41
   Jan H. Slavenburg

4. Unused Opportunities for Behaviour Therapy in Education 53
   Henck P.J.G. van Bilsen

5. Cognitive Behavior Modification of ADHD: A Family System Approach 65
   Harry van der Vlugt, Huub M. Pijnenburg, Paul M. A. Wels, and Aly Koning

6. Competency-Based Treatment for Antisocial Youth 77
   N. W. Slot

7. Behaviour Therapy with Learning Problems 87
   Chris Struiksma

8. Treating Children Who Lack Social Skills in a Pedological Institute School 95
   Ria Swager

9. Stop Think Do: Improving Social and Learning Skills for Children in Clinics and Schools 103
   Lindy Petersen

10. Cognitive and Behavioral Treatment of Childhood Depression 113
    Kevin D. Stark and Anne Smith

11. Cognitive Behavioral Therapy of Aggressive Children: Effects of Schemas 145
    John E. Lochman and L. Lenhart

12. Motivation as a Precondition and Bridge between Unmotivated Client and
        Overmotivated Therapist 167

        Henck P.J.G. van Bilsen

Index 175

COGNITIVE-BEHAVIORAL THERAPIES WITH CHILDREN AND ADOLESCENTS
An Integrative Overview

Philip C. Kendall, Susan M. Panichelli-Mindel, and Michael A. Gerow

Temple University
Dept. of Psychology
Weiss Hall Room 478 (265-67)
Philadelphia, Pennsylvania 19122

In general, psychological theory and underlying world views guide psychological therapy. One begins with ontological and epistemological assumptions about the world and how humans operate within it (stated either explicitly or implicitly), and from these assumptions, one constructs either a theory of human behavior or a research paradigm to study human behavior or both. In the field of clinical child psychology there has been an increasing interest in the formulation of cognitive-behavioral theories, especially as they relate to psychopathology and psychotherapy. These theories, tied to empirical data (i.e., observations of phenomena), attempt to identify concepts that generalize to broader circumstances. This chapter provides an overview of the emerging and evolving cognitive-behavioral position, especially as it relates to psychosocial therapy with children. We will begin by briefly discussing the theoretical framework on which the cognitive-behavioral position is based. Next, we will illustrate how this theory guides the therapeutic posture of the cognitive-behavioral therapist. In a brief review of the extant literature, we consider cognitive-behavioral applications with a variety of clinical problems in youth. Finally, we suggest future directions for theory and practice.

BRIEF HISTORY AND THEORETICAL OVERVIEW

Cognitive-behavioral theory is a mediational theory and represents a hybrid of behavioral and cognitive research and theory. In integrating these two approaches, theorists have removed the doctrinaire attitude of strictly behavioral theorists by incorporating the cognitive activities of the child into the equation. Strict behavioral theory (e.g. Skinner, 1987) recommends the shunning of "internal" (i.e., not visible to direct observation) variables. Observable behavior represents, according to behaviorists, the only possible domain for scientific psychological research. In clinical realms, this translated into therapies, for example systematic desensitization and flooding (e.g. Wolpe, 1958), where the focus of

Behavioral Approaches for Children and Adolescents, Edited by
H. P. J. G. van Bilsen et al., Plenum Press, New York, 1995

1

attention was primarily on changing observable behavior. This direction radically conflicted with the historically-dominant psychodynamic view of psychology, which held that intrapsychic forces were responsible for behavior and therefore the crux of therapeutic effort lay in "working through" internal conflict.

The theoretical revolution which brought behaviorism into a dominant position of several recent decades lead to a counter-revolution. Cognitive theorists re-introduced "internal" variables into research and clinical practice and built a body of research suggesting that cognition (i.e. thought) influenced behavior. The so-called cognitive revolution proceeded in several directions (e.g. information-processing, connectionist theory, etc.), the details of which we omit here (see Ingram, 1986; Kendall and Hollon, 1979; Varela, Thompson, and Rosch, 1991, and others for details), and created a space for an integration of the two approaches. Cognitive-behavioral theory, as described here, represents an integration of cognitive and behavioral positions in the realm of information-processing and social learning theories (Kendall and Bacon, 1988).

The cognitive-behavioral position, when applied to psychopathology and its treatment, consists of several components. First, it posits that psychological problems (e.g., disorders, difficulties) result from behavioral and cognitive antecedents. For example, the distress of an anxious youth is associated with both behavioral avoidance and/or the contingencies surrounding the feared event(s) as well as cognitive appraisal, attitudes, and beliefs surrounding the behavioral events. In other words, a child who worries about interacting with peers does so because of past learning history (e.g., distress when with peers) and cognitive appraisal of the past events and anticipatory appraisal of future events (e.g., a self-statement such as "They will criticize/reject me," reflecting a belief such as "people are to be feared because peer failure is unavoidable").

Given this framework, a therapeutic pathway becomes clear. Remedy occurs within both behavioral and cognitive realms. It does not suffice, cognitive-behavioral theory states, to have a socially anxious child to face numerous social situations; nor does it suffice to simply teach coping skills. Rather, the combination represents the preferred route where behavioral *and* cognitive dysfunctions are addressed. Cognitive-behavioral therapy is a skill-building approach that uses knowledge of developmental trajectories to affect necessary change, adjusting the dysfunctional path of a troubled youth. A cognitive-behavioral intervention involves both the teaching of coping skills and the practice of these skills in actual situations, with opportunity for feedback from the therapist.

While the theory has garnered much support from practitioners and researchers alike, cognitive-behavioral theory continues to have its critics (e.g. Lee, 1990). For example, strict behaviorists criticize cognitive-behavioral theory because it relies on "undefined and unobservable variables in order to explain behavior" (Lee, 1990, p. 143). This position arises from the belief that while "human behavior is complex...it is determined by material events" (Lee, 1990, pp. 144). We maintain that human behavior is complex and multi-determined. We are sceptical that behavior will find simple, linear explanations in material causes. Although so-called "internal" causes are not observable, we believe that cognition and emotion influence behavior in ways that simple stimulus-response relationships often cannot explain.

Because of its stress on cognitive and behavioral factors, one could argue that cognitive-behavioral theory and practice fails to take emotion into account. Kendall (1991) described how cognitive-behavioral theory includes emotion. Cognitive appraisal of affect, for example, is critical in the etiology of many childhood and adolescent disorders. Nevertheless, cognition and affect are interrelated: the variance in etiology of some disorders may be best accounted for by cognitive assessments and analyses (Kendall, 1991) while other disorders may find best explanation from within other perspectives (e.g. emotional, behavioral). This position underscores the cognitive-behaviorist's belief in the multi-determined nature of human behavior.

Cognitive-behavioral theory considers context such as the social/interpersonal world of the child. These contexts provide the behavioral settings in which events impact the functioning of children and youth. Unfortunately, the precise role of these contexts has yet to be well researched. For example, although parents are considered important in the etiology of several childhood problems, we remain uncertain of the specific role(s) they play. The cognitive-behavioral theorist and therapist seeks to determine the effect of the familial (school, peer) contexts on the development (both "normal" and maladaptive) of youth.

Consideration of developmental pathways represents an under-investigated but critical arena that cognitive-behavioral theorists and therapists have begun to explore. Cognitive-behavioral theory allows for a broader framework within which to study psychological problems. Cognitive-behavioral interventions are designed with at least two developmental considerations in mind. First, the current developmental level of the child (i.e. cognitive ability, current developmental challenges) is assessed to affect the thrust and inform the intervention to be used. For example, a young, cognitively immature child might benefit less from long, didactic sessions and would be better served by brief, active sessions, often with the cognitive content of the session occurring in vivo. Second, the intervention is best when it occurs in the context of the developmental challenges facing the child. Therefore, a cognitive-behavioral therapist seeing a child dealing with separation anxiety at age nine intervenes within the appropriate developmental challenge (i.e. issues of autonomy).

Cognitive-behavioral theory represents an amalgam of behavioral and cognitive positions with an integration of emotional and contextual factors: the theory remains flexible to reformulation in accord with data. However, the flexible nature of the cognitive-behavioral position leaves the theory vulnerable to the criticism that it fails to take a true position. Because we do not maintain that the theory can explain all of human behavior, the theory's weaknesses are acknowledged from the start. In this sense, cognitive-behavioral theory is not so much a theory as its is an approach to theory formulation and, more importantly to this paper, an approach to therapy. It is a data-driven, hypothesis-testing approach, combining cognitive and behavioral interventions into a new - and hopefully more useful - hybrid.

THERAPISTS' ROLES AND COGNITION

Posture of the Therapist

The cognitive-behavioral therapist plays a number of roles when treating children and adolescents. These roles can be described as consultant, diagnostician, and educator. As a *consultant*, the therapist helps the child to develop skills to think independently rather than providing specific solutions to the child's problems. Both therapist and child collaborate in this problem-solving effort, together generating ideas to try and to evaluate in an effort to help the child handle difficulties he or she is experiencing. The therapist provides suggestions for the child to think about and describes experiments to use to determine whether these ideas have value for the individual child. The child is given the opportunity to "test-out" these ideas, implement and practice those that seem most helpful, and in the process examine and correct dysfunctional beliefs. The therapist and child share experiences, and the therapist helps the child to make sense of the experiences - all without telling the child what to do. In this way the therapist facilitates the process of problem-solving, without providing specific solutions to problems. The therapist fosters the child's independence and affords opportunities for the child to think and problem-solve on his or her own.

The therapist, as a *diagnostician*, gathers information on the child from many sources. In addition to the child's own report, parents and teachers are requested to help the therapist gain a better understanding, and the therapist additionally observes the child's behavior. The therapist integrates the information with his or her own knowledge and expertise about normal development and psychopathology to determine the nature of the problem and how best to handle it. A teacher may report that the child has an Attention-deficit Hyperactivity Disorder (ADHD), based on the child's classroom behavior, displaying impulsivity and an inability to concentrate. A cognitive-behavioral therapist weighs this opinion with other data - including his or her own expertise, knowledge, and experience, and the input of others. Explanations other than a diagnosis of ADHD are possible. What expectations does the teacher hold regarding appropriate classroom behavior? Perhaps the child is quite bright and becomes bored easily by simple schoolwork. The cognitive-behavioral therapist uses all available resources in determining the nature of the disorder and in planning the most appropriate intervention for the child.

As an *educator*, the cognitive-behavioral therapist is concerned about teaching skills—skills that help the child think and act independently. Not all children need to learn the same behavioral or cognitive repertoire: rather the therapist attempts to maximize each individual child's strengths and reduce hindrances. The role of educator benefits from the therapist's attending to the child's internal dialogue - creating an educational context that impacts the child's interpretations of current and future experiences.

Cognitive-behavioral therapists guide children through their cognitive processing, attend to their emotional states, and provide them with social experiences and opportunities to broaden their perspectives. Therapists determine the most appropriate intervention for the individual child, yet they problem-solve collaboratively with the child. This posture is intended to facilitate the child's development of healthier ways of interpreting experiences and making sense of the world.

Coping, Cognition, and the Coping Template

Treatment generally has beneficial effects, and these effects may best be seen after treatment is completed - when new ideas have been given time to cultivate and flourish, and the child uses some of the concepts discussed in therapy to actively cope. As treatment builds to success, the child begins to see its merits and uses the approach as part of his or her everyday coping style. The case of Donna, an extremely shy 10-year-old girl, provides an illustration of this process. She avoided people as much as possible and did not participate in activities that would require her to have interactions with strangers. Almost two months after treatment, Donna and her mother were in their car stopping at a supermarket to pick up a gallon of milk. To Donna's mother's surprise, Donna said she wanted to go inside the store herself and buy the milk. This was something she had always refused to do, fearing interaction with strangers. She went into the store by herself and came back five minutes later with a gallon of milk in hand and a big smile of triumph on her face. Donna was able to recall, and test out, the skills she learned in therapy and use them appropriately.

Therapists do not expect therapy to completely eliminate life problems. Rather, we conceptualize treatment as a way of providing children with strategies to help them *manage* and *cope* (Kendall, 1989). The goal of therapy is to offer a more effective mode of coping in place of the child's current unsuccessful approaches. Although behavior changes may be evident with treatment, it is important for treatment to provide maintenance skills concerning decision making and coping to help the child when he or she is no longer in treatment. The therapist accepts and anticipates future difficulties for the child. These are addressed as part of therapy so the child does not attribute failure to him or herself, and as a means of relapse prevention. The therapeutic process is a process of continual management and practising of coping skills. The specific outcomes of treatment in terms of maintenance and generalizability vary across severity of presenting problems (presence of comorbidity) but research has demonstrated adjustment to be poorest without treatment, and best after intervention (e.g. Kendall, 1994).

A primary focus of a cognitive-behavioral therapist lies in understanding client cognition. Cognition has been described as having four distinguishable components: structure, content, processes, and product (Ingram and Kendall, 1986; Kendall, 1991). These four components are not separate entities, rather they are interrelated and together compose what is often referred to simply as cognition. *Cognitive structure* refers to memory and how information is represented in memory. It serves as a template that filters certain cognitive processes. *Cognitive content* is the specific information stored in memory. Content also refers to one's self-talk and internal speech. *Cognitive process* is how we perceive and interpret our experiences. *Cognitive products* are the thoughts an individual experiences as a result of the interaction between content, structure, and process - the conclusion one reaches as a result of cognitive processing.

As an illustration of this complex system, imagine a child knocking on the door of a neighbourhood playmate to ask her to come out and play. The playmate responds by saying she can not come out. The child begins to process this experience - and his conclusions will affect the behavioral and emotional consequences. The child may think that the neighbour doesn't like him - an attribution that is not justified by the experience. Or may think she just doesn't feel like playing outside today. This later attribution would have different emotional consequences. After the experience, conclusions are drawn regarding the other child saying she does not want to come out and play - cognitive products. Some children may attribute the girl's refusal to themselves, perhaps thinking the girl does not like him because he is not fun to be around. This often characterizes the cognitive products of depressed people (Abramson, Seligman, and Teasdale, 1979). An aggressive child may attribute the negative response to someone's purposeful act such the child was scheming with another child who told her not to go out and play (Dodge, 1985). An anxious child might focus on the threat of embarrassment and future difficulties - "Everyone in the neighbourhood is going to know I wanted to play with her and she said no. I'm not going to ask her to play again because she might say no like she did this time."

Individuals experience and observe the world through their own unique cognitive structures - schema (Beck, 1976; Kendall, 1991). Cognitive structures serve to filter what is perceived as well as trigger automatic cognitive content and information processing about behavioral events. Cognitive structures both screen new experiences and incorporate past events to influence current processing. Children with psychological problems have problems in the way they interpret the world, and therapists help to build a new schema or what we call a "coping template." The role of the therapist is to pay attention to the child's cognition before, during, and after an event (Kendall et al., 1991). Therapeutically, cognitive-behavioral interventions seek to provide experiences that attend to the cognitive content, process, and product so that the child can build a new structure that will have a positive influence on future experiences. Building a coping template can be achieved by teaching new skills, providing new experiences to test out dysfunctional - as well as healthy - beliefs, and guiding the child through the processing of these experiences. The new coping template is then brought to bear on future experiences.

Cognitive Distortions and Deficiencies

All cognitive dysfunction is not the same. Within the realm of cognitive processing, a distinction can be made between *distortions* and *deficiencies* (Kendall, 1985; Kendall and MacDonald, 1993). *Cognitive distortion* is an active but misguided way of processing.

Children who distort are able to process information, but do so in a biased, dysfunctional way. For example, they may misperceive the demands of the environment. This type of dysfunctional processing is mostly seen in children with internalizing disorders such as depression and anxiety (Kendall, Stark, and Adam, 1990). In contrast, *cognitive deficiency* is the lack of information processing in which children do not think about the situation or plan for it. They may misperceive environmental demands because they do not take the time to pay attention or process social cues and information. Hyperactive and impulsive youth, and those with externalizing disorders, demonstrate this type of cognitive processing dysfunction. Aggressive children appear to demonstrate both types of processing difficulties (Kendall, Ronan, and Epps, 1991). They react without thinking and do not use all the environmental cues provided (Dodge, 1985) to accurately make sense of social experiences. In addition, they process in a distorted fashion, usually distorting the cause of ambiguous outcomes by seeing the cause as intentional and provocative (Milich and Dodge, 1984).

The distinction between distortion and deficiency has been directly tested with a group of depressive youth (Kendall, Stark, and Adam, 1990). In a series of three studies, diagnosed depressed children, based on a structured interview, completed a number of self-report measures. Teachers were also required to describe and rate the children. The first two studies found that depressed children evidenced a negative, distorted style of processing self-evaluative information. They evaluated themselves less favourably, although both depressed and nondepressed children reported the same standards. They did not differ from the nondepressed in the total number of errors or latency to respond on the Matching Familiar Figures Test (Kagan, 1966), demonstrating no evidence of a deficiency in their information processing. In the third study, childrens' perceptions of themselves were judged in comparison to their teacher's perceptions of the same children. Depressed children rated themselves more negatively than the nondepressed children, where as the teachers reported no discrepancies. This supports the idea that depressed children demonstrate a distorted style of processing self-evaluative information, being more critical of themselves than their own teachers. The significance of different cognitive processing dysfunctions suggests that future research should investigate the differences in the specific cognitive processing difficulties associated with a particular disorder to create treatment programs for children and adolescents that will address these difficulties.

COGNITIVE-BEHAVIORAL TREATMENT STRATEGIES: GENERAL STRATEGIES AND SPECIFIC PROGRAMS

There are a variety of cognitive-behavioral intervention procedures that are used and said to be effective across disorders. The strategies/procedures are altered and individualized for each disorder and each child, but the basic strategies remain the same. The techniques arise from social learning and information processing models of behavior and illustrate the integrative nature of cognitive-behavioral therapy. Rather than discuss each strategy as it is applied for different disorders, we first present an overview of the basic strategies.

General Cognitive Behavioral Strategies

Modelling (Bandura, 1969) is an effective way of influencing behavior (Bandura, 1986; LaGreca and Santogrossi, 1981; Morris and Kratochwill, 1983). When perceived as a respected, liked individual, the therapist can be a potent model for nondistorted thinking, careful reasoning, and reasonable behavior (Kendall and Siqueland, 1989). The child observes the therapist as a model, imitates the model's behavior, and receives feedback and

reinforcement for the performance. Numerous studies of modelling repor
someone to a model who demonstrates desired behaviors (as well as less desi
increases the likelihood that observers will perform similarly in the futu.
Brush, Hollon, and Rimm, 1987).

Not all models are of equal potency. Therapists may model a mastery model in which ideal or fearless behavior is demonstrated. In participant modelling the therapist encourages and guides the child to problem-solve through a situation independently. The therapist can also serve as a "coping model." Instead of demonstrating an error-free performance, the therapist as a coping model exhibits behavior that is, like the client's, maladaptive (e.g. lack of attention; cognitive misperceptions) but then also models a strategy to address and correct these difficulties.

As a coping model the therapist displays some of the child's difficulties as well as a strategy for self-catching and self-correcting the difficulties. The therapist uses problem-solving techniques and models different strategies to help overcome the distress (Panichelli and Kendall, 1995). In solving a problem, the coping model breaks down and thinks through the problem and solutions out loud so the child can observe the problem-solving process. The problem-solving process can be understood in a number of steps: identifying the problem, generating a number of solutions, choosing one of these strategies or solutions which seems most efficacious, implementing the strategy, and then evaluating its effectiveness. Via coping model, the child witnesses the use of coping strategies in action and can try them and use them to self-correct his or her own difficulties. A coping model appears to be more effective than a mastery model in helping clients overcome avoidance (e.g. Ginther and Roberts, 1982; Kazdin, 1974), perhaps because the observer can relate better to the coping model.

Role playing is a technique used in therapy which gives the child an opportunity to practice coping and to experience use of the alternative solutions generated for specific problems. The therapist guides the experience for the child and reinforces progress. This reinforced practice is important in the remediation of cognitive, behavioral, and emotional difficulties (Kendall and Siqueland, 1989).

Role-playing involves the creation of interactive scenes and is a way to practice in simulated situations in a nonthreatening way. For younger children, imagery may be necessary to help guide the child in playing a specific role. Imagery can be used to describe a situation in concrete detail so the child can follow along (Ollendick, 1986).

In-vivo exposure is similar to role-playing, but the child is given the opportunity to practice, with the therapist's guidance, coping in real-life situations. A hierarchy is constructed to gradually introduce experiences to the individual that require greater coping efforts. With each successful experience, the client ascends the hierarchy to new situations with higher levels of provocation. With regard to anxiety disorders, for example, research suggests that exposure to the once feared objects or situations is an active component of treatment (Barlow, 1988). Through in vivo exposure the child is able to gain mastery and be more able and willing to attempt to conquer a new and more difficult situation. In-vivo exposures are more effective than imagery for younger children because the younger children may not have the cognitive capacity necessary for effective imaging (Hughes, 1993; Ultee, Griffiaen, and Schellekens, 1982).

Another important feature of therapy is the use of contingencies and reinforcements. In cognitive-behavioral therapy, children can earn rewards for appropriate behavior. Research has provided more than ample evidence that reinforced behaviors are more likely to occur again and that reinforced adaptive behaviors can come to replace maladaptive ones. By applying positive and negative reinforcement, behavior can be shaped, maintained, and altered. Some children, particularly those with internalizing disorders, find it very difficult to accept rewards or reward themselves unless they complete a task perfectly. These youth tend to be harsh on themselves and tend to fail to process and attend to positive experiences. Therefore, the therapist emphasizes rewards for partial success and for the child's effort, even if the result is less than preferred.

For some children, particularly externalizing disordered youth, contingent consequences are needed to control maladaptive behavior. The child receives reinforcement for appropriate behavior, but at the same time is given direction for controlling and modifying inappropriate behavior (DuPaul, Guevremont and Barkley, 1991). Token economies involve both reinforcements and consequences by having children earn tokens to be exchanged for rewards or privileges for desired behaviors, and lose tokens for undesirable behaviors. Token economies have been found to be effective, particularly in classroom settings, for controlling and altering behavior and improving overall levels of client functioning (McLaughlin and Williams, 1988).

Relaxation training is used to help children learn how to monitor their own levels of stress and anxiety (Ollendick and Cerny, 1981). The child is taught relaxation training (Ollendick, 1986) to learn to relax, and to provide an activity which can be substituted in place of an undesirable response. By using deep breathing exercises and imagery, children learn how to recognize their own body signals of distress and how to calm themselves down. Relatedly, affective education helps children to recognize different feelings and that different feelings can result from different experiences. It is also used to help children develop empathy.

The techniques described thus far represent a sample of the strategies implemented in a cognitive-behavioral treatment plan. We now turn to a review of how cognitive-behavioral therapy has been applied to a variety of clinical problems in youth (i.e., chronic pain, depression, aggression, ADHD, and anxiety disorders).

Chronic Pain

Though research on chronic pain is limited, Keefe and Williams (1989) discuss how cognitive-behavioral therapy can alter the behavioral, cognitive, and physiological responses to pain. More specifically, Varni (1983) defined different types of cognitive-behavioral techniques in helping children cope with chronic pain. Children are taught to relax through deep breathing and through imagery of pleasant distracting scenes. Children are also taught to cope by imagining the opposite of what they feel. In one report, Elliott and Olsen (1983) found a multicomponent stress management intervention able to reduce the distress of children in pain. When children are given some control, they report less distress and pain (Tarnowski, McGrath, Calhoun, and Drabman, 1987). Behavioral programs can be set up to monitor behavior important for the child medically, such as visits to the doctor or hospital stays (Walco and Dampier, 1987; Walco and Varni, 1991). Positive reinforcement has also been helpful, along with breathing and imagery, in helping children handle chronic pain (Jay, Elliott, and Varni, 1986). In addition, social skills can be used to facilitate social support for the child.

Depression

Depressed youth are often characterized as having cognitive distortions (Stark, Rouse, Livingston, 1991) that reflect negative perceptions about themselves and global, stable, and internal attributions about negative events (Laurent and Stark, 1993; Seligman, Peterson, Kaslow, Tanenbaum, Alloy, and Abramson, 1984). They have low levels of self-esteem and social and academic confidence (Asarnow, Carlson, and Guthrie, 1987), and evaluate their own performance stringently (Rehm and Carter, 1990) leading to negative self-perceptions (Asarnow and Bates, 1988; Hammen, 1988; Kendall et al., 1990).

Unfortunately, there are only a few studies investigating the efficacy of cognitive-behavioral treatment for clinically depressed children. Stark, Rouse, and Livingston (1991) describe a cognitive-behavioral program for treating depressed children - a program that includes the same range of strategies previously discussed. Problem-solving techniques are used to help the depressed children overcome the sense of hopelessness they often feel. The therapist works to restructure and modify the children's patterns of distorted thinking, assumptions, and perceptions. Results of one outcome study indicated that cognitive-behavioral therapy demonstrated greatest improvement in comparison to traditional counselling.

Reynolds and Coats (1986) conducted a study where significant decreases in depression were found in the youth who received cognitive-behavioral treatment and relaxation training as compared to a waitlist control group. Stark, Reynolds, and Kaslow (1987) compared the efficacy in treating depression with self-control techniques, behavioral problem-solving or a waitlist condition. Decreases in depression were demonstrated in those who received treatment. Similar to the results with depressed adults, though with many fewer studies, cognitive-behavioral procedures seem applicable in the treatment of depressed youth.

Aggression

Mild forms of aggression is common in youth, but it can become a problem when it occurs across settings with high intensity (Loeber and Dishion, 1983). Aggression, when not treated, has been found to be stable over time (Huesmann, Eron, Lefkowitz and Walker, 1984) and is associated with substance abuse, delinquency, and school failure (Pepler and Rubin, 1991).

Aggressive children can be characterized as suffering from cognitive distortions and deficiencies (Kendall, Ronan and Epps, 1991). They attend to aggressive environmental cues more than to nonaggressive cues. As described by Milich and Dodge (1984), they have a hostile attributional bias in which they overestimate the degree of hostility of intent by peer provocation. Aggressive children also have a response decision bias in which they generate more aggressive incompetent solutions to provoking situations. Finally, they demonstrate a biased recall towards aggression (Dodge, Pettit, McClaskey and Brown, 1986). This lends support to the idea that aggressive kids cognitively distort the processing of information (Kendall and MacDonald, 1993).

Aggressive children also demonstrate cognitive deficiencies in their limited problem-solving abilities (Lochman, Lampron and Rabiner, 1990), and overuse of quick action-oriented solutions (Perry, Perry and Rasmussen, 1986). They do not utilize all the cues given to them regarding the processing of information, and have difficulty in generating alternate, nonaggressive, solutions to problems. The solutions they generate tend to be ineffective and hostile (Dodge, 1985; Richard and Dodge, 1982).

Research suggests that cognitive-behavioral therapy can be promising for aggressive children (Kazdin, 1987). In a clinical study by Kazdin, Esveldt-Dawson, French, and Unis (1987a), a 20-session problem-solving skills training program was reported to decrease aggression as verified by teachers and parents. This study was replicated in conjunction with parent training (Kazdin, Esveldt-Dawson, French, and Unis, 1987b), and with antisocial children (Kazdin, Bass, Siegel, and Thomas, 1989). Lochman and colleagues demonstrated a decrease in aggression and disruptive behavior using a cognitive-behavioral based anger-coping program (Lochman, Burch, Curry, and Lampron, 1984). Lochman and Lenhart (1993) reported more success in treating aggressive children when a parent training program was incorporated into treatment. In addition to parent training, they suggest improving treatment outcome studies by making the treatment more lengthy, more intensive, and including follow-up booster sessions to maintain treatment effects.

The strategies previously discussed can be used with aggressive youth. Of particular benefit for aggressive youth seems to be modelling problem-solving. Emphasis is placed on identifying problems, generating solutions, and evaluating the outcomes of the solutions. Additionally, social perspective-taking is applied to provide opportunities to gain empathy and to better infer the intention and thoughts of others. Role-playing can aid in the process of social perspective-taking. Contingencies and rewards are also used and recommended.

Attention-Deficit Hyperactivity Disorder (ADHD)

Children with ADHD have been characterized as having deficiencies in problem-solving abilities, in modulation of behavior to match environmental demands, and in overall self-control and regulation (Douglas, Barr, Amin, O'Neill and Britton, 1988; Hinshaw and Erhardt, 1991). They have difficulty focusing on tasks and find it particularly challenging paying attention when there are appealing distracters (Zentall, 1985; Radosh and Gittelman, 1981; Ceci and Tishman, 1984).

Medications help to alleviate hyperactivity (Abikoff and Klein, 1992), but do not always address the cognitive processing deficits. Cognitive-behavioral therapy may be a good method of treating these difficulties in cognitive functioning. However, data suggest that cognitive-behavioral therapy can aid in the reduction of impulsivity, but has not always been successful in treating other symptoms of ADHD (Kendall and Braswell, 1982; 1985). Bloomquist, August, and Ostrander (1991) conducted a school-based study involving a ten-week, two-hour a week, treatment intervention. Problem-solving skills were taught and then generalized to be used in everyday situations such as interpersonal interactions. Role playing and modelling were used in the session to help the children gain better expertise in problem-solving. Teachers were also taught these skills in a separate seminar. Children following this treatment were then compared to children who received no treatment and were on a waitlist and children who did not receive individual treatment, but whose teachers received the training. Although their were reported gains, the results did not indicate significant differences across the groups after treatment.

Hinshaw and Melnick (1992) discussed that perhaps treatment is not as effective with children suffering form ADHD because the disorder encompasses such a wide range of symptoms. Often children with ADHD are also aggressive, have problems in school both academically and with peers, are hyperactive, and have very short attention spans. Before cognitive issues can be addressed through cognitive-behavioral therapy, many other factors should be considered and implemented (i.e., medication, behavioral strategies, help with academics) which may be prerequisite to cognitive changes). Cognitive-behavioral therapy can work to get the child to change his or her ways of thinking and acting, but it is also essential to address issues of parenting (Whalen and Henker, 1991). Perhaps future research can include a full array of behavioral and cognitive components specifically geared towards the child and place greater emphasis on parent training to aid in treatment (Braswell and Bloomquist, 1991; Kendall and Reber, 1987). Although the evidence to date is not universally supportive, researchers need to experiment with treatments other than medication because medication can not be given to everyone, it can have unwanted side effects, and when the child stops taking it, the child is left alone without strategies to help cope with everyday functioning (Whalen and Henker, 1991).

Anxiety Disorders

Anxiety is a universal human experience, but when it is persistent and intense, it can interfere in everyday functioning and become maladaptive. Although there is limited research on children with anxiety disorders, studies of anxious youth have been informative.

For example, anxiety has been shown to be connected to negative self-referent speech (Prins, 1985). Prins (1986) reported that children's self-talk in anxiety provoking situations was correlated with the amount of fear they experienced with those who were most anxious reporting more negative self-talk and negative expectations. Anxious children have a tendency to report more threat-related self-statements (Ronan, Kendall and Rowe, 1994) and provide more coping self-talk, although this coping talk does not appear to relieve their distress (Kendall and Chansky, 1991). In test taking situations, those children considered to be anxious performed at a lower level than those who were not anxious (Zatz and Chassin, 1983; 1985). Perhaps both on- and off-task thoughts demonstrated by the test anxious children distracted them from the cognitive processing needed to successfully complete the test. Bell-Dolan and Wessler (1994) describe anxious individuals as having low outcome expectations and expectations of failure, hence they tend to attribute failure to themselves. In stressful situations such as medical and dental procedures, when children were prepared with coping strategies, they were more able to cope with the stressful procedure and demonstrated less anxiety (Siegel and Peterson, 1980; 1981).

While physiological signs of anxiety have received little empirical attention (Barrios and Hartmann, 1988), Beidel (1988) reported differences in the autonomic activity of anxious versus nonanxious children. Physiological components of anxiety can increase anxiety, therefore reduction of these symptoms or learning a new way of coping with them may be helpful. Relaxation training is one means which is an effective way of coping with these symptoms (Ollendick and Cerny, 1981).

Other strategies, as discussed earlier, are useful in helping the child cope with anxiety. Anxious children are described as having cognitive processing distortions (Kendall, 1993) and therefore it is important for the child to be able to generate solutions, problem-solve through many different situations, and test out these alternate strategies. This treatment approach allows the child to test out his or her dysfunctional beliefs and help to build a new schema or coping template. In vivo exposure experiences are particularly useful in disputing and correcting misperceptions.

The outcomes of a preliminary study of cognitive-behavioral therapy with anxiety disordered youth (Kane and Kendall, 1989), demonstrated the effectiveness of treatment. Changes in levels of anxiety were demonstrated in parent report, child self-report, and independent clinicians ratings. Based on these results, a randomized clinical trial for children diagnosed with overanxious disorder, separation anxiety, and avoidant disorder was undertaken (Kendall, 1994). Subjects received 16-20, hour long, individual treatment sessions. The treatment itself trained children to use cognitive strategies as well as behavioral relaxation techniques to manage their anxiety. Treatment provided practice opportunities to further build and develop the newly learned skills. The treatment helped children to recognize their anxious feelings and somatic responses to anxiety, recognize their thoughts in anxiety provoking situations, problem-solve and develop a plan to cope with the anxious situation, and evaluate their ability to cope with the situation and reward themselves as appropriate (see treatment manual; Kendall, Kane, Howard and Siqueland, 1989, available from the author).

Combinations of strategies such as relaxation training, imagery, problem solving, modelling, role playing, and homework assignments were used to modify anxious and threatening thoughts. These skills were practised through exposure experiences, presented in a hierarchical fashion, where children were given the opportunity to cope with threatening situations. After successful exposure, self-efficacy is increased and other challenges are seen as less demanding. It is our argument that the exposure occur after children are given the skills to handle the situations more effectively so that the in vivo exposures will be successful experiences for them (Kendall and Panichelli-Mindel, 1995).

Results of the Kendall (1994) study were favourable. Across self- and parent-report and behavioral observations, therapy was shown to reduce maladaptive and distressing anxiety. In terms of clinical significance, approximately two-thirds of clients were found to be without their primary diagnosis after treatment and to be within normal limits on several measures. For example, according to a structured diagnostic interview, 64% did not meet criteria for their primary diagnosis at completion of treatment. On self- report of anxiety and depression, a significantly greater number of subjects fell within the normal range after treatment on measures which they once reported clinical levels of disturbance. Coders blind to condition observed and coded videotapes of pretreatment and post-treatment behavior - these observations indicated a visible reduction in total anxious behavior. These results were maintained at one year follow-up, and were again found to have been maintained at a 3.5 year follow-up (Kendall and Gerow, 1994).

FUTURE DIRECTIONS

We neither propose nor advocate a monolithic approach to child therapy. Indeed, the human experience is marked for its diversity not for its conformity. In our discussion of cognition and behavior, we discourage narrow notions of "normalcy" and avoid any hint that there is only one "normal" way to think and act (e.g., Kendall, 1992). Instead, we suggest broad notions of diverse, adaptive functioning. There are maladaptive cognitive processing styles and high-cost behavior patterns - both needing to be rectified - but it is not the case that a singular pattern of thinking or behavior is the necessary or required solution.

Our coverage of interventions, whose focus lies primarily in the realm of cognition and behavior, underscores these aspects of human behavior and behavior change. However, highlighting cognitive processing and behavioral performance does not preclude the importance of more contextual and/or affective factors in intervention. True to its empirical roots, the approach welcomes additional integration as research data and outcome studies are reported.

Future work in the cognitive-behavioral arena would benefit from several new directions. First, current and projected future need for psychological services for youth requires that time and effort be expended toward the development and evaluation of treatments aimed at not only the remedy of distress but also the prevention of psychological problems. Cognitive-behavioral theory permits considerable flexibility when approaching the multifaceted problems in youth from both preventative as well as remedial perspectives.

Cognitive-behavioral approaches have begun to change their individual focus and attend to the wider context of family, social milieu, and school setting (see Kendall, MacDonald and Treadwell, in press). In this way, researchers are answering Kazdin and Kagan's (1994) call for the examination of other than single pathways to disorders. Causes of and treatments for disorders do not necessarily reside within a single individual. For example, Howard and Kendall (1995) used a multiple-baseline design to examine the efficacy of a family-based cognitive-behavioral treatment for anxiety-disordered youth. The outcomes at post-treatment and follow-up evidenced significant and clinically meaningful gains - changes that were not seen over the baseline periods. Current research also suggests that a broader perspective is necessary in the treatment of aggressive and ADHD youth (see Braswell and Bloomquist, 1991). For example, treatment of aggressive youth is enhanced when a combined parent training and problem-solving skills training approach are used (e.g., Kazdin, Siegel and Bass, 1992; for review, see Gerow and Kendall, 1995). Additionally, with ADHD youth, combined approaches are recommended to address the multiple levels of problems these children experience (e.g., academic, family, and social problems). Finally, though the paucity of the treatment outcome research with depressed children does not allow for any definitive statements, it is likely that a broad perspective, encompassing school and family (Stark, 1990) and interpersonal approaches (e.g., Mufson, Moreau, Weissman and Klerman, 1993) will be valued additions to work that is directed toward the amelioration of these children's problems and to the advancement of the field.

Although it is apparent that we recommend "broader" applications, the need remains for the bases of breadth to be evaluated on at least two fronts. First, the need for the broader applications must be validated. The important role (adaptive and maladaptive) of the family in the development of children has long been maintained, yet the research evidence concerning the interaction of familial contributions and, for example, child cognitive functioning to child psychopathology is far from extensive. The future will benefit greatly from studies in this arena. Second, once a basis has been established, empirical evaluations of interventions are required to assess the efficacy of a broader intervention versus a more individually-focused one. Although it is theoretically appealing (and tempting at the practical level) to believe that a broader intervention will be superior, there are intriguing rationales for the opposite conclusion. For example, Weisz, Weiss, and Donenberg (1992) reported that outcomes of therapies provided in research settings, whose treatments tend to be focused and relatively narrow, were superior to outcomes achieved in service-providing clinics, whose approaches are presumably more "broad." Thus, it remains an empirical question whether more focused approaches or broader ones are more efficacious in the amelioration of psychological problems of youth.

The comparative assessment of treatment outcomes produced by various approaches to child and adolescent therapy will be useful on a number of levels. We maintain that while cognitive-behavioral theory appears to have utility and power in explaining certain aspects of several childhood psychological problems, this does not preclude other theories from having similar explanatory and applied power. Thus, studies comparing the relative effects of, for example, a cognitive-behavioral therapy versus a strictly behavioral one or a family therapy versus a child-focused approach, will be useful from both a theoretical as well as an applied perspective.

Additionally, treatments with less empirical validation but widespread use in some applied settings (e.g., psychodynamic) are encouraged to develop research programs. Work along these lines has been accomplished in the adult literature (e.g., Luborsky, Crits-Christoph, Mintz and Auerbach, 1988). However, few studies have addressed this in the child literature. Szapocznick et al. (1989) compared a structural family treatment with a psychodynamic treatment and found the psychodynamic treatment more effective than a control group but less effective overall than the structural family intervention. More recently, Smyrnios and Kirkby (1993) reported that a time-unlimited psychodynamic approach with children and their families was not more effective than a time-limited psychodynamic approach. Thus, while investigators have begun to examine the effectiveness of a psychodynamic approach, the results are not uniformly supportive and additional research remains warranted.

As comparative treatment outcome studies become more prevalent, examinations of "active" components of the treatments will be more plausible. For example, are the cognitive strategies employed in cognitive-behavioral more effective when employed in conjunction with behavioral strategies? While cognitive-behavioral therapy is based on the assumption that the answer is yes, research has yet to verify this assertion. Additionally, differences among treatment approaches can be explored. Work along these lines has suggested some interesting findings. For example, in studying adult treatments, Kerr, Goldfried, Hayes, Castonguay, and Goldsamt (1992) found that cognitive-behavioral therapists placed more emphasis on interpersonal as opposed to intrapersonal factors contrary to what some readers see as cognitive-behavioral's theoretical emphasis on cognitive (i.e., internal) factors. Comparative treatment designs offer many advantages in a search for active ingredients and we look forward to the advances our field will provide as such studies are completed and published.

Finally, we acknowledge that whereas the cognitive-behavioral position outlined here has included no formal discussion of nonspecific factors (e.g., Strupp and Hadley, 1979), we consider them important to all forms of therapy. For example, a trusting relationship between child and therapist provides the proper milieu for the experimentation with new ways of thinking which plays a central role in cognitive-behavioral approaches. A recent report from our clinic (Kendall, 1994) found that all clients reported highly positive relationships with their therapists, precluding correlations between relationship and outcome. Because all therapeutic approaches rely on a therapeutic relationship, teasing out its relative contribution (in fact, even measuring the strength of such a relationship) is fraught with difficulty. Kazdin and his colleagues (Kazdin, Esveldt-Dawson, French, and Unis, 1987) compared a "relationship" therapy (i.e., a Rogerian style, supportive intervention) versus a cognitive-behavioral therapy in an attempt to determine if the relationship alone is responsible for treatment's positive effects. They found the cognitive-behavioral treatment superior to the relationship therapy. However, one study does not settle the issue. We are hopeful that nonspecific factors can be more fully specified and their contribution to treatment's effectiveness more extensively examined.

The cognitive-behavioral framework is an expanding and promising one. Many treatments derived from the theory have demonstrated efficacy in rigorous clinical trials and the theory has spawned a proliferation of research in the treatment of clinical problems in youth. We do not argue that cognitive-behavioral theory and therapy offers a panacea for all the clinical problems of all youth. We do believe, however, that the approach has advanced our understanding of child psychopathology and psychotherapy and in doing so, the approach has itself expanded in response to data. In the end, the cognitive-behavioral theorist, like the cognitive-behavioral therapist, tests out his/her hypotheses and modifies the framework in order to explain more and more of the problems facing youth. In this way, we hope that the services that children need, sometimes desperately, will be delivered in the most sensitive and efficacious manner.

REFERENCES

Abikoff, H. and Klein, R.G. (1992). Attention-deficit hyperactivity and conduct-disorder: Comorbidity and implications for treatment. *Journal of Consulting and Clinical Psychology, 60,* 881-892.

Abramson, L.Y., Seligman, M.E.P. and Teasdale, J.D. (1978). Learned helplessness in humans: Critique and reformulation. *Journal of Abnormal Psychology, 87,* 49-74.

Asarnow, J.R. and Bates, S. (1988). Depression in child psychiatric inpatients: Cognitive attributional patterns. *Journal of Abnormal Child Psychology, 16,* 601-615.

Asarnow, J.R., Carlson, G.A. and Guthrie, D. (1987). Coping strategies, self perceptions, hopelessness, and perceived family environments in depressed and suicidal children. *Journal of Consulting and Clinical Psychology, 55,* 361-366.

Bandura, A. (1969). *Principles of behavior modification.* New York: Holt, Rinehart and Winston.

Bandura, A. (1986). *Social foundation of thought and action: A social cognitive theory. Englewood Cliffs, NJ: Prentice-Hall.*

Barlow, D. (1988). *Anxiety and its disorders.* New York: Guilford Press.

Barrios, B.A. and Hartmann, D.B. (1988). Fears and anxieties. In: E.J. Mash and L. G. Terdal (Eds.), *Behavioral assessment of childhood disorders.* (2nd ed., pp. 196-264). New York: Guilford Press.

Beck, A.T. (1976). *Cognitive therapy and emotional disorders.* New York: International Universities Press.

Beidel, D.C. (1988). Psychophysiological assessment of anxious emotional states in children. *Journal of Abnormal Psychology, 97,* 80-82.

Bell-Dolan, D. and Wessler, A.E. (1994). Attributional styles of anxious children: Extensions from cognitive theory and research on adult anxiety. *Journal of Anxiety Disorders, 8,* 79-96.

Bloomquist, M.L., August, G.J. and Ostrander, R. (1991). Effects of a school-based cognitive-behavioral intervention for attention deficit hyperactivity disordered children. *Journal of Abnormal Child Psychology, 19*, 591-605.

Braswell, L. and Bloomquist, M. (1991). *Cognitive-behavioral therapy with ADHD children: Child, family, and school intervention.* New York: Guilford Press.

Ceci, S.J. and Tishman, J. (1984). Hyperactivity and incidental memory: Evidence for attentional diffusion. *Child Development, 55*, 2192-2203.

Dodge, K.A. (1985). Attributional bias in aggressive children. In: P.C. Kendall (Ed.), *Advances in cognitive-behavioral research and therapy* (Vol. 4). New York: Academic Press.

Dodge, K.A., Pettit, G.S., McClaskey, C.L. and Brown, M.M. (1986). Social competence in children. *Monographs of the Society for Research in Child Development, 51*, (2, Serial No. 213).

Douglas, V.I., Barr, R.G., Amin, K., O'Neill, M.E. and Britton, B.G. (1988). Dosage effects and individual responsivity to methylphenidate in attention deficit disorder. *Journal of Child Psychology and Psychiatry, 29*, 453-475.

DuPaul. G.J., Guevremont, D.C. and Barkley, R.A. (1991). Attention-Deficit Hyperactivity Disorder. In: T.R. Kratochwill and R.J. Morris (Eds.), *The practice of child therapy-second edition.* New York: Pergamon Press.

Elliott, C.H. and Olsen, R.A. (1983). The management of children's distress in response to painful medical treatment for burn injuries. *Behavior Research and Therapy, 21*, 675-683.

Gerow, M.A. and Kendall, P.C. (in press). The psychosocial treatment of antisocial behavior in children and adolescents. In: D. Stoff, J. Breiling and J. Maser (Eds.) *Handbook of antisocial behavior.*

Hammen, C.L. (1988). Self-cognitions, stressful events, and the prediction of depression in children of depressed mothers. *Journal of Abnormal Child Psychology, 16*, 347-360.

Hinshaw, S.P. and Erhardt, D. (1991). Attention-deficit hyperactivity disorder. In: P.C. Kendall (Ed.), *Child and adolescent therapy: Cognitive-behavioral procedures* (pp. 98-130). New York: Guilford Press.

Hinshaw, S.P. and Melnick, S. (1992). Self-management therapies and attention-deficit hyperactivity disorder: Reinforced self-evaluation and anger control interventions. *Behavior Modification, 16*, 253-273.

Howard, B. and Kendall, P.C. (1994). Cognitive-behavioral family therapy for anxiety disordered children: Multiple-baseline evaluation. Manuscript submitted for publication, Temple University, Phila., PA.

Huesmann, L.R., Eron, L.D., Lefkowitz, M.M. and Walker, L.O. (1984). Stability of aggression over time and generations. *Developmental Psychology, 20*, 1120-1134.

Hughes, J. (1993). Behavior therapy. In: T.R. Kratochwill and R.J. Morris (Eds.) *Handbook of psychotherapy with children and adolescents.* Boston: Allyn and Bacon.

Ingram, R.E. (1986). *Information processing approaches to clinical psychology.* New York: Academic Press.

Ingram, R.E. and Kendall, P.C. (1986). Cognitive clinical psychology: Implications of an information processing perspective. In: R.E. Ingram (Ed.), *Information processing approaches to clinical psychology* (pp. 3-21). New York: Academic Press.

Jay, S., Elliott, C. and Varni, J. (1986). Acute and chronic pain in adults and children with cancer. *Journal of Consulting and Clinical Psychology, 54*, 601-607.

Kane, M.T. and Kendall, P.C. (1989). Anxiety disorders in children: A multiple-baseline evaluation of a cognitive-behavioral treatment. *Behavior Therapy, 20*, 499-508.

Kazdin, A.E. (1974). Covert modelling, model similarity, and reduction of avoidance behavior. *Behavior Therapy, 5*, 325-340.

Kazdin, A.E. (1987). Treatment of antisocial behavior in children: Current status and future directions. *Psychological Bulletin, 102*, 187-203.

Kazdin, A.E., Bass, D., Siegel, T. and Thomas, C. (1989). Cognitive-behavioral therapy and relationship therapy in the treatment of children referred for antisocial behavior. *Journal of Consulting and Clinical Psychology, 57*, 522-535.

Kazdin, A.E., Esveldt-Dawson, K., French, N.H. and Unis, A.S. (1987a). Effects of parent management training and problem-solving skills training combined in the treatment of antisocial child behavior. *Journal of the American Academy of Child and Adolescent Psychiatry, 26*, 416-424.

Kazdin, A.E., Esveldt-Dawson, K., French, N.H. and Unis, A.S (1987b). Problem-solving skills training and relationship therapy in the treatment of antisocial child behavior. *Journal of Consulting and Clinical Psychology, 55*, 76-85.

Kazdin, A.E. and Kagan, J. (1994). Models of dysfunction in developmental psychopathology. *Clinical Psychology: Science and Practice, 1*, 35-52.

Kazdin, A.E., Siegel, T.C. and Bass, D. (1992). Cognitive problem-solving skills training and parent management training in the treatment of antisocial behavior in children. *Journal of Consulting and Clinical Psychology, 60*, 733-740.

Keefe, F.J. and Williams, D.A. (1989). New directions in pain assessment and treatment. *Clinical Psychology Review, 9,* 549-568.

Kendall, P.C. (1985). Toward a cognitive-behavioral model of child psychopathology and a critique of related interventions. *Journal of Abnormal Child Psychology, 13,* 357-372.

Kendall, P.C. (1989). The generalization and maintenance of behavior change: Comments, considerations, and the "no-cure" criticism. *Behavior Therapy, 20,* 357-364.

Kendall, P.C. (1991). Guiding theory for therapy with children and adolescents. In: P.C. Kendall, (Ed.), *Child and adolescent therapy: Cognitive-behavioral procedures.* NY: Guilford.

Kendall, P.C. (1992). Healthy thinking. *Behavior Therapy, 23,* 1-11.

Kendall, P.C. (1993). Cognitive-behavioral therapies with youth: Guiding theory, current status, and emerging developments. *Journal of Consulting and Clinical Psychology, 61,* 235-247.

Kendall, P.C. (1994). Treating anxiety disorders in youth: Results of a randomized clinical trial. *Journal of Consulting and Clinical Psychology, 62,* 100-110.

Kendall, P.C. and Bacon, S.F. (1988). Cognitive behavior therapy. In: D.B. Fishman, F. Rotgers and C.M. Franks (Eds.), *Paradigms in behavior therapy: Present and promise.* New York: Springer Publishing.

Kendall, P.C. and Braswell, L. (1982). Cognitive-behavioral self-control therapy for children: A components analysis. *Journal of Consulting and Clinical Psychology, 50,* 672-690.

Kendall, P.C. and Braswell, L. (1985). *Cognitive-behavioral therapy for impulsive children.* New York: Guilford Press.

Kendall, P.C. and Chansky, T.E. (1991). Considering cognition in anxiety-disordered children. *Journal of Anxiety Disorders, 5,* 167-185.

Kendall, P.C., Chansky, T., Freidman, M., Kim, R., Kortlander, E., Sessa, F. and Siqueland, L. (1991). Treating anxiety disorders in children and adolescents. In: P.C. Kendall, (Ed.), *Child and adolescent therapy: Cognitive-behavioral procedures.* NY: Guilford.

Kendall, P.C. and Gerow, M.A. (1994). *Long-term follow-up of a cognitive-behavioral therapy for anxiety-disordered youth.* Manuscript submitted for publication, Temple University, Phila., PA 19122.

Kendall, P.C. and Hollon, S.D. (1979). Cognitive-behavioral interventions: Overview and current status. In: P.C. Kendall and S.D. Hollon (Eds.), *Cognitive-behavioral interventions: Theory, research, and procedures* (pp. 1-13). New York: Academic Press.

Kendall, P.C., Kane, M., Howard, B. and Siqueland, L. (1989). *Cognitive-behavioral therapy for anxious children: Treatment manual.* (Available from P.C. Kendall, Psychology Department, Temple University, Philadelphia, PA 19122.)

Kendall, P.C. and MacDonald, J.P. (1993). Cognition in the psychopathology of youth and implications for treatment. In: K.S. Dobson and P.C. Kendall (Eds.), *Psychopathology and Cognition.* San Diego, CA: Academic Press Inc.

Kendall, P.C., MacDonald, J.P. and Treadwell, K.R.H. (in press). The treatment of anxiety disorders in youth: Future directions. In: A.R. Eisen, C.A. Kearney and C.E. Schaefer (Eds.), *Clinical handbook of anxiety disorders in children.* New York: Jason Aronson.

Kendall, P.C. and Panichelli-Mindel, S.M. (1995). Cognitive-behavioral treatments. *Journal of Abnormal Child Psychology, 23,* (in press).

Kendall, P.C. and Reber, M. (1987). Reply to Abikoff and Gittelman's evaluation of cognitive training with medicated hyperactive children. *Archives of General Psychiatry, 8,* 77-79.

Kendall, P.C., Ronan, K.R. and Epps, J. (1991). Aggression in children/adolescents: Cognitive-behavioral treatment perspective. In: D.J. Pepler and K.H. Rubin (Eds.), *The development and treatment of childhood aggression* (pp. 341-360). Hillsdale, NJ: Erlbaum.

Kendall, P.C. and Siqueland, L. (1989). Child and adolescent therapy. In: A.M. Nezu and C.M. Nezu (Eds.), *Clinical decision making in behavior therapy: A problem-solving perspective.* Champaign, Illinois: Research Press Company.

Kendall, P.C., Stark, K. and Adam, T. (1990). Cognitive deficit or cognitive distortion in childhood depression. *Journal of Abnormal Child Psychology, 18,* 267-283.

Kerr, S., Goldfried, M.R., Hayes, A.M., Castonguay, L.G. and Goldsamt, L.A. (1992). Interpersonal and intrapersonal focus in cognitive-behavioral and psychodynamic-interpersonal therapies. A preliminary analysis of the Sheffield project. Psychotherapy Research, 2, 266-276.

LaGreca, A.M. and Santogrossi, D.A. (1981). Social skills training with elementary school students: A behavioral group approach. *Journal of Consulting and Clinical Psychology, 48,* 201-227.

Laurent, J. and Stark, K.D. (1993). Testing the cognitive content-specificity hypothesis with anxious and depressed youngsters. *Journal of Abnormal Psychology, 102,* 226-237.

Lee, C. (1990). Theoretical weaknesses: Fundamental flaws in cognitive-behavioral theories are more than a problem of probability. *Journal of Behavior Therapy and Experimental Psychiatry, 21,* 143-145.

Lochman, J.E., Burch, P.R., Curry, J.F. and Lampron, L.B. (1984). Treatment and generalization effects of cognitive-behavioral and goal-setting interventions with aggressive boys. *Journal of Consulting and Clinical Psychology, 52*, 915-916.

Lochman, J.E., Lampron, L.B. and Rabiner, D.L. (1990). Format and salience effects in the social problem-solving of aggressive and nonaggressive boys. *Journal of Consulting and Clinical Psychology, 18*, 230-236.

Lochman, J.E. and Lenhart, L.A (1993). Anger coping intervention for aggressive children: Conceptual models and outcome effects. *Clinical Psychology Review, 13*, 785-805.

Loeber, R. and Dishion, T.J. (1983). Early predictors of male delinquency: A review. *Psychological Bulletin, 94*, 68-99.

Luborsky, L. Crits-Christoph, P., Mintz, J. and Auerbach. A. (1988). *Who will benefit from psychotherapy? Predicting therapeutic outcomes*. New York: Basic Books.

Masters, J.C., Brush, T.G., Hollon, S.D. and Rimm, D.C. (1987). *Behavior Therapy* (3rd ed.). New York: Harcourt, Brace Jonanovich.

McLaughlin, T.F. and Williams, R.L. (1988). The token economy. In: J.C. Witt, S.N. Elliott and F.M. Gresham (Eds.), *Handbook of Behavior Therapy in Education*. New York: Plenum Press.

Milich, R. and Dodge, K.A. (1984). Social information processing in child psychiatric populations. *Journal of Abnormal Child Psychology, 12*, 471-490.

Morris, R.J. and Kratochwill, T.R. (1983). *Treating children's fears and phobias: A behavioral approach*. Elmsford, New York: Pergamon Press.

Mufson, L., Moreau, D., Weissman, M.M. and Klerman, G.L. (1993). *Interpersonal psychotherapy for depressed adolescents*. New York: Guilford Press.

Ollendick, T.H. (1986). Behavior therapy with children and adolescents. In: S.L. Garfield and A. E. Berger (Eds.), *Handbook of psychotherapy and behavior change* (3rd ed.). New York: Wiley.

Ollendick, T.H. and Cerny, J.A. (1981). *Clinical behavior therapy with children*. New York: Plenum Press.

Panichelli, S.M. and Kendall, P.C. (in press). Therapy with children and adolescents. In: B. Bongar and L.E. Beutler, (Eds.), *Foundations of Psychotherapy: Theory, Research, and Practice*, (in press). Oxford University Press.

Pepler, D.J. and Rubin, K.H. (Eds.) (1991). *The development and treatment of childhood aggression*. Hillsdale, NJ; Erlbaum Associates.

Pepper, S.C. (1942). *World hypotheses*. Berkeley, CA; University of California Press.

Perry, D.G., Perry, L.C. and Rasmussen, P. (1986). Cognitive social learning mediators of aggression. *Child development, 57*, 700-711.

Prins, P.J. (1985). Self-speech and self-regulation of high-and low-anxious children in the dental situation: An interview study. *Behavior Research and Therapy, 23*, 641-650.

Prins, P.J. (1986). Children's self-speech and self-regulation during a fear provoking behavioral test. *Behavior Research and Therapy, 24*, 181-191.

Radosh, A. and Gittelman, R. (1981). The effect of appealing distracters on the performance of hyperactive children. *Journal of Abnormal Child Psychology, 9*, 179-189.

Rehm, L.P. and Carter, A.S. (1990). Cognitive components of depression. In: M. Lewis and S.M. Miller (Eds.), *Handbook of developmental psychopathology* (pp. 341-351). New York: Plenum.

Reynolds, W.M. and Coats, K.I. (1986). A comparison of cognitive-behavioral therapy and relaxation training for the treatment of depression in adolescents. *Journal of Consulting and Clinical Psychology, 54*, 653-660.

Richard, B.A. and Dodge, K.A. (1982). Social maladjustment and problem-solving in school aged children. *Journal of Consulting and Clinical Psychology, 50*, 226-233.

Ronan, K., Kendall, P.C. and Rowe, M. (1994). Negative affectivity in children: Development and validation of a self-statement questionnaire. *Cognitive Therapy and Research, 18*, 509-528.

Seligman, M.E.P., Peterson, C., Kaslow, N.J., Tanenbaum, R.L., Alloy, L.B. and Abramson, L.Y. (1984). Attributional style and depressive symptoms among children. *Journal of Abnormal Psychology, 93*, 235-238.

Siegel, L.J. and Peterson, L. (1980). Stress reduction in young dental patients through coping skills and sensory information. *Journal of Consulting and Clinical Psychology, 48*, 785-787.

Siegel, L.J. and Peterson, L. (1981). Maintenance effects of coping skills and sensory information on young children's response to repeated dental procedures. *Behavior Therapy, 12*, 530-535.

Skinner, B.F. (1987). Whatever happened to psychology as the science of behavior? *American Psychologist, 42*, 780-786.

Smyrnios, K.X. and Kirkby, R.J. (1993). Long-term comparison of brief versus unlimited psychodynamic treatments with children and their parents. *Journal of Consulting and Clinical Psychology, 61*, 1020-1027.

Stark, K.D. (1990). *Childhood depression: School-based intervention.* New York: Guilford Press.

Stark, K.D., Reynolds, W.M. and Kaslow, N.J. (1987). A comparison of the relative efficacy of self-control therapy and a behavioral problem-solving therapy for depression in children. *Journal of Abnormal Child Psychology, 15*, 91-113.

Stark, K.D., Rouse, L.W. and Livingston, R. (1991). Treatment of depression during childhood and adolescence: Cognitive-behavioral procedures for the individual and family. In: P.C. Kendall, (Ed.). *Child and adolescent therapy: Cognitive-behavioral procedures* (pp. 165-206). New York: Guilford.

Strupp, H.H. and Hadley, S.W. (1979). Specific vs. nonspecific factors in psychotherapy: A controlled study of outcome. *Archives of General Psychiatry, 36*, 1125-1136.

Szapocznik, J., Rio, A., Murray, E., Cohen, R., Scopetta, M., Rivas-Vasquez, A, Hervis, O, Posada, V. and Kurtines, W. (1989). Structural family versus psychodynamic child therapy for problematic Hispanic boys. *Journal of Consulting and Clinical Psychology, 57*, 571-578.

Tarnowski, K.J., McGrath, M.L., Calhoun, M.B. and Drabman, R.S. (1987). Pediatric burn injury: Self-versus therapist-medicated debridement. *Journal of Pediatric Psychology, 12*, 567-579.

Ultee, C.A., Griffiaen, D. and Schellekens, J. (1982). The reduction of anxiety in children: A comparison of the effects of systematic desensitization in vitro and systematic desensitization in vivo. *Behavior Therapy and Research, 20*, 61-67.

Varela, F.J., Thompson, E. and Rosch, E. (1991). *The embodied mind: Cognitive science and human experience.* Cambridge, MA: MIT Press.

Varni, J.W. (1983). *Clinical behavioral paediatrics: An interdisciplinary bio-behavioral approach.* New York: Pergamon Press.

Walco, G.A. and Dampier, C.D. (1987). Chronic pain in adolescent patients. *Journal of Pediatric Psychology, 12*, 215-225.

Walco, G.A. and Varni, J.W. (1991). Cognitive-behavioral interventions for children with chronic illnesses. In: P.C. Kendall (Ed.), *Child and adolescent therapy: Cognitive-behavioral procedures* (pp. 209-244). New York: Guilford Press.

Weisz, J.R., Weiss, B. and Donenberg, G.R. (1992). The lab versus the clinic: Effects of child and adolescent psychotherapy. *American Psychologist, 47*, 1578-1585.

Whalen, C.K. and Henker, B. (1991). Therapies for hyperactive children: Comparisons, combinations, and compromises. *Journal of Consulting and Clinical Psychology, 59*, 126-137.

Wolpe, J. (1958). *Psychotherapy by reciprocal inhibition.* Stanford, CA: Stanford University Press.

Zatz, S. and Chassin, L. (1983). Cognitions of test-anxious children. *Journal of Consulting and Clinical Psychology, 51*, 526-534.

Zatz, S. and Chassin, L. (1985). Cognitions of test-anxious children under naturalistic test-taking condition. *Journal of Consulting and Clinical Psychology, 53*, 393-401.

Zentall, S.S., (1985). Stimulus-control factors in search of performance of hyperactive children. *Journal of Learning Disabilities, 18*, 480-485.

2

SOME NEW DIMENSIONS OF BEHAVIOUR ANALYSIS AND THERAPY

Dennis C. Russo and Carryl P. Navalta

The May Institute Inc.
Health and Rehabilitative Services
35 Parcella Park Drive
Randolph, Massachusetts 02368

ABSTRACT

Clinical approaches based on the principles of behaviour modification and behaviour therapy have evolved into an experimental literature that demonstrates the benefit and efficacy of these approaches in mental illness, mental retardation, autism, and special education. Significant advantages of these learning-based therapies have reduced reliance on traditional psychodynamic models. Indeed, over the past 30 years, behavioural services have not only become a cornerstone of clinical psychology but have led to the development of new models of care for a host of other disorders and problems. This paper summarizes the historical perspectives and new directions in the field of behaviour analysis and therapy. Focusing on applications to paediatric medicine, we will trace the development of behavioural applications in this field and explore new extensions of the behavioural paradigm. By way of review of one of the newest areas of endeavour for behavioural medicine, traumatic brain injuries, we suggest future directions for the growth of behavioural approaches.

INTRODUCTION

Since the development of clinical approaches based on the principles of behaviour modification and behaviour therapy in the 1960's, a steadily growing experimental literature has documented the benefit and efficacy of these approaches in ameliorating or significantly reducing a host of problems in both adults and children. Early applications to long standing problems in mental illness, mental retardation, autism, and special education demonstrated the significant advantages of learning-based therapies over traditional psychodynamic models.

Early workers in behaviour analysis (Baer, Wolf, and Risley, 1968) identified clear differences between practices of the day and behavioural, usually applied behaviour analytic, formulations and treatments. The behavioural philosophy was extremely useful to provide quick resolution and scientific documentation of efficacy to a host of human needs which

Behavioral Approaches for Children and Adolescents, Edited by
H. P. J. G. van Bilsen et al., Plenum Press, New York, 1995

had not previously been associated with satisfactory outcome. Founding centres or enclaves developed in the United States, Europe, Australia, and South America during the late 60's and early 70's continue to espouse a strong behavioural philosophy (Kazdin, 1977). Behaviour analysis and therapy spread from these centres to the extent that behavioural approaches have today become a major force within the mainstream of international clinical psychology.

Behavioural organizations have enjoyed phenomenal growth over this period as well. Internationally, organizations such as the Australian Behaviour Modification Association (ABMA), ALAMOC in South America, and the European Association for Behaviour Therapy (EABT) enjoyed tremendous growth through the 1980's. In the United States, the Association for Advancement of Behavior Therapy (AABT) and the Association for Behavior Analysis International (ABA) provide a primary identity for their members and foster the science through highly ranked psychological journals and annual conventions. Most of these organizations have recently changed their names or their mastheads in recognition of new approaches and data and the changing identities of their memberships (Craighead, 1990), seeking to integrate the whole range of behaviour analysis, behaviour therapy, and cognitive approaches within one continuum. Many leaders of our behavioural organizations today hold appointment to the boards or to editorships of major psychology journals or hold elective office in national and international psychology organizations.

Their emphasis on *behaviour* and empiricism makes these approaches and individuals unique in the field of psychology. As students of behaviourism are well aware, change in overt, operationalizable, and thus measurable, behaviour was the one fundamental value which defined this approach. The premise was simple: If behaviour change (i.e., learning) is observed to occur, agents that effect change are assumed to be identifiable and, if identified, are operationalized as cues or stimuli that mark the time and place of the reinforcement, punishment, or extinction contingencies. Conceptually and empirically, such agents are found in the environment. Functionally, behaviour is referred to as a *respondent* if the behaviour is changed by the stimuli that precede it and as an *operant* if the behaviour is changed by the stimuli that follow it. To some such an approach might seem a bit myopic in eschewing mediary constructs such as thoughts, feelings, and motivation that are assumed to be important aspects of psychological functioning, but one cogent argument is that such singularity of the model was necessary for the development of the field (Russo, 1990, 1993).

A brief review of literature in the behavioural sciences documents the significant advances in producing desirable and adaptively functional benefits. Applications of behavioural technology have resulted in significant behaviour change across different behaviours, problems, and nosologies; even a frequent lack of generality was attacked as a problem to be solved (Baer, 1986; Lovaas, Koegel, Simmons, and Long, 1974; Stokes and Baer, 1976).

Given this enormous early success in modifying behaviour, our purpose here is to address the utility of behavioural approaches to other, more contemporary applications and problems. How well has the traditional behavioural paradigm withstood the rigors of time? Given increasing attention to cognitive models and behaviour therapy approaches, does the three-term contingency (S^D-R-S^R) still hold the same utility and heuristic value as in the past?

The Extension of Behavioural Analysis and Therapy to Pediatrics

In the late 1970's, many practitioners of behaviour analysis began to recognize that new needs were emerging in the general population that might be well served by behavioural approaches. As behaviourists and others looked at children and adults with medical diseases and at the health care system in general, sweeping changes were occurring in the delivery of services, the nature of disabilities, the course of disease, and the importance of prevention that spoke to the potential importance of learned or behavioural factors in disease genesis, maintenance, and treatment (Engel, 1977; Russo and Varni, 1982).

Early scientific work in this area began to explore the biobehavioural interface, that is, how people's behaviour could influence disease expression or symptom management. A new literature with the label of *behavioural medicine* began to appear that documented the utility of a partnership between behaviourists and medical specialists in the treatment of disease in both adults and children (Schwartz and Weiss, 1978; Russo and Varni, 1982).

In this chapter, we shall use one aspect of medicine, pediatrics, to address the utility of applying behavioural paradigms to new fields. While many of our demographics and examples will be drawn from healthcare and social issues in the United States, the problems we will identify are of worldwide concern. Our goal here is to suggest as well that new incarnations of our tried methodologies require careful attention to the nature of the problems to which they are applied.

Pediatrics and Psychology: An Overview

Behavioural approaches that have been shown to be successful with children with developmental and other severe behaviour disorders have crossed over to the field of paediatric medicine. Within this area has evolved the subspecialty of behavioural pediatrics. In fact, training in behavioural-developmental pediatrics is now required for residency in accredited paediatric training programs (Residency Review Committee for Pediatrics, 1992). Varni and Dietrich (1981) defined behavioural pediatrics as "the interdisciplinary integration between biobehavioural science and paediatric medicine, with emphasis on multidimensional and comprehensive diagnosis, prevention and treatment, and rehabilitation of physical disease and disabilities in children and adolescents".

Cataldo (1986) outlined three phases of behavioural pediatrics' evolution: 1) liaison psychiatry and child psychiatry; 2) psychosomatic medicine for adults; and 3) application of findings from psychological research to paediatric problems. Even though operant behavioural approaches to paediatric problems have not been widely adopted in clinical paediatric practice (Cataldo, 1986), behavioural methods that are, in fact, utilized are popular due to the reliable and valid assessment of process and outcome variables - the hallmark characteristic of behavioural interventions (Gross and Drabman, 1990). In fact, the focus on assessment and empirical process-outcome data rather than theory or technique in behavioural pediatrics research and practice was espoused by clinical researchers in the earlier days of the field (e.g., Russo and Varni, 1982). In regard to the present state of health care and health care finance, empirically validated methods, based on well-established principles of learning and with high rates of success in their clinical application, are indeed clearly attractive selling points.

One of the preeminent journals that bridges the two areas of pediatrics and psychology is the *Journal of Paediatric Psychology*, a bi-monthly publication. To gain a perspective on the range of disorders and problems currently addressed in the literature, an analysis was conducted on the Journal regarding its content. Citations were collected from PsycLIT CD-ROM (SilverPlatter 3.11; American Psychological Association, 1994) dated January 1987 to June 1994. Specifically, the last 100 citations that were referenced specific to the Journal were obtained, which covered the period from December 1991 to February 1994 (see Table 1).

As seen in Table 1, HIV infection/AIDS was the most prevalent disorder found in the analysis (11%). However, this finding must be tempered by the fact that five of the eleven references came from a special issue on paediatric AIDS, which inflated the disorder's prevalence in the Journal, and that HIV infection/AIDS is a "hot" topic in both research circles and the public. The next two most prevalent disorders, diabetes and cancer, typically

Table 1. Paediatric disorders or problems identified in the last 100 citations of the *Journal of Pae-diatric Psychology* referenced in PsycLIT CD-ROM (December 1991 to February 1994)

HIV infection/AIDS (11)*	Diabetes (9)
Cancer (8)	Injury (5)
Brain injury (5 total):	Rheumatic disease (4)
hydrocephalus (2)	Sickle cell disease (4)
tumor	Cystic fibrosis (4)
intracranial hemorrhage	Rheumatic disease (4)
epilepsy	Cystic fibrosis (4)
Physical disabilities (3)	Premature infants (2)
Leukemia (2)	Prenatal drug exposure (2)
Spina bifida (2)	Asthma (2)
Mental retardation	Drug regimen refusal
Migraine	Sleep disorders
Reactions to injections	Presurgical anxiety
Failure to thrive	High risk infants
Intestinal parasites	Substance use
Personal safety	Invasive medical procedures
Pain	Sleep-disturbed infants
Otitis media	Hypothyroidism
Nocturnal enuresis	Feeding disorders
Attention deficit hyperactivity disorder	

* Total number of citations are found in parentheses

fall under the rubric of chronic illness/disease. In addition, sickle cell disease, cystic fibrosis, and rheumatic disease were found to be equally prevalent in the Journal - all three being chronic diseases. This emphasis on chronic conditions is timely given that recent data suggest that children with chronic physical disorders have twice the risk of psychosocial maladjust-ment as compared to children who are healthy (Pless and Nolan, 1991). The remaining conditions or problems found in Table 1 can be loosely categorized under the following headings: physical disabilities, children at-risk, acute conditions, negative responses to treatment protocol, sleep disorders, pain-related disorders, health-risk behaviours, elimina-tion disorders, feeding disorders, developmental disorders, and responses to invasive/painful medical procedures.

The above findings nicely parallel the current status of pediatrics in general. That is, because children of today no longer die in significant numbers from acute infectious disease, the practice of paediatric medicine has undergone a shift in focus to the effects of behaviour, lifestyle, and environment on the health and development of children (Russo and Varni, 1982). For those children who live with chronic, overt, and symptomatic diseases, treatment is now focused on the management of the disease process. Russo (1986) summarized the area and stated that interventions geared toward reduction of symptomatology, maintenance of internal homeostasis, and improved comfort for the child comprise disease management. In addition, attention to the disease itself; the environment of care; significant others in the environment; and the patient's behaviour, biochemistry, and beliefs must be incorporated as integral aspects of the total treatment package. Such a formulation could not have come to fruition, as Russo (1986) pointed out, without the occurrence of a change in the philosophy of science in medicine from linear "either-or" logic (e.g., the germ model – single entities produce single outcomes) to contextual or organismic methodologies (e.g., the biopsychoso-cial model – multiple causative factors, multiple settings, and multiple outcome variables). Thus, because behavioural pediatrics is typically involved with a complex web of various interrelated factors that potentially impact on the child's functioning (e.g., biomaturational, cognitive, and socioemotional developmental factors), precise assessment strategies and methodologies are necessary prerequisites for effective and efficient interventions.

Fortunately, during the 1980's, the extension of psychological assessment concepts and practices into health care settings of behavioural pediatrics occurred (Mash and Terdal, 1988; Russo, Bird, and Masek, 1980), including general psychological assessment techniques, illness and health-oriented assessments, and assessments reflecting the conceptual and methodological tenets of behavioural analysis and behavioural assessment (Mash and Terdal, 1990). Potential areas of assessment in behavioural pediatrics include the following: 1) characteristics of the illness; 2) characteristics of medical/social interventions; 3) characteristics of the child; and 4) characteristics of the environment. That is, behavioural independent and dependent variables; biological independent and dependent variables; and dependent performance measures at the interface between organism and environment are all possible targets for assessment (Brady, 1986).

Such a framework implies that the focus of assessment exclusively on the illness is both incomplete and inaccurate because greater emphasis is given to physical causes and potential environmental factors of equal importance are ignored. With chronic illness, for example, effects from the initial onset of the disease or problem cannot be assumed to be more significant contributors to the child and family's difficulties than current physical conditions and social processes. Furthermore, although behavioural-analytic formulations of the problem in relation to possible operant and respondent functions are an integral part of assessment in behavioural pediatrics (Gross and Drabman, 1990), currently updated information used for behavioural assessment purposes should be evaluated within a broader temporal and social context (Mash and Terdal, 1990). Accordingly, assessment strategies in behavioural pediatrics must be 1) both flexible and sensitive to the specific areas of concern that differentiate childhood illnesses; 2) sensitive to those common features that cut across diagnoses; and 3) focused on the needs of children and their families at the idiographic level, with the assumption that variability exists among children with similar diagnoses. Such an approach has been argued to be best served by an ongoing decision-making framework (Mash and Terdal, 1990).

Specific to operant research and practice in the area of disease, Russo and Budd (1987) made four general observations:

- 1) disease processes often are characterized by multiple factors interacting in variable patterns;
- 2) biological factors restrict the extent of available behavior change for some conditions more markedly than was previously understood;
- 3) numerous physiological responses previously thought to be beyond the individual's control can be trained as voluntary responses through behavioral interventions; and
- 4) many mechanisms of control are idiosyncratic, both in the extent to which known factors affect the individual case and in the extent to which they are modifiable by external events.

More specifically, behaviour is only one of the key variables that can potentially impact on health and illness. Other potent stimuli include some or all of the following: genetic/constitutional, developmental, cognitive, personality, environmental, behavioural, pharmacological, and physiological. For example, in terms of intervention efficacy, the consideration that pharmacological effects may decrease treatment effectiveness must be entertained. Given the scientific developments that continually occur (e.g., novel pharmacotherapeutics), communication of findings across disciplines and integration of new discoveries into behavioural models are required to aide in enhancing the adequacy of behavioural analyses and to ensure patient safety. That is, reliance on "traditional" behaviour analyses or packaged treatment protocols is risky when attempting to ameliorate or reduce disease-related symptomatology in that the distinction between medical and behavioural disorders is often unclear.

A more complete functional analysis of disease processes is necessary and can be provided by considering distal and indirect factors within behaviour analyses, searching for differential effects among variables, and continuing to conduct careful, broadly based assessment. In sum, expanding beyond traditional behaviour analysis in the area of disease involves 1) gaining knowledge from other disciplines; 2) working in collaboration and referencing with these disciplines; 3) integrating new variables in behaviour analyses; and 4) applying new methodology while maintaining the basic tenets of a functional analysis (Russo and Budd, 1987).

This approach to the application of behavioural science to problems found in medical practice and disease management has led to the development of a significant literature documenting the efficacy and value of behavioural input to medicine. To gain a more current perspective on behaviourists' work in pediatrics, four journals (*Behavior Therapy, Behavioral Assessment, Behavior Modification*, and *Journal of Applied Behavior Analysis*) were reviewed to determine the scope of paediatric-related research in publications known to be behavioural-oriented. Again, citations were collected from PsycLIT CD-ROM from 1990 to November 1994 (SilverPlatter 3.11; American Psychological Association, 1994). In order to identify articles that were child-focused, the title of each journal and the term *child** were used as keywords for the search - the keyword *child** purportedly identifies all words in which the main word *child* is present (i.e., *child, child*'s, *child*ren, *child*ren's, and *child*hood).

The articles identified in the last five years indicate that behavioural work continues to be successfully conducted with a wide range of paediatric problems. For example, a significant amount of behavioural-focused research was found in such areas as feeding disorders (Greer, Dorow, Williams, and McCorkle, 1991; Hoch, Babbitt, Coe, and Krell, 1994; Johnson, and Babbitt, 1993); responses to invasive/stressful/painful medical procedures (Blount, Bachanas, Powers, and Cotter, 1992; Blount, Sturges, and Powers, 1990; Derrickson, Neef, and Cataldo, 1993); children at-risk (Ammerman, 1990; Burke, 1991; Dew, Penkower, and Bromet, 1991); physical/sexual abuse (Cone, 1991; Fantuzzo, 1990; Harbeck, Peterson, and Starr, 1992); and personal safety (Kolko, Watson, and Faust, 1991; Lavelle, Hovell, West, and Wahlgren, 1992; Lehman and Geller, 1990).

In contrast, fewer articles were identified with respect to the following areas: adherence to treatment protocol (Ross, Friman, and Christophersen, 1993); injury (Peterson and Schick, 1993); cytomegalovirus (Finney, Miller, and Adler, 1993); cystic fibrosis (Stark, Knapp, Bowen, and Powers, 1993); cancer (Blount, Powers, Cotter, and Swan, 1994; Lombard, Neubauer, Canfield, and Winett, 1991); sleep disorders (Durand and Mindell, 1990; France, and Hudson, 1990); stuttering (Gagnon, and Ladoucuer, 1992; Wagaman, Miltenberger, and Arndorfer, 1993); recurrent abdominal pain (Edwards, Finney, and Bonner, 1991); high-risk behavior (Church, Forehand, Brown, and Holmes, 1990); tourette syndrome (Azrin and Peterson, 1990); obesity (de Luca and Holborn, 1992); and colic (Sosland, and Christophersen, 1991). Interestingly, even research in the area of elimination disorders - an area in which behaviourists had much early success - was found to be in small numbers in this sample (enuresis - Hagopian, Fisher, Piazza, and Wierzbicki, 1993; Houts, 1991; and encopresis - Boon and Singh, 1991).

The above results, however, are not completely representative of the accomplishments of behaviourists who indeed work and publish in the application of behavioural principles to pediatrics. For example, a significant number of them have published in journals that are appropriate to the medical subject matter although not necessarily behavioural (e.g., *Pediatrics* and *Journal of Developmental and Behavioral Pediatrics*). However, taken together, this literature suggests the wide applicability of behavioural procedures to medical practice and that as new problems arise in the health care arena, assessment of the utility of behavioural approaches should be a first thought.

Brain Injury: A New Morbidity

Taken together, extracranial and brain injury accounted for 10% of the citations that were analyzed from the *Journal of Paediatric Psychology* mentioned above, making this one of the most prevalent conditions found, just behind HIV infection/AIDS. This finding is consistent with the fact that injury, in general, is the leading cause of disability among children between birth and age 19 years (Savage, 1993). In regard to traumatic brain injury (TBI), over one million children in the United States are injured annually, with 165,000 of them requiring hospitalization. Sixteen to twenty-thousand of those children experience severe, life-long sequelae as a result of their injury.

Since 1985, the National Paediatric Trauma Registry (NPTR; 1993) has gathered data on the causes, circumstances, and consequences of children's injuries in the United States. By Spring 1993, the records of 28,692 children who were admitted to 61 children's hospitals or trauma centres were summarized. Although the children typically had multiple injuries that resulted in several diagnoses, TBI was the most frequent diagnosis (28%), followed by fractures to the bones of extremities and torso; and open wounds. TBI was also three times more likely to result in four or more functional limitations (i.e., vision, hearing, speech, self-feeding, bathing, dressing, walking, cognition, and behavior).

Causes of TBI in children include such events as motor vehicle collisions, falls, hit as pedestrian, near drowning, other trauma, gunshot wounds, and physical abuse. In regard to classification, TBI is differentiated according to whether the injury is penetrating (i.e., a foreign object enters the brain) or closed (i.e., blunt trauma is caused by mechanical force relayed to the brain). In all, TBI contributes significantly to the neurologically-based etiologies of disease and illness in children. Advances in medical trauma care have greatly reduced mortality, producing a generation of 'survivors' of brain injury with severe cognitive, behavioural, and physical deficits. A brief review below should help to elucidate some of these issues.

A diverse, growing, and fairly sophisticated literature identifies the complex nature of the impairment, disability, and handicap associated with brain injury and begins to document longitudinal courses of recovery (e.g., Bach-y-Rita, 1989; Bagnato and Feldman, 1989; Bigler, 1990; Dalby and Obrzut, 1991; Ewing-Cobbs, Fletcher and Levin, 1986; Ewing-Cobbs and Miner, 1989; Kreutzer and Wehman, 1990; Lehr, 1990; Perrott, Taylor, and Montes, 1991; Shaffer, Bijur, Chadwick and Rutter, 1980; Ylvisaker, 1985). Among the themes of this work are a number of controversies as well as some consensus. For example, the nature of injury severity and, in particular, the extent to which "mild" injury should be considered a major or priority concern are yet to be resolved.

Recovery and secondary problems are influenced by a host of factors (Fletcher and Levin, 1988). Injury severity is the one factor that best predicts the extent of recovery; however, factors such as post-traumatic amnesia, longer periods of coma, brainstem abnormalities, seizures, and higher levels of intracranial pressure are associated with poorer outcomes (Jaffe, Fay, Polissar, Martin, Shurtleff, Rivara, and Winn, 1993; Rivara, Jaffe, Fay, Polissar, Martin, Shurtleff, and Liao, 1993). Severity of TBI does not always predict residual impairment whether the initial trauma is a severe (Lieh-Lai, Theodorou, Sarnaik, Meert, Moylan, and Canady, 1992) or a mild injury (Beers, 1992). Generally, lower intelligence scores are obtained with children following TBI. However, the use of standardized tests can be misleading, suggesting that more fine grained tests should be used (Goldstein and Levin, 1985; Jaffe et al., 1992, 1993).

Physical and cognitive deficits are frequent long term outcomes. Problems in fine motor skills (Chaplin, Deitz, and Jaffe, 1993); hearing (Cockrell and Gregory, 1992), sensorimotor functioning (Haley, Baryza, Lewin, and Cioffi, 1991); problem solving skills (Goldstein and Levin, 1985); memory (Donders, 1993); impaired adaptive functioning (Asarnow, Satz, Light, Lewis, and Neumann, 1991; Fletcher, Ewing-Cobbs, Miner, and Levin, 1990); and attention (Kaufmann, Fletcher, Levin, and Miner, 1993; Timmermans and Christensen, 1991) are common. Language processing deficits (e.g., word retrieval, verbal organization, comprehension, and verbal learning) are also likely (Ylvisaker, 1986), especially in social contexts (Ylvisaker, 1993). School reentry and educational achievement are often made difficult by TBI (Boyer and Edwards, 1991). Successful school performance is hampered as well by post traumatic behavioural disorders (Michaud, Rivara, Jaffe, Fay, and Dailey, 1993).

Severe brain injury is associated with a marked increase in the rate of behaviour disorder (Brown, Chadwick, Shaffer, Rutter, and Traub, 1981) as compared to mild brain injury, with behavioural adjustment often worsened by preinjury disturbance and changes in the family as a consequence of the injury (Barry, and Clark, 1992; Hartman, 1987; Waaland and Kreutzer, 1988). Behavioural problems which frequently accompany TBI, whether mild or severe, include aggression, poor anger control, hyperactivity, and social skills (Asarnow et al., 1991). The nature of behavioural deficit may be significantly determined by the location of the injury as well (Sollee and Kindlon, 1987).

Although hypotheses exist that children's recovery after brain injury is superior to that of adults, such as greater plasticity of the brain during childhood (Rosner, 1974), children may actually be more vulnerable to the effects of brain injury as compared to adults (Isaacson, 1975). Because brain injury causes not only new deficits but affects the performance and learning of new skills as well, injury to a child hampers development and makes more difficult the learning of complete skill repertoires. Professional perceptions of the impact of brain injury on children may be inaccurate (Hart and Faust, 1988) and lead to incorrect treatment or in not providing treatment at all. However, other factors (e.g., injury severity as mentioned above) appear to be more predictive of future functioning. Poor premorbid factors such as substance abuse, psychiatric history, and dysfunctional families (Rivara et al., 1993) is also likely to cause greater greater post traumatic behaviour disorders.

We face a crisis in paediatric care for these children with traumatic injuries. As the above literature review suggests, even those children with more minor TBI may experience secondary problems in learning, memory, attention, or mood that will require the continued provision of educational and medical services. Traditional models of clinical service delivery, provided in hospital and ward settings, do much to promote physical recovery. However, for many children and families, these strong gains made during recovery in hospital and acute rehabilitation may be attenuated or even lost in the return to the community, home, and school. Programs are needed to develop the skills, behaviours, and adaptations that children and their families require to cope with chronic physical or psychological handicap. Developing new environments and technologies of care designed to extend our current paediatric rehabilitation continuum and maintain adaptive behavior in a real world context holds significant promise to reduce morbidity, improve outcome, and simultaneously reduce the costs of providing health care services.

Behavioural Approaches to TBI. Given that impairment remains, at least at some minimal level, following TBI, one heuristic approach to guide possible assessment and treatment of children with TBI can be extrapolated from the concepts of chronicity and normality with respect to chronic disease, as initially outlined by Russo (1986). Specifically, TBI can be conceptualized as a chronic *condition*, which emphasizes the long-term impact of TBI on children's functioning. Consequently, intervention efforts need to be focused on long-term psychosocial functioning, in addition to short-term medical rehabilitation. In addition, the child with the brain injury may be perceived as *different* by those in his environment. Such perceptions can be influenced by the physical side effects of treatment (e.g., pharmacotherapy for seizures), altered social histories, and cognitive or neurobehavioural sequelae or physical limitations of the original trauma. From a behavioural-analytic perspective, the presence of TBI together with long-term intervention efforts become potent setting events for learning - both adaptive and maladaptive. Thus, the behavior of children with TBI may be viewed within a learning framework as a *normal* outcome of the process of chronicity. In other words, "chronicity teaches" (Russo, 1986; p. 529).

Under the assumptions of chronicity and normality, interventions geared toward children with TBI requires alterations of behaviour and the environment within the context of care. Given the potential impact of TBI on children's functioning, care may include such services as therapy (physical, occupational, speech), psychological counselling, special education/vocational programming, and medical services (e.g., doctor's visits). The mission of professionals who work with a child with TBI should thus be seen as the prevention of secondary psychopathology arising out of TBI as a chronic condition, the environment, and the reactions of individuals to the child. Such efforts can be better effected when further knowledge is ascertained on the impact of TBI on learning, behaviour, and development.

As previously mentioned, TBI in children occurs in the context of incomplete behavioural repertoires and impacts on the natural course of development. Thus, the developmental level of a child with TBI, as with any other condition, is perhaps her/his most fundamental characteristic, which implies that developmental considerations need to be taken into account in terms of both habilitation and rehabilitation of the child. If an absence of clear developmental data exists, appropriate decision-making with respect to assessment and interventions becomes hampered, which underscores the need for other sources. One possible source is increased integration between the areas of child development and child health, especially in terms of the interaction between the two. Although some have argued against the exclusive use of any one developmental conceptual framework (e.g., Ferrari, 1990), a developmental theory such as that of Bijou and Baer (1978) is much more likely to be espoused by behaviourists, who are well-known, perhaps overly so, to be more comfortable with concepts that are in concert with their philosophy of science. Use of such a theory could potentially guide developmental research, such as identifying the variables that influence the development of health/illness behaviours, that in turn could lead to practical applications of novel behavioural technologies to children with TBI and consequently could result in more effective and useful research on prevention and treatment.

Educational Services for Children with Brain Injury. Annually in the United States, 1 out of every 500 school children is hospitalized with a brain injury. The vast majority of these will eventually return to school (Krauss, Fife, and Conroy, 1987). Health, education, and rehabilitation professionals, as well as parents, need condition-appropriate information, curricula, and systems for addressing the educational, social, and family needs of these children, and access to appropriate concessions, accommodations, and modifications (National Head Injury Foundation Task Force, 1989; Tyler and Mira, 1993).

Reentry into the school setting has been recognized as a critical phase in recovery for children with TBI (e.g., Carney and Gerring, 1990) with assessment, especially functionally-based assessment (Haley, Hallenborg, and Gans, 1989); research-based educational programming (Ewing-Cobbs et al., 1986); and behaviour management strategies acknowledged as important factors (Cohen, 1986). The use of behavioral change strategies with children with brain injury is not new (e.g., see Deaton, 1987) and its extension to teaching academic skills (e.g., direct instruction techniques) has been shown as promising (Glang, Singer, Cooley, and Tish, 1992). Few present day educational systems have the training, funds, or a comprehensive plan necessary to meet the needs of children with TBI (Cooley and Singer, 1991). However, efforts to at least educate professionals regarding school-related issues are increasing (e.g., Blosser and DePompei, 1991).

Many of these children are at present maintained in public and private schools with little awareness on the part of educators or psychologists of the nature of their injuries or the limitations that they produce. An ever growing number, however, enters the social milieu each year in need of specialized and intensive educational and family support services. Indeed, many children with brain injuries are labelled with existing, but inappropriate, diagnoses such as LD, ADDH, EH, or even TMR. This mislabelling leads to placement in available treatment and education environments without any specific programming for their unique and dynamic disabilities: a course which seldom allows for the provision of appropriate services and often leads to poor or detrimental outcomes (Blosser and Depompei, 1991; Cohen, 1986; DePompei and Blosser, 1987; Lehr, 1990). These children are in desperate need of an approach to treatment that features an integration of the most progressive medical and psychoeducational services, enabling practitioners to not only assess, diagnose, and treat these children, but to monitor the generalization and long-term maintenance of the effects of such interventions.

Recent revision of the U.S. Federal right-of-education statutes (P.L. 101-456) to categorically include children with TBI requires the development of programs and curricula to meet the needs of these children within the education system. The revised law clearly states that children and youth with traumatic brain injuries have a right to "appropriate public education which emphasizes special education and related services designed to meet their unique needs." Unfortunately, public schools will be faced with a formidable challenge to train personnel and to design curricula when very little information is currently available to guide them. Similar laws are unlikely to be enacted internationally and the availability of brain injury programs are scarce.

Despite staggering statistics on the number of children affected each year, instructional materials relevant to the community integration and education of young children with congenital and acquired neurological disorders is sparse. Furthermore, current models of service delivery often fail to offer specific strategies for successfully transitioning children from hospitals and acute rehabilitation centres to home and public school placements. As a result, far too often parents and teachers are unable to cope with the significant physical and psychological handicaps of a child with a neurological disorder.

Behavioural practitioners can provide significant input to all aspects of the rehabilitation process both acute and post acute. As with paediatric medicine, this new area of need

Table 2. Paediatric disorders or problems identified in the last 100 citations of the *Journal of Clinical Child Psychology* referenced in PsycLIT CD-ROM (December 1991 to February 1994)

Inattention/hyperactivity/impulsivity (11)*	Developmental disorders (5)
Sexual abuse (3)	Sickle-cell disease (2)
Primary care (2)	Spina bifida
Brain injury (3 total):	Daily injury events
tumor	Effects of perinatal complications
hydrocephalus	Failure to thrive
Haemophilus influenzae Type b meningitis	Rheumatic disease
Premature and ill full-term infants	Pain
Diabetes	Lymphocytic leukemia
Substance use	Personal safety

* Total number of citations are found in parentheses

will require careful attention to the methodologies of behaviour as well as the conditions of the injury itself to develop adequate clinical programs.

Next Steps in Pediatrics

Table 2 shows the results of an analysis of the last 100 references of the *Journal of Clinical Child Psychology* cited in PsycLIT CD-ROM (SilverPlatter 3.11; American Psychological Association, 1994) dated January 1987 to June 1994. This journal was examined to sample the range of paediatric disorders or problems that are currently being addressed by clinical child psychologists. Results indicate that 37% of the articles concerned paediatric-related work. Although this finding is a significant percentage of the types of disorders or problems found in the psychological literature, this proportion pales in comparison to the fact that psychiatric conditions comprise only about 10% of the general population. In other words, almost two-thirds of the work found in this restricted sample was dedicated toward a very small minority of individuals. Thus, behavioural child psychologists, in general, appear to place a relative de-emphasis on medical and typical behavioural and developmental problems seen in children whose conditions are primarily nonpsychiatric.

Fortunately, in the area of behavioural pediatrics, the trends have been toward prevention, the development of well-child care interventions, health risk reduction, and assessment and treatment of illness and health-related behaviour (Gross and Drabman, 1990). As an example, Finney and Weist (1992) reviewed behavioural assessment of children and adolescents in the context of primary care visits and argued that better identification of children's behavioural and developmental problems would result in such settings with the aide of behaviour assessment methodologies, which could potentially lead to an improved health care system that is responsive to all aspects of children's health. In addition, psychosocial/behavioural approaches that take environmental considerations into account have been seen in such areas as somatic disorders (e.g., obesity and nocturnal enuresis; Larsson, 1992); children at-risk (Aylward, 1992); pain (Walker, Garber, and Greene, 1993; Zeltzer, Barr, McGrath, and Schechter, 1992); rheumatic disease (Miller, 1993); asthma (Creer, Stein, Rappaport, and Lewis, 1992; Evans and Mellins, 1991); cancer (Chang, 1991); and injury (Grossman and Rivara, 1992; Irwin, Cataldo, Matheny, and Peterson, 1992).

With respect to child health behavior, Horowitz and O'Brien (1986) predicted that mechanisms need to be placed such that programmatic and systematic research essential to advancing our knowledge base in a significant manner (e.g., longitudinal studies) can be supported. One possible outcome that the authors proposed is the development of core research teams that work together over a period of years in laboratory or field setting groups. Behaviourists in such a setting may demonstrate to medical professionals their competence and knowledge about their technology and how they, as empiricists, can provide additional expertise in the area of pediatrics (Allen, Barone, and Kuhn, 1993). One such set of research teams can be found at the *Research and Training Center in Rehabilitation and Childhood Trauma*, which focuses on the rehabilitation of children who have been injured. The teams include medical professionals (e.g., paediatric physiatrists and nurses), a biostatistician, social worker, education specialist, consumer, pre- and post-doctoral fellows (both medical and nonmedical), various research assistants and associates, and *behavioural scientists*. The teams at the Center are an exemplary example of how future collaborative activities can be fostered by training behaviourists early in their careers in effecting collaboration (Davidson, 1988; Drotar, 1993).

The goals of the Center are three-fold: 1) conduct research to increase knowledge about the causes, treatment, and outcomes of injuries among children; 2) improve the delivery of services to enhance the physical, developmental, psychological, social, educational, and vocational competence of children and families; and 3) disseminate information to families, their children, and multidisciplinary professionals working in hospitals, schools, vocational programs, and other community settings. In addition, the research and training activities of the Center are based on a partnership among children who have been injured, their families or guardians, and various providers. The research projects at the Center have been designed in direct response to the identification by parents and professionals of major gaps in knowledge and services for the rehabilitation of children who have been injured (e.g., Lash, Russo, Navalta, and Baryza, 1994). In all, the Center strives to insure that the goals, instruments, measures, and outcomes are relevant and responsive to the changing needs of recovering children and their families.

This focus on families, in addition to the child, appears to be a major factor in the current literature. For example, additional analysis of the *Journal of Paediatric Psychology* indicates that 41% of the articles surveyed included family-related variables. An emphasis on these variables is important given recent findings concerning families indicating that the adjustment of children is dependent on the type of illness and who is reporting (i.e., child, mother, or teacher; Perrin, Ayoub, and Willett, 1993) and that families with children who are at risk have great difficulty in securing mental health services (Tarnowski, 1991). Furthermore, given that children's adherence to medical treatment protocols continues to be problematic, the impact of the family needs to be addressed. Indeed, behavioural approaches to address such family issues have been documented (e.g., behavioural systems perspective; Wahler and Hann, 1986).

Behaviourists have a great opportunity to make a profound impact in the area of pediatrics and medical care in general. For example, one of the current challenges in pediatrics is to develop evaluation models that adequately represent complex clinical concerns and that translate the empirical rigor of the behavioural approach into clinical practice in a cost-efficient manner (Mash and Terdal, 1990). The achievement of success in pediatrics may result in the promotion of behaviour analysis within medicine in general (Allen et al., 1993). As we have seen, such integration into new areas requires careful attention to the nature of new problems and the thoughtful application of behavioural approaches with an eye toward inherent limitations of the approach and conditions imposed upon behaviour change by the problems under study. Brain injury represents one of the newest areas of endeavour, born out of the increasingly capable science of emergency medical care. The promise of behavioural applications must be met by empirical study and the development of clinical methodologies for care during the acute and postacute phases of this now most common disorder.

NEW APPLICATIONS ARE THE FUTURE

It would be remiss to congratulate ourselves for our successes thus far. Indeed, new disorders, disabilities, and ills beg for intelligent behavioural solution. As behavioural scientists and practitioners, we should constantly seek to employ the same zealous curiosity that led to the founding of our field. As we have seen in applications to medicine, the utility of the behavioural paradigm is vast. However, as a field, we have often been slow to identify new opportunities. Understanding the epidemiology and demographics of human needs in the health care and social arenas allows us to look forward and identify new areas which would likely benefit from behavioural study. We would therefore like to close this chapter with a preview of some of the areas that we feel are particularly promising for behavioural study and treatment.

New Medical Issues for Behaviour Analysis

While behavioural approaches have made profound impact on medical practice and the health of children, new diseases and threats to the public health are constantly emerging.

Fetal Exposure to Toxic Substances. A need exists to develop, evaluate, and disseminate a comprehensive, behavioural-based program to assist physicians, human service agencies, parents, and schools in providing for the medical, educational, and social habilitation/rehabilitation of young children with neurobehavioural disorders resulting from in utero or early exposure to alcohol and drugs. To date, these populations have been severely undeserved. The need for such methods is urgent. For example, approximately 375,000 children are born annually in the United States to mothers actively engaged in drug abuse during their pregnancy with estimates that between 1.4 and 16% of live births are positive for maternal cocaine use, with the greatest incidence seen in inner-city or teaching hospitals (Matera, Warren, Moomjy, Fink, and Fox, 1990; McCalla, Minkoff, Feldman, Delke, Salwin, Valencia, and Glass, 1991; Streissguth, Grant, Barr, Brown, Martin, Mayock, Ramey, and Moore, 1991; VanDyke and Fox, 1990). A number of studies have also reported significant physical and cognitive dysfunction secondary to cocaine exposure including developmental delay and congenital cerebral anomalies (Dominguez, Villa-Coro, Slopis, and Bohan, 1991), necrotizing, enterocolitis (Czyrko, Del Pin, O'Neill, Peckham, and Ross 1991), intrauterine growth retardation (Chasnoff 1991; Tabor, Smith-Wallace, and Yonekura, 1990) and, postnatally, significant neurological symptoms (Smart 1991) or death (Michandani, Michandani, Helman, English-Rider, Rosen, and Laposata, 1991) in infants resulting simply from the passive exposure to crack cocaine smoke.

While little is yet known about the development course of these children or their educational or learning capabilities, studies do suggest that drug exposed children may experience problems with language development (vanBaar, 1990) and that alcohol exposed children may face lower IQ and learning and behavior problems in the early school years (Streissguth, Barr, and Sampson, 1990). Encouragingly, Johnson, Glassman, Fiks, and Rosen (1990) report that with proper placement in enriched social and academic environments, some children born to methadone mothers appear to be resilient and show improved development as compared to controls.

With respect to Fetal Alcohol Syndrome (FAS) and Alcohol Related Birth Defects (ARBD), the US numbers are similarly staggering with FAS and ARBD outranking Down's Syndrome and spina bifida as the leading known cause of mental retardation (Warren and Bast, 1988). Incidence estimates of FAS and ARBD are 1 per 300 births, with seven to tenfold increases in mortality and an eightfold increase in significant associated problems such as low birth weight, preterm delivery, and small for gestational age (Olegrard, Sabel, Aronsson, Sandin, Johanssen, Carlsson, Kyllerman, Iversen, and Hrbek, 1979). Fetal exposure to alcohol may result as well in severe disorders such as facial, joint, limb, and cardiac anomalies (Abel, 1984), psychomotor retardation (Autti-Ramo and Granstrom, 1991), or low birth weight (Burkett, Yasin, and Palow, 1990).

As a result of advances in neonatology, these children are able to be kept alive despite enormous physical damage. Children with severe neurological deficit due to birth defects of known etiology (fetal alcohol syndrome, crack cocaine, or other maternal substance abuse, etc.) may face a lifetime of medical care and present significant special needs with respect to education and living. The treatment of these children, from a biopsychosocial perspective, is underdeveloped, invalidated, and generally is unavailable to many who need services. No current model of clinical service delivery exists for these children that provides the necessary medical/psychosocial coordination or the training technology to develop the skills, behaviours, and adaptations that these children and their families need to cope with the chronic physical or psychological handicaps that result.

Community Based Service Provision. As health service models move from the traditional hospital environments of care to more community-based, point-of-need services, behavioural procedures are necessary to 'push-down' the implementation of procedures from traditional, expensive, disciplinary care to paraprofessionals and family members. Problems such as ventilator care (Parrish, 1994), home infusion, and community based convalescence will require extension of traditional models for teaching parents and others to provide services to developmentally disabled populations in the community in areas where behaviourism has had past successes, such as integration into typical school and community settings with nondisabled peers (Anderson, Avery, DiPietro, Edwards, and Christian, 1987; Koegel, Russo, and Rincover, 1977); systematic programming for generalization and maintenance of educational and treatment gains (Christian, Hannah, and Glahn, 1984; Luce, Anderson, Thibadeau, and Lipsker, 1984; Luce and Christian, 1981); systematic planning for the transition of children into less restrictive, community-based placements (Anderson, Christian, and Luce, 1986; Christian et al., 1984; Luce et al., 1984) and intensive home-based training and support with parents as active participants (Anderson, 1989; Anderson et al., 1987).

Consumer Empowerment. An increasing trend is being seen toward the making the consumer of health care services central to the process of both service delivery and health care research (Klein, 1992). New models are being evolved for the conduct of research in areas such as mental health (Rapp, Shera, Kisthart, 1993) that emphasize consumer involvement in all phases of the research process. Labelled Consumer-Oriented Research and Dissemination (CORD) (Barlow, Hayes and Nelson, 1984; Fenton, Batavia, and Roody, 1993) or Participatory Action Research (PAR) (Graves, 1991; Whyte, 1991), these approach promise unparalleled consumer input to the process of science. Behaviour analysts have developed excellent methodologies for sampling consumer need and satisfaction (Barrish, Saunders, and Wolf, 1969; Minkin, Braukmann, Minkin, Timbers, Timbers, Fixsen, Phillips, and Wolf, 1976). Expansion of our methodology to encompass broader areas of the health care sector is appropriate and timely.

SOCIAL ISSUES

We would be remiss in limiting our examination of future opportunities to the health care area alone. Behaviour analysis has significant opportunity to impact the broad population in a variety of social issues as well. For example, in all parts of the world, many families live in poverty, which is a growing problem. In the US, approximately 25% of families with children under 3 live in poverty of 100,000 children in the US who are homeless, nearly 1/2 are under age six. Problems of poverty and homelessness may benefit from the input of behaviourists. Studies of job development skills, parenting techniques, and other pragmatic programs used in conjunction with other, more traditional services (e.g., primary care settings; Roberts and Lyman, 1990; Tarnowski, 1991) for these populations may provide improved outcomes.

Other areas of human need including, violence prevention, physical and sexual abuse and neglect, cultural and gender issues, teenage pregnancy, and accident prevention and safety, are but a few of the issues likely to continue to derive benefit from the broad range of behavioural approaches.

Taken together, these new areas represent suggestions for the further development of our science and new directions for behaviour analysis. We must not neglect, as well, the fact that many interventions in these areas will be derived from the continuum of behavioural and cognitive therapies. While our methods should run the range from discrimination, to desensitization, to thought-stopping, we must not forget that the basis of our success has been our insistence on the primacy of the scientific method in evaluating experimental and clinical outcomes. That behavioural approaches will continue as a central vehicle in meeting the needs of our population is clear.

REFERENCES

Abel, G.L. (1984). Prenatal effects of alcohol. *Drug and Alcohol Dependence, 14*, 1-10.

Allen, K.D., Barone, V.J. and Kuhn, B.R. (1993). A behavioral prescription for promoting applied behavior analysis within pediatrics. *Journal of Applied Behavior Analysis, 26*, 493-502.

Ammerman, R.T. (1990). Etiological models of child maltreatment: A behavioral perspective. *Behavior Modification, 14*, 230-254.

Anderson, S.R. (1989). Training parents of autistic children. In: B.L. Baker (Ed.), *Parent training and developmental disabilities. Monograph of the American Association on Mental Deficiency, No. 13.*

Anderson, S.R., Avery D.L., DiPietro E.K., Edwards G.L. and Christian, W.P. (1987). Intensive home-based early intervention with autistic children. *Education and Treatment of Children, 10*, 352-366.

Anderson, S.R., Christian, W.P. and Luce, S.C. (1986). Transitional residential programming for autistic individuals. *The Behavior Therapist, 9*, 205-211.

Asarnow, R.F., Satz, P., Light, R., Lewis, R. and Neumann, E. (1991). Behavior problems and adaptive functioning in children with mild and severe closed head injury. *Journal of Paediatric Psychology, 16*, 543-555.

Autti-Ramo, I. and Granstrom, M.L. (1991). The psychomotor development during the first year of life of infants exposed to intrauterine alcohol of various duration. *Neuropediatrics, 22*, 59-64.

Aylward, G.P. (1992). The relationship between environmental risk and developmental outcome. *Journal of Developmental and Behavioral Pediatrics, 13*, 222-229.

Azrin, N.H., and Peterson, A.L. (1990). Treatment of Tourette Syndrome by habit reversal: A waiting-list control group comparison. *Behavior Therapy, 21*, 305-318.

Bach-y-Rita, P. (1989). *Traumatic Brain Injury.* New York: Demo Publications.

Baer, D.M. (1986). Advances and gaps in a behavioral methodology of paediatric medicine. In: N.A. Krasnegor, J.D. Arasteh and M.F. Cataldo (Eds.), *Child health behavior* (pp. 54-69), New York: John Wiley and Sons.

Baer, D.M., Wolf, M.M. and Risley, T.R. (1986). Some current dimensions of applied behavior analysis. *Journal of Applied Behavior Analysis, 1*, 91-97.

Bagnato, S. and Feldman, D. (1989). Closed head injury in infants and preschool children: Research and practice issues. *Infants and Young Children, 2*, 1-13.

Barlow, D.H., Hayes, S.C. and Nelson, R.O. (1984). *The scientist practitioner: Research and accountability in clinical and educational settings.* New York: Pergamon Press.

Barrish, H.H., Saunders, M. and Wolf, M.M. (1969). Good Behavior Game: Effects of individual contingencies for group consequences on disruptive behavior in a classroom, *Journal of Applied Behavior Analysis, 2*, 119-124.

Barry, P. and Clark, D. (1992). Effects of intact versus non-intact families on adolescent head injury rehabilitation. *Brain Injury, 6*, 229-232.

Beers, S.R. (1992). Cognitive effects of mild head injury in children and adolescents. *Neuropsychology Review, 3*, 281-320.

Bigler, E.D. (1990). *Traumatic brain injury: Mechanisms of damage, assessment, intervention, and outcome.* Austin, TX: Pro-Ed.

Bijou, S.W. and Baer, D.M. (1978). *Behavior analysis of child development.* Englewood Cliffs, NJ: Prentice-Hall.

Blosser, J.L. and DePompei, R. (1991). Preparing educational professionals for meeting the needs of students with traumatic brain injury. *Journal of Head Trauma Rehabilitation, 6*, 73-82.

Blount, R.L., Bachanas, P.J., Powers, S.W. and Cotter, M.C. (1992). Training children to cope and parents to coach them during routine immunizations: Effects on child, parent, and staff behaviours. *Behavior Therapy, 23*, 689-705.

Blount, R.L., Powers, S.W., Cotter, M.W. and Swan, S. (1994). Making the system work: Training paediatric oncology patients to cope and their parents to coach them during BMA/LP procedures. *Behavior Modification, 18*, 6-31.

Blount, R.L., Sturges, J.W. and Powers, S.W. (1990). Analysis of child and adult behavioral variations by phase of medical procedure. *Behavior Therapy, 21*, 33-48.

Boon, F.F. and Singh, N.N. (1991). A model for the treatment of encopresis. *Behavior Modification, 15*, 355-371.

Boyer, M.G. and Edwards, P. (1991). Outcome 1 to 3 years after severe traumatic brain injury in children and adolescents. *Injury, 22*, 315-320.

Brady, J.V. (1986). A behavioral perspective on child health. In: N.A. Krasnegor, J. D. Arasteh and M.F. Cataldo (Eds.), *Child health behavior* (pp. 31-53), New York: John Wiley and Sons.

Brown, G., Chadwick, O., Shaffer, D., Rutter, M. and Traub, M. (1981). A prospective study of children with head injuries: III. Psychiatric sequelae. *Psychological Medicine, 11*, 63-78.

Burke, P. (1991). Depression in paediatric illness. *Behavior Modification, 15*, 486-500.

Burkett, G., Yasin, S. and Palow, D. (1990). Perinatal implications of cocaine exposure. *Journal of Reproductive Medicine, 35*, 35-42.

Carney, J. and Gerring, J. (1990). Return to school following severe closed head injury: A critical phase in paediatric rehabilitation. *Paediatrician, 17*, 222-229.

Cataldo, M.F. (1986). Research strategies and future directions in behavioral pediatrics. In: N.A. Krasnegor, J.D. Arasteh and M.F. Cataldo (Eds.), *Child health behavior* (pp. 559-574). New York: John Wiley and Sons.

Cataldo, M.F., Finney, J.W., Madden, N.A. and Russo, D.C. (1982). Behavioral approaches to lead ingestion. In: J.J. Chisolm and D. O'Hara (Eds.), *Lead absorption in children: Management, clinical, and environmental aspects* (103-112). Baltimore: Urban and Schwartzenburg.

Cataldo, M.F., Russo, D.C. and Freeman, J.M. (1980). Behavior modification of a 4 1/2 year old child with myoclonic and grand mal seizures. *Journal of Autism and Developmental Disorders, 9*, 413-427.

Chang, P.N. (1991). Psychosocial needs of long-term childhood cancer survivors: A review of literature. *Paediatrician, 18*, 20-24.

Chaplin, D., Deitz, J. and Jaffe, K.M. (1993). Motor performance in children after traumatic brain injury. *Archives of Physical Medicine and Rehabilitation, 74*, 161-164.

Chasnoff, I.J. (1991). Cocaine and pregnancy: Clinical and methodologic issues. Clinical *Perinatology, 18*, 113-123.

Christian, W.P., Hannah, G.T. and Glahn, T.J. (1984). *Programming effective human services: Strategies for institutional change and client transition*. New York: Plenum Press.

Church, P., Forehand, R., Brown, C. and Holmes, T. (1990). Prevention of drug abuse: Examination of the effectiveness of a program with elementary school children. *Behavior Therapy, 21*, 339-347.

Cockrell, J.L. and Gregory, S. A. (1992). Audiological deficits in brain-injured children and adolescents. *Brain Injury, 6*, 261-266.

Cohen, S.B. (1986). Educational reintegration and programming for children with head injuries. *Journal of Head Trauma Rehabilitation, 1*, 22-29.

Cone, J.D. (1991). Child sexual abuse assessment: Contributions from behavioral assessment. *Behavioral Assessment, 13*, 241-243.

Cooley, E. and Singer, G. (1991). On serving students with head injuries: Are we reinventing a wheel that doesn't roll? *Journal of Head Trauma Rehabilitation, 6*, 47-55.

Craighead, W.E. (1990). There's a place for us: All of us. *Behavior Therapy, 21*, 3-23.

Creer, T.L., Stein, R.E., Rappaport, L. and Lewis, C. (1992). Behavioral consequences of illness: Childhood asthma as a model. *Pediatrics, 90*, 808-815.

Czyrko, C., Del Pin, C.A., O'Neill, A.A. Jr., Peckham, G.J. and Ross, A.J. 3rd, (1991). Maternal cocaine abuse and necrotizing enterocolitis: Outcome and survival. *Journal of Paediatric Surgery, 26*, 414-418.

Dalby, P.R. and Obrzut, J.E. (1991). Epidemiologic characteristics and sequelae of closed head injured children and adolescents. *Developmental Neuropsychology, 7*, 35-68.

Davidson, C.V. (1988). Training the paediatric psychologist and the developmental-behavioral paediatrician. In: D.K. Routh (Ed.), *Handbook of paediatric psychology* (pp. 507-537). New York: Guilford Press.

Deaton, A.V. (1987). Behavioral change strategies for children and adolescents with severe brain injury. *Journal of Learning Disabilities, 20*, 581-589.

De Luca, R.V., and Holborn, S.W. (1992). Effects of a variable-ratio reinforcement schedule with changing criteria on exercise in obese and nonobese boys. *Journal of Applied Behavior Analysis, 25*, 671-679.

DePompei, R. and Blosser, J. L. (1987). Strategies for helping head-injured children successfully return to school. *Language, Speech, and Hearing Services in Schools, 18*, 292-300.

Derrickson, J.G., Neef, N.A. and Parrish, J.M. (1991). Teaching self-administration of sanctioning to children with tracheostomies. *Journal of Applied Behavior Analysis, 24*, 563-570.

Dew, M.A., Penkower, L. and Bromet, E.J. (1991). Effects of unemployment on mental health in the contemporary family. *Behavior Modification, 15*, 501-544.

Dominguez, R., Villa-Coro, A.A., Slopis, J.M. and Bohan, T.P. (1991). Brain and ocular abnormalities in infants with in utero exposure to cocaine and other street drugs. *American Journal of Diseases in Children, 145*, 688-695.

Donders, J. (1993). Memory functioning after traumatic brain injury in children. Brain *Injury, 7*, 431-437.

Drotar, D. (1993). Influences on collaborative activities among psychologists and paediatricians: Implications for practice, training, and research. *Journal of Paediatric Psychology, 18*, 159-172.

Durand, V.M. and Mindell, J.A. (1990). Behavioral treatment of multiple childhood sleep disorders: Effects on child and family. *Behavior Modification, 14*, 37-49.

Edwards, M.C., Finney, J.W. and Bonner, M. (1991). Matching treatment with recurrent abdominal pain symptoms: An evaluation of dietary fiber and relaxation treatments. *Behavior Therapy , 22*, 257-267.

Engel, G.L. (1977). The care of the patient: Art or science? *The Johns Hopkins Medical Journal, 140*, 222-232.

Evans, D. and Mellins, R.B. (1991). Educational programs for children with asthma. *Paediatrician, 18*, 317-323.

Ewing-Cobbs, L., Fletcher, J.M. and Levin, H.S. (1986). Neurobehavioral sequelae following head injury in children: Educational implications. *Journal of Head Trauma Rehabilitation, 1*, 57-65.

Ewing-Cobbs, L. and Miner M. E. (1989). Intellectual, motor, and language sequelae following closed head injury in infants and preschoolers. *Journal of Paediatric Psychology, 14*, 531-547.

Fantuzzo, J.W. (1990). Behavioral treatment of the victims of child abuse and neglect. *Behavior Modification, 14*, 316-339.

Fenton, J., Batavia, A. and Roody, D. (1993, November). Constituency-oriented research and dissemination (CORD): Proposed policy statement for the National Institute on Disability and Rehabilitation Research.

Ferrari, M. (1990). Developmental issues in behavioral pediatrics. In: A.M. Gross and R.S. Drabman (Eds.), *Handbook of clinical behavioral pediatrics*. New York: Plenum Press.

Finney, J.W., Miller, K.M. and Adler, S.P. ((1993). Changing protective and risky behaviours to prevent child-to-parent transmission of cytomegalovirus. *Journal of Applied Behavior Analysis, 26*, 471-472.

Finney, J.W. and Weist, M.D. (1992). Behavioral assessment of children and adolescents. *Paediatric Clinics of North America, 39*, 369-378.

Fletcher, J.M., Ewing-Cobbs, L., Miner, M.E. and Levin, H.S. (1990). Behavioral changes after closed head injury in children. *Journal of Consulting and Clinical Psychology, 58*(1), 93-98.

Fletcher, J.M. and Levin, H.S. (1988). Neurobehavioral effects of brain injury in children. In: D.K. Routh (Ed.), *Handbook of paediatric psychology* (pp. 258-296). New York: Guilford Press.

France, K.G. and Hudson, S.M. (1990). Behavior management of infant sleep disturbance. *Journal of Applied Behavior Analysis, 23*, 91-98.

Gagnon, M., Ladouceur, R. (1992). Behavioral treatment of child stutterers: Replication and extension. *Behavior Therapy, 23*, 113-129.

Glang, A., Singer, G., Cooley, E. and Tish, N. (1992). Tailoring direct instruction techniques for use with elementary students with brain injury. *Journal of Head Trauma Rehabilitation, 7*, 93-108.

Goldstein, F.C. and Levin, H.S. (1985). Intellectual and academic outcome following closed head injury in children and adolescents: Research strategies and empirical findings. *Developmental Neuropsychology, 1*, 195-214.

Graves, W.H. (1991, May). *Participatory action research: A new paradigm for disability and rehabilitation research*. Paper presented at the Annual Meeting of National Association of Rehabilitation Research and Training Centres, Washington, DC.

Greer, R.D., Dorow, L., Williams, G. and McCorckle, N. (1991). Peer-mediated procedures to induce swallowing and food acceptance in young children. *Journal of Applied Behavior Analysis, 24*, 783-790.

Gross, A.M. and Drabman, R.S. (1990). Clinical behavioral pediatrics: An introduction. In: A.M. Gross and R.S. Drabman (Eds.), *Handbook of clinical behavioral pediatrics*. New York: Plenum Press.

Grossman, D.C. and Rivara, F.P. (1992). Injury control in childhood. *Paediatric Clinics of North America, 39*, 471-485.

Hagopian, L.P., Fisher, W., Piazza, C.C. and Wierbicki, J.J. (1993). A water-prompting procedure for the treatment of urinary incontinence. *Journal of Applied Behavior Analysis, 26*, 473-474.

Haley, S.M., Baryza, M.J., Lewin, J.E. and Cioffi, M.I. (1991). Sensorimotor dysfunction in children with brain injury: Development of a data base for evaluation research. *Physical and Occupational Therapy in Pediatrics, 11*, 1-26.

Haley, S.M., Hallenborg, S.C. and Gans, B.M. (1989). Functional assessment in young children with neurological impairment. *Topics in Early Childhood Special Education, 9*, 106-126.

Harbeck, C., Peterson, L. and Starr, L. (1992). Previously abused child victims' response to a sexual abuse prevention program: A matter of measures. *Behavior Therapy, 23*, 375-387.

Hart, K.J. and Faust, D. (1988). Prediction of the effects of mild head injury: A message about the Kennard Principle. *Journal of Clinical Psychology, 44*, 780-782.

Hartman, S. (1987). Patterns of change in families following severe head injuries in children. *Australian and New Zealand Journal of Family Therapy, 8*, 125-130.

Hoch, T.A., Babbitt, R.L., Coe, D.A. and Krell, D.M. (1994). Contingency contacting: Combining positive reinforcement and escape extinction procedures to treat persistent food refusal. *Behavior Modification, 18*, 106-128.

Horowitz, F.D. and O'Brien, M. (1986). Developmental determinants and child health behavior: Research priorities. In: N.A. Krasnegor, J.D. Arasteh, and M.F. Cataldo (Eds.), *Child health behavior* (pp. 129-145), New York: John Wiley and Sons.

Houts, A.C. (1991). Nocturnal enuresis as a biobehavioral problem. *Behavior Therapy, 22*, 133-151.

Irwin, C.E. Jr., Cataldo, M.F., Matheny, A.P. Jr. and Peterson, L. Health consequences of behaviours: Injury as a model. *Pediatrics, 90*, 798-807.

Isaacson, R.L. (1975). The myth of recovery from early brain damage. In: N. Ellis (Ed.), *Aberrant development in infancy*. London: Wiley.

Jaffe, K.M., Fay, G.C., Polissar, N.L., Martin, K.M., Shurtleff, H.A., Rivara, J.B. and Winn, H.R. (1992). Severity of paediatric traumatic brain injury and early neurobehavioral outcome: A cohort study. *Archives of Physical Medicine and Rehabilitation, 73*, 540-547.

Jaffe, K.M., Fay, G.C., Polissar, N.L., Martin, K.M., Shurtleff, H.A., Rivara, J.B. and Winn, H.R. (1993). Severity of traumatic brain injury and neurobehavioral recovery at one year: A cohort study. *Archives of Physical Medicine and Rehabilitation, 74*, 587-595.

Johnson, C.R. and Babbitt, R.L. (1993). Antecedent manipulation in the treatment of primary solid food refusal. *Behavior Modification, 17*, 510-521.

Johnson, H.L., Glassman, M.B., Fiks, K.B. and Rosen, T.S. (1990). Resilient children: Individual differences in developmental outcome of children born to drug abusers. *Journal of Genetic Psychology, 151*, 523-539.

Kaufmann, P.M., Fletcher, J.M., Levin, H.S. and Miner, M. (1993). Attentional disturbance after paediatric closed head injury. *Journal of Child Neurology, 8*, 348-353.

Kazdin, A.E. (1977). *The history of behavior modification: Experimental foundations of contemporary research.* Baltimore: University Park Press.

Klein, S.D. (1992, May). *The challenge of communicating with parents.* Paper presented at "Creating family-professional partnerships: Educating physicians and other health professionals to care for children with chronic and disabling conditions", Pittsburgh, PA.

Koegel, R.L., Russo, D.C. and Rincover, A. (1977). Assessing and training teacher use of behavior modification procedures with autistic children. *Journal of Applied Behavior Analysis, 10*, 197-205.

Kolko, D.J., Watson, S. and Faust, J. (1991). Fire safety/prevention skills training to reduce involvement with fire in young psychiatric inpatients: Preliminary findings. *Behavior Therapy, 22*, 269-284.

Krauss, J.F., Fife, D. and Conroy, D. (1987). Paediatric brain injuries: The nature, clinical course, and early outcomes in a defined United States population. *Pediatrics, 79*, 501-507.

Kreutzer, J. and Wehman, P. (1990). *Community integration following traumatic brain injury.* Baltimore, MD: Paul H. Brookes Publishing Co.

Larsson, B. (1992). Behavioural treatment of somatic disorders in children and adolescents. *European Child and Adolescent Psychiatry, 1*, 68-81.

Lash, M., Russo, D.C., Navalta, C.P. and Baryza, M.J. (1994). Families of children with traumatic injuries identify needs for research and training. Neurorehabilitation. (submitted for publication).

Lavelle, J.M., Hovell, M.F., West, M.P. and Wahlgren, D.R., (1992). Promoting law enforcement for child protection: A community analysis. *Journal of Applied Behavior Analysis, 25*, 885-892.

Lehman, G.R. and Geller, E.S. (1990). Participative education for children: An effective approach to increase safety belt use. *Journal of Applied Behavior Analysis, 23*, 219-225.

Lehr, E. (1990). *Psychological management of traumatic brain injuries in children and adolescents.* Rockville: Aspen Publishers.

Lieh-Lai, M.W., Theodorou, A.A., Sarnaik, A.P., Meert, K.L., Moylan, P.M. and Canady, A.I. (1992). Limitations of the Glasgow Coma Scale in predicting outcome in children with traumatic brain injury. *Journal of Pediatrics, 120*, 195-199.

Lombard, D., Neubauer, T.E., Canfield, D. and Winett, R.A. (1991). Behavioral community intervention to reduce the risk of skin cancer. *Journal of Applied Behavior Analysis, 24*, 677-686.

Lovaas, O.I., Koegel, R.L., Simmons, J.Q. and Long, J.S. (1973). Some generalization and follow-up measures on autistic children in behavior therapy. *Journal of Applied Behavior Analysis, 6*, 131-166.

Luce, S.C., Anderson, S.R., Thibadeau, S.F. and Lipsker, L.E. (1984). Preparing the client for transition to the community. In: W.P. Christian, G.T. Hannah and T.J. Glahn (Eds.), *Programming effective human services: Strategies for institutional change and client transition.* New York: Plenum Press.

Luce, S.C. and Christian, W.P. (Eds.) (1981). *How to work with autistic and severely handicapped youth: A series of eight training manuals.* Lawrence, Kansas: H and H Enterprises.

Madden, N.A., Russo, D.C. and Cataldo, M.F. (1980). Environmental influences on mouthing in children with lead intoxication. *Journal of Paediatric Psychology, 5*, 207-216.

Mash, E.J. and Terdal, L.G. (1988). Behavioral assessment of child and family disturbance. In: E.J. Mash and L.G. Terdal (Eds.), *Behavioral assessment of childhood disorders* (2nd ed., pp. 3-65). New York: Guilford Press.

Mash, E.J. and Terdal, L.G. (1990). Assessment strategies in clinical behavioral pediatrics. In: A.M. Gross and R.S. Drabman (Eds.), *Handbook of clinical behavioral pediatrics*. New York: Plenum Press.

Matera, C., Warren, W.B., Moomjy, M., Fink, D.J. and Fox, H.E. (1990). Prevalence of use of cocaine and other substances in an obstetric population. *American Journal of Obstetrics and Gynaecology, 163*, 797-801.

McCalla, S., Minkoff, H.L., Feldman, J., Delke, I., Salwin, M., Valencia, G. and Glass, L. (1991). The biologic and social consequences of perinatal cocaine use in an inner-city population: Results of an anonymous cross-sectional study. *American Journal of Obstetrics and Gynaecology, 164*, 625-630.

Michandani, H.G., Michandani, I.H., Helman, F., English-Rider, R., Rosen,S. and Laposata, E.A. (1991). Passive inhalation of free-base cocaine (crack) smoke by infants. *Archives of Pathological Laboratory Medicine, 115*, 494-498.

Michaud, L.J., Rivara, F.P., Jaffe, K.M., Fay, G. and Dailey, J.L. (1993). Traumatic brain injury as a risk factor for behavioral disorders in children. *Archives of Physical Medicine and Rehabilitation, 74*, 368-375.

Miller, J. J. 3rd. (1993). Psychosocial factors related to rheumatic diseases in childhood. *Journal of Rheumatology Supplements, 38*, 1-11.

Minkin, N., Braukmann, C.J., Minkin, B.L., Timbers, G.D., Timbers, B.J., Fixsen, D.L., Phillips, E.L. and Wolf, M.M. (1976). The social validation and training of conversation skills. *Journal of Applied Behavior Analysis, 9*, 127-139.

National Head Injury Foundation Task Force (1989). *An educators manual: What educators need to know about students with traumatic brain injuries*. Framingham, MA: National Head Injury Foundation.

National Paediatric Trauma Registry. (1993, October). *Facts from the National Paediatric Trauma Trauma Registry - Fact sheet #1*. Boston: Research and Training Center in Rehabilitation and Childhood Trauma.

Olegrard, R., Sabel, K.C., Aronsson, M., Sandin, D., Johanssen, P.R., Carlsson, C., Kyllerman, M., Iversen, K. and Hrbek, A. (1979). Effects on the child of alcohol abuse during pregnancy. Retrospective and prospective studies. *Acta Paeditrica Scandinavia, 275*, 112-121.

Perrin, E.C., Ayoub, C.C. and Willett, J.B. (1993). In the eyes of the beholder: Family and maternal influences on perceptions of adjustment of children with chronic illness. *Journal of Developmental and Behavioral Pediatrics, 14*, 94-105.

Perrott, S.B., Taylor, H.G. and Montes, J.L. (1991). Neurological sequelae, familial stress, and environmental adaptation following paediatric head injury. *Developmental Neuropsychology, 7*, 69-86.

Peterson, L., and Schick, B. (1993). Empirically derived in jury prevention rules. *Journal of Applied Behavior Analysis, 26*, 451-460.

Pless, I.B. and Nolan, T. (1991). Revision, replication, and neglect: Research on maladjustment in chronic illness. *Journal of Child Psychology and Psychiatry, 32*, 347-365.

Rapp C.A., Shera W. and Kisthart , W. (1993). Research strategies for consumer empowerment of people with severe mental illness. *Social Work, 38*, 727-735.

Residency Review Committee for Pediatrics. (1992). Essentials of accredited residencies. In: S.L. Etzel (Ed.), *Directory of graduate medical education programs: 1992-1993* (p. 97). Chicago: American Medical Association.

Rivara, J.B., Jaffe, K.M., Fay, G.C., Polissar, N.L. Martin, K.M., Shurtleff, H.A. and Liao, S. (1993). Family functioning and injury severity as predictors of child functioning one year following traumatic brain injury. *Archives of Physical Medicine and Rehabilitation, 74*, 1047-1055.

Roberts, M.C. and Lyman, R.D. (1990). The psychologist as a paediatric consultant: Inpatient and outpatient. In: A.M. Gross and R.S. Drabman (Eds.), *Handbook of clinical behavioral pediatrics*. New York: Plenum Press.

Rosner, B.S. (1974). Recovery of function and localization of function in historical perspective. In: D.G. Stein, J.J. Rosen and N. Butters (Eds.), *Plasticity and recovery of function in the central nervous system* (pp. 1-29). New York: Academic Press.

Ross, L.V., Friman, P.C. and Christophersen, E.R. (1993). An appointment-keeping improvement package for outpatient pediatrics: Systematic replication and component analysis. *Journal of Applied Behavior Analysis, 26*, 461-467.

Russo, D.C. (1986). Chronicity and normalcy as the basis for research and treatment in chronic disease in children. In: N.A. Krasnegor, J.D. Arasteh and M.F. Cataldo (Eds.), *Child health behavior: A behavioral pediatrics perspective* (pp. 521-536). New York: John Wiley and Sons.

Russo, D.C. (1990). A requiem for the passing of the three-term contingency. *Behavior Therapy, 21*, 153-165.

Russo, D.C. (1993). The primacy of an independent behaviour therapy community in the evolution of clinical psychology. *Behaviour Change, 10*, 13-15.

Russo, D.C., Bird, B.L. and Masek, B.J. (1980). Assessment issues in behavioral medicine. *Behavioral Assessment, 2*, 1-18.

Russo, D.C. and Budd, K.S. (1987). Limitations of operant practice in the study of disease. *Behavior Modification, 11*, 264-285.

Russo, D.C. and Varni, J.W. (1982). *Behavioral Pediatrics: Research and Practice.* New York: Plenum Press.

Savage, R.C. (1993). Children with traumatic brain injury. *TBI Challenge. Summer*, 4-5.

Schwartz, G. E. and Weiss, S. M. (1978). Yale conference on behavioral medicine: A proposed definition and statement of goals. *Journal of Behavioral Medicine, 1*, 3-12.

Shaffer, D., Bijur, P., Chadwick, O.F.D. and Rutter, M. (1980). Head injury and later reading disability. *Journal of the American Academy of Child Psychiatry, 19*, 592-610.

Smart, R.B. (1991). Crack cocaine use: A review of prevalence and adverse effects. *American Journal of Drug and Alcohol Abuse, 17*, 13-26.

Sollee, N.D. and Kindlon, D.J. (1987). Lateralized brain injury and behavior problems in children. *Journal of Abnormal Child Psychology, 15*, 479-491.

Sosland, J.M. and Christophersen, E.R. (1991). Does SleepTight work? A behavioral analysis of the effectiveness of SleepTight for the management of infant colic. *Journal of Applied Behavior Analysis, 24* , 161-166.

Stark, L.J., Knapp, L.G., Bowen, A.M. and Powers, S.W. (1993). Increasing calorie consumption in children with cystic fibrosis: Replication with 2-year follow-up. *Journal of Applied Behavior Analysis, 26*, 435-450.

Stokes, T.F. and Baer, D.M. (1976). An implicit technology of generalization. *Journal of Applied Behavior Analysis, 10*, 349-367.

Streissguth, A.P., Barr, H.M. and Sampson, P.D. (1990). Moderate prenatal alcohol exposure: Effects on child IQ and learning problems at age 7 1/2 years. *Alcohol Clinical and Experimental Research, 14*, 662-669.

Streissguth, A.P., Grant, T.M., Barr, H.M., Brown, Z.A., Martin, J.C., Mayock, D.E., Ramey, S.L. and Moore, L. (1991). Cocaine and use of alcohol and other drugs during pregnancy. *American Journal of Obstetrics and Gynaecology, 164*, 1239-1243.

Tabor, B.L., Smith-Wallace, T. and Yonekura, M.L. (1990). Perinatal outcome associated with PCP versus cocaine use. *American Journal of Drug and Alcohol Abuse, 16*, 337-348.

Tarnowski, K.J. (1991). Disadvantaged children and families in paediatric primary care settings: I. Broadening the scope of integrated mental health service. *Journal of Clinical Child Psychology, 20*, 351-359.

Timmermans, S.R. and Christensen, B. (1991). The measurement of attention deficits in TBI children and adolescents. *Cognitive Rehabilitation, 9*, 26-31.

Tyler, J.S. and Mira, M.P. (1993). Educational modifications for students with head injuries. *Teaching Exceptional Children, Spring*, 24-27.

VanBaar, A. (1990). Development of infants of drug dependent mothers. *Journal of Child Psychology and Psychiatry, 31*, 911-920.

VanDyke, D.C. and Fox, A.A. (1990). Fetal drug exposure and its possible implications for learning in the preschool and school-age population. *Journal of Learning Disabilities, 23*, 160-163.

Varni, J.W., Bessman, C.B., Russo, D.C. and Cataldo, M.F. (1980). Behavioral treatment of paediatric chronic pain. *Archives of Physical Medicine and Rehabilitation, 61*, 375-379.

Varni, J.W. and Dietrich, S.L. (1981). Behavioral pediatrics: Towards a reconceptualization. *Behavioral Medicine Update, 3*, 5-7.

Waaland, P.K. and Kreutzer, J.S. (1988). Family response to childhood traumatic brain injury. *Journal of Head Trauma Rehabilitation, 3*, 51-63.

Wagaman, J.R., Miltenberger, R.G. and Arndorfer, R.E. (1993). Analysis of a simplified treatment for stuttering in children. *Journal of Applied Behavior Analysis, 26*, 53-61.

Wahler, R.G. and Hann, D.M. (1986). A behavioral systems perspective in childhood psychopathology: Expanding the three-term operant contingency. In: N.A. Krasnegor, J.D. Arasteh, and M.F. Cataldo (Eds.), *Child health behavior* (pp. 146-170), New York: John Wiley and Sons.

Walker, L.S., Garber, J. and Greene, J.W. (1993). Psychosocial correlates of recurrent childhood pain: A comparison of paediatric patients with recurrent abdominal pain, organic illness, and psychiatric disorders. *Journal of Abnormal Psychology, 102*, 248-258.

Warren, K.R. and Bast, R.J. (1988). Alcohol related birth defects: An update. *Public Health Reports, 103*, 630-642.

Whyte, W.F. (1991). *Participatory action research.* Newbury Park, CA: Sage.

Ylvisaker, M. (1985). *Head injury rehabilitation: Children and adolescents.* San Diego: College-Hill.

Ylvisaker, M. (1986). Language and communication disorders following paediatric head injury. *Journal of Head Trauma Rehabilitation, 1*, 48-56.

Ylvisaker, M. (1993). Communication outcome in children and adolescents with traumatic brain injury. *Neuropsychological Rehabilitation, 3,* 367-387.

Zeltzer, L.K., Barr, R.G., McGrath, P.A. and Schechter, N.L. (1992). Paediatric pain: Interacting behavioral and physical factors. *Pediatrics, 90,* 816-821.

3

BEHAVIOUR THERAPY AND EDUCATIONAL REFORM

A Review of Study Findings

Jan H. Slavenburg

Centrum Educatieve Dienstverlening/Pedologisch Instituut
PO Box 8639
3009 AP Rotterdam
The Netherlands

THE EFFECTS OF BEHAVIOUR MODIFICATION

There are all kinds of behaviour modification methods and techniques - whether cognitive in approach or not - which from scientific study have been found to be effective. A significant number of these effective treatments were also maintained over the long term and became generalised or transferred to new situations. This type of effectiveness has been found in particular among mentally normal and slightly mentally disabled children who have shown modified behaviour in the classroom.

For the sake of clarity the effects shown can be divided into three categories. First, a reduction in the behavioural problems of individual pupils and all-round improvement in their social and emotional development. Secondly, a general improvement in pupils' academic performance and thirdly, improvement in the cognitive skills of disadvantaged children.

Rutherford and Nelson (1988) have widely documented the use of behaviour modification to reduce behavioural problems in individual pupils and improve social and emotional development. This was not only used for mentally normal and slightly mentally disabled children between 4 and 15, but also for profoundly mentally disabled children and young adults between 4 and 22 years of age. Of 5,300 studies analysed by the authors, 103 were studied for lasting and generalised effects. Such effects were found in 98 cases and a significant number of these were related to reducing behavioural problems and improving social and emotional development.

Regarding behaviour modification techniques in improving academic performance, as far as we know there are no review studies and meta-analyses available. However, there are extensive meta-analyses available on the effects of diverse variables on academic performance and several of these are closely related to behaviour modification studies. It is useful for this discussion to divide academic performance into two groups: academic performance measured by programme-related tests and academic performance measured by

Behavioral Approaches for Children and Adolescents, Edited by
H. P. J. G. van Bilsen et al., Plenum Press, New York, 1995

transfer tests. Programme related tests precisely measure subject matter taught, while transfer tests measure the extent to which the material taught has become generalised and transferred or applied to new situations. In education everything hinges on this transfer value. In meta-analyses of variables that effect academic performance this important distinction is largely ignored. Thus we do not know whether the variables from these analyses affect the achievement of short-term programme objectives or the achievement of longer term transfer ones. I will come back to this later.

Fraser et al. (1987) carried out a meta analysis of 134 individual meta analyses, based on a total of 7,827 separate studies in which the effects of hundreds of variables on academic performance were looked at. The average correlation between all these variables and academic performance was .20. Variables in the meta analysis related to, or arising from, behaviour modification studies and their correlation with academic performance are:

- programmed instruction: .04 to .13
- mastery learning (PS1): .21 to .29
- reinforcement: .43 to .54
- programme goals in behavioural terms: .06
- corrective feedback: .22 to .43.

There are also indirect significant variables related to social and emotional development such as time-on-task (in the sense of attitude towards work), concentration and various aspects of motivation. The correlation between these and academic performance is .26 to .38.

From the review of these behaviour modification related variables it was found that a number of these were seen as having more than average significance on academic performance: all those variables that correlated higher than .20. Here it is namely reinforcement and corrective feedback that positively relate as well as the more social and emotional aspects such as motivation and time on task. These are all variables that are influenced by - and which also represent - behaviour modification methods and techniques.

The third group of effects of behaviour modification methods and techniques are linked to improving the cognitive skills of disadvantaged pupils. These methods and techniques are mainly incorporated into compensatory and family intervention programmes. Compensatory education programmes are often combined with programmes aimed at stimulating social and emotional development (whether or not they have positive and indirect effects on cognitive development). Here cognitive development is understood as the developing of intelligence, the cognitive stages as Piaget describes them and school progress, including academic performance, resitting a class, receiving special education and secondary school type attended. From a review of the effectiveness of these programme types in the Netherlands (Slavenburg, 1989a; 1991a), it was found that they resulted in fewer children having to resit classes or attend special schools and more children attending higher types of secondary education. Academic performance measured by transfer tests hardly increased, while attainment measured by programme-related tests generally conformed to the programme's average norms. The effect on intelligence and cognitive development stages is limited and ebbs after a few years. There is no clear type of programme that shows the best transfer effects. It is evident however that well structured programmes - the learning material split into small steps, frequent testing, re-learning and so on - lead to good results. Programmes more explicitly based on behaviour modification principles show no more clear-cut and better effects than other programme types. Also the more effective programmes have much in common with the features of mastery learning (Block et al., 1989; Creemers, 1991) and direct instruction (Kneedler and Meese, 1988).

According to studies published this far, the effectiveness of family intervention programmes is even more patchy than that of compensatory education programmes. These have only short-term positive effects and diminishing long-term ones - and then only among the most successful programmes (White, Taylor and Moss, 1992). Moreover these effects are only predicted when programmes use continuous family visits by semi-skilled professionals during the pre-school or infant school phase. From the methods used on these visits to influence parents, 'modelling' works particularly well (Slavenburg, 1992; Wallace and Walberg, 1991).

An important category of behaviour modification effects that cannot be overlooked concerns the treatment of special problems such as phobias, serious mental disorders and so on. These effects however generally fall outside those that can be achieved using behaviour modification within education, so will not be dealt with here.

At first glance most effects of behaviour modification methods and techniques appear to be encouraging. Effects have been found that positively relate to reducing behavioural problems and improving social and emotional development. Significant variables directly linked to behaviour modification that also positively relate to academic performance include reinforcement and corrective feedback, while indirect ones include motivation and time-on-task. Behaviour modification used in intervention programmes for disadvantaged pupils appears to be less significant, although certain features of the more successful programmes can be traced to behaviour modification principles. These include programme structuring (small steps, feedback and reinforcement) in compensatory education programmes and modelling in the family intervention programmes. Structuring here is closely tied in with ideas on direct teaching and mastery learning.

The picture appears less rosy if we distinguish between generalised effects and more short-term ones, directly linked to education programmes. While the former have been found with regard to reducing behavioural problems and improving social and emotional improvement, they are not shown in compensatory and intervention programmes when academic performace is measured by transfer tests and in general cognitive development. Regarding significant variables that directly affect academic performance, we are hampered by the fact that these meta analyses do not distinguish between programme-linked academic performance and transfer-linked academic performance.

Notwithstanding, it is still possible to say something about this. It has already been mentioned that mastery learning is a teaching approach not directly based on behaviour modification principles. Its designer (Bloom, 1976) took as starting point a summary of relevant educational research and Carroll's learning model. However, in practice a number of relevant behaviour modification principles can be found in mastery learning, including reinforcement, corrective feedback and re-learning.

From available analyses, we know that mastery learning produces good programme-linked results, though for transfer tests it is also somewhat disappointing: the results are no better or worse than for other teaching methods. (For a review of the discussion, see Slavenburg, 1991b.) We obviously do not know whether the same holds true regarding the effectiveness of the remaining variables related to factors found in behaviour modification research. We can see however that this fits amazingly well with the effects of intervention programmes. These too are short-term and have no impact or diminishing impact on longer term transfer tests.

From this brief review of the effects of behaviour modification methods and techniques, we can conclude that, generally speaking, lasting transfer effects are namely found in the reduction of problem behaviour and the improvement in social and emotional development. In relation to increasing academic performance, this behaviour modification has mainly positive effects on programme tests and no impact or ebbing effect on transfer tests (or on cognitive development generally). While the effects of behaviour modification strategies are not positive on every front, there are still enough successful outcomes to justify their use.

Successfully Implementing Primary School Reforms

The aforementioned behaviour modification methods and techniques used in education and the welfare sectors may be seen as an innovation or reform. Within the limitations of this paper, we can examine the conditions that provide the best chance of successfully implementing reform, specifically in education. In other words the best conditions under which behaviour modification methods and techniques can be implemented within schools.

As a working yardstick we assume that a reform has been sufficiently implemented if those involved - usually the teachers - have practically implemented at least 70 per cent of its written directives, and no more than ten per cent of what has been implemented has been amended (for a discussion on implementation criteria see Slavenburg, 1986 and Klaasman, 1989).

To implement a reform, written information on it needs to be available, for instance via an educational publisher, and made known to prospective target groups via various publications. This is the so-called dissemination phase of a reform. Schools then have to decide whether to acquire the relevant manuals and so on needed to implement the reform and from this decide on whether to introduce it. Having decided, the actual implementation phase then follows. Once a reform is implemented, the school then monitors standards and progress while newly appointed teachers are familiarised with it.

Dissemination

In his study of the dissemination of 12 Dutch educational reforms, Stokking (1989) found that familiarising target groups in education with a new reform (between 80 and 95 per cent reached) and supplying them with the information (between 65 and 80 per cent) was for the most part successful. The information was then studied by between 30 and 50 per cent and was final used by between 5 and 35 per cent. Thus there is a big gap between being made aware of a reform and actually implementing it.

The awareness of a reform is largely dependent on factors such as:

- whether it is attractively 'packaged' and available in sufficient quantities (a task for educational publishers, here);
- the reinforcement of background information, for instance in the trade press;
- free mailing of background information to schools and enlisting the help of intermediary bodies such as support services and teacher centres etc.
- publicity in a general sense.

As far as is known there has been no research into the degree of dissemination of behaviour modification methods and techniques in the Netherlands, so it is difficult to judge wether they contain the earlier mentioned features. As long as materials such as in-house publications of an institute or research group are not widely available and insufficient use made of existing distribution sources such as educational publishers, support services and the like, then the spread of information will be unsatisfactory. Of the written material available from the Rotterdam project Education and Social Milieu (OSM) (Slavenburg and Peters, 1989), based on behaviour modification theories, which includes *Problem behaviour in School* (Constandse and Magito, 1981), *Problem behaviour in the Family* (Van der Horst, 1989) and *Child development and Education Programme* (Constandse and Van Velzen, 1983), only the *Problem behaviour in School* programme has been published and distributed via an educational publisher. Some 3,000 examples of the programme were sold and about 15 per cent of Dutch primary schools acquired it. (A summary of the findings of various pilot projects of other OSM programmes is given in Slavenburg, 1989b.)

Thus if *Problem behaviour in School* is anything to go by, existing distribution channels do 'work' and if behaviour modification programmes are to become more widely known and disseminated in the Netherlands this can be realised via existing possibilities.

Adopting Reform

An awareness of an education reform and even a school acquiring all the relevant information, does not mean the reform will actually be implemented. The decision on this is taken during the so-called adoption phase. Some extremely important criteria that influence this include the reform's perceived effectiveness, whether the objectives, components and so on are described in concrete terms and its practical workability in terms of time scale, degree of in-service training/support etc required. (For a review of literature on this and other aspects of reform see Holt (1990)). As far as I am aware there are no such reviews on adopting behaviour modification available with regard to the Dutch situation, only American ones. Elliott's analysis of acceptability studies (1988) shows that behaviour modification methods and techniques are more acceptable the more they are perceived to be effective, the less time needs to be spent on them and the more the emphasis is on positive methods and techniques rather than repressive ones such as punishment, time-out and so on. A Dutch example here is the earlier mentioned *Problem behaviour in School* programme. Of the schools that had this, 60 per cent did not use it at all, while only between 2 and 8 per cent of schools used it consistently (Slavenburg, 1989). Some data is also available for a related programme *Focus on yourself and others*, which was acquired by schools in the province of South Holland. Of these, 28 per cent used it occasionally, while 25 per cent were in the initial stages of using it consistently (see Schuurman, 1986, on the basis of findings by Van Zuuren and Martens, 1988).

When behaviour modification methods and techniques are considered according to the three aspects of a reform that lead to a school deciding on its implementation, it is clear that while their effectiveness has been proven (particularly in reducing problem behaviour and stimulating social and emotional development), it is doubtful whether behaviour modification strategies are so perceived by teachers or whether teachers are sufficiently familiar with these effectiveness findings. This brings us back to the problem of dissemination as well as workability. Behaviour modification programmes usually demand a great deal of a teacher's time, including consultations with advisors, observing before, during and after treatment, tailoring the methods and techniques on top of all the other heavy demands required of a teacher. We have an idea that these factors for instance contributed to the *Problem behaviour in School* programme being hardly used.

Few problems are liable to occur concerning the clarity with which behaviour modification strategies are described. In keeping with their scientific background, behaviour is depicted in extremely concrete terms. On the other hand, the use of repressive techniques will not inspire implementation in the Netherlands, where behaviour modification and cognitive behaviour therapy still has to contend with the effects of their behaviourist image.

Implementation

Assuming that dissemination has been successful, the reform meets the required criteria for success and a school has actually decided to implement a behaviour modification programme, what is the next step? What is the most effective means of implementation?

This question needs to be prefaced by another: what are the pre-conditions necessary for a school to implement a reform successfully? These can be summed up as school organisation features (see Holt's summary of research literature, 1990) and are:

a. working systematically
b. monitoring progress and standards
c. forceful leadership (both from the head teacher and school governing body)
d. a climate of positive collaboration
e. didactic and management skills among teachers
f. individual teacher's ability to work systematically and monitor progress.

While this paper does not intend to go deeply into these features, it must be mentioned that if too many are missing then implementation has little chance of success. For instance if school policy lacks any systematic planning then the situation often arises where there are so many reforms and reforms in progress that not many actually result in succeeding. If there is no monitoring of progress, then reforms can be implemented in such a way that while the new materials appear to be used, they are still used in the same manner as the old materials (so-called non-implementation). However let us assume that a reform is implemented in a school where most of the features of good organisation are in place, for if this is not the case the exercise is pointless.

Implementing a reform to the level described earlier in this paper requires an effective implementation strategy, which includes both a preparatory and an execution phase. In both instances there are a number of strategies (Rotterdam School Advisory Service, 1990; Holt, 1990) that positively effect the level of implementation.

In the preparatory phase these include:

- information sessions on the reform for the entire school staff
- drawing-up a concrete and long-term plan for implementing the proposed reform in which the roles of the school authority, school management, teachers and school advisor are clearly designated
- scheduling a series of evaluation/progress talks
- tailoring the reform to the actual school situation
- visits to schools who have already successfully implemented the reform
- appropriate in-service training run by local support services.

In the implementation phase these include:

- regular evaluation meetings chaired by the team leader and school advisor
- tailoring the reform to the concrete school situation where problems arise (teachers and school advisor)
- resolving practical problems that hamper the reform being implemented (school governing body, school management, teachers and school advisor)
- inspiring enthusiasm for the reform (school governing body, school management, teachers and school advisor)
- classroom consultation in the form of teacher observation and feedback (school advisor)
- monitoring progress (school governing body and school management)
- final, end-of-school-year evaluation plus any necessary amendments to planning schedule (school management, teachers and school advisor)
- mutual support among teachers and support from the school head as needed.

It is obvious that introducing educational reforms is a fairly complex matter and involves much time and energy if they are to be effectively implemented. Depending on the nature of the reform and the number of classes involved, a time span of two or three years per class year seems reasonable, as well as some 90 hours of school back-up per year. The most important task of the school advisor within all this is to provide class consultation for teachers, a method that by and large produces positive results (Snippe, 1991). This essentially concerns the school advisor observing the teachers while they implement the reform and then supplying feedback.

Regarding implementation studies of behaviour modification methods, we again have to turn to American literature. In their summary of 50 studies of the subject, Anderson & Kratochwill (1988) conclude it is quite possible to teach teachers behaviour modification strategies and the principles behind them. Modelling, role play and feedback combined with printed materials, discussion groups and so on is particularly effective. The researchers also emphasise that much time should be spent on the implementation *process* - or dissemination phase as they call it - as many reforms fail through paying too little attention to this. They regard in-service training as an outstanding means of achieving successful implementation, though this should not only be limited to workshops, but should include observing the implementation process and its results.

When implementing the *Problem Behaviour in School* programme, we opted for a course/workshop for the teachers in which they were taught the principles of the programme and then shown practically how these could be applied to certain pupils with behavioural problems. The teachers were then expected to carry out the programme independently with a behaviour therapy specialist - school advisor or psychologist - on hand for advice. Classroom observation and other related strategies were not used at the time, and in view of what has been said on effective implementation strategies, we did not expect the programme to be properly introduced. In the eight-year longitudinal follow-up of OSM pupils, as part of a summary evaluation, only a handful of them had been given the *Problem Behaviour in School* programme. Taking the entire OSM sample of 6,000 pupils, on average only 65 pupils per year used the programme and in 75 per cent of cases the treatment was successful. The most likely conclusion from these findings is that the programme was not properly implemented within the 23 OSM schools (Slavenburg, 1989c).

Consolidation Phase

In general when introducing behaviour modification programmes much attention needs to be given to the implementation phase. Much more attention then has been the case until now. At the same time school organisation features should also be kept continually in mind, otherwise implementing reforms makes little sense. One of the central activities of successful implementation is the oft-repeated feedback via classroom consultation as well as the other factors that have already been mentioned.

The final stage of implementing a reform is the period of consolidation. By now support has discontinued, monitoring progress and standards has been handed over to the school management or school governing body, the reform has been absorbed into the curriculum and training and supporting for newly appointed teachers are provided. The period when the reform is absorbed into normal school routine is an important one, for its very survival depends on it. Notwithstanding, we know little about this phase, let alone being able to name the precise strategies that help to sustain a reform. Certain study findings show that while the school governing body and head teachers should be responsible for monitoring the progress and academic standards of reforms, school heads do not generally do this, even if they have followed the appropriate management courses. School governing bodies too make little use of the opportunities given them to monitor results. For the most part they neglect the educational side of their duties (Braster and Leune, 1986). Reforms are usually recorded in the formal school curriculum, but for most schools this is not the most important document on which they base school policy (Van der Werf and Reezigt, 1983).

Little is known about the way in which newly appointed teachers are made familiar with reforms. In fact the OSM project is one of the few that gave attention to this by developing audiovisual courses, though their use among newly appointed teachers was minimal (Peters, 1989). These findings tie in with the picture that emerges from effective schools studies, another traditional research area (e g Scheerens, 1989), namely that Dutch school heads play an insignificant role in educational reforms, apart from the initial phase and provide no guidance at all for teachers, for instance via classroom consultation (Vandenberghe, 1989). The lack of internal school support for monitoring progress and standards is a difficult problem to resolve. One solution already in use is to bring in a consultant (over and above classroom consultations) or other specialist help who are on call whenever the teachers need advise. This strategy is effective as far as it concerns individual pupils with problems (see literature review in Meijer's dissertation, 1991). Even so the teachers must already possess behaviour modification skills and know how to use them. Thus bringing in consultants at the implementation stage is pointless, though they can help to maintain the reforms during the incorporation phase. We have been unable to trace any reviews on incorporating behaviour modification programmes, including any findings from the *Problem behaviour in school* programme, although as this was not properly implemented in the first place this is not entirely unexpected.

Conclusions on incorporating behaviour modification methods and techniques remain confused. It is evident that school management and governing bodies should be made part of the process, but exactly how is still a matter for debate. At the very least they should be responsible for making sure newly appointed teachers are trained in the reforms. Whether the reform is included in the school curriculum is a formality and does not in any way affect assimilation. Schools working with consultants can produce results providing the behaviour modification programme has already been properly implemented. Thus it is obvious that the necessary research and development work still needs to be done concerning the assimilation phase.

Implementing Behaviour Modification

We have just discussed the conditions necessary for effective educational reforms. These were borrowed from various educational research as well as from studies on implementing behaviour modification programmes - in as far as they are available. On the basis of these conditions, we now need to assess what needs to be done to stimulate the use of behaviour modification in education.

During the dissemination phase behaviour-modification based reforms should be drawn to the attention of potential users and be widely available and distributed. Here we run up against the first problem, as there are virtually no such reforms available to education in a practical form in the Netherlands, i e manuals, implementation/instruction programmes and so on. The *Problem behaviour in school* programme is the only one that has been distributed to any extent and it is no longer available from the publisher. Still available however is the *Focus on yourself and others* programme in which Engelen and Krab give examples of behaviour therapy programmes now sporadically used in primary education.

There are of course education programmes available that incorporate behaviour modification ideas, such as those based on direct teaching, mastery learning and so on, but these can hardly be regarded as typical behaviour modification programmes. In Van Lieshout's review (1992) of diagnostic, policy orientated and nationwide programmes aimed at stimulating social and emotional development, not one of the fifteen studied were based on behaviour modification aside from the aforementioned OSM programmes. The recently successfully distributed programmes of the Harmonisation Strategy project (Stevens et al, 1990) aimed at reducing problems related to motivation and attention span are not directly linked to behaviour modification. It is however an example of a clearly documented education reform in the form of manuals, disseminated by an education support service and supported by trade press articles as well as gatherings for school advisors, psychologists etc. All these facilities still need to be in place for behaviour modification programmes so it is hardly surprising they are hardly known within schools, let alone used.

It has already been mentioned that whether a school adopts a reform depends on its perceived effectiveness and workability as well as the concreteness of the goals and core elements. Due to behaviour therapy's essential nature, theoretically it has concreteness but in practice this is missing due to the aforementioned lack of clear-cut programmes, manuals etc which are needed to flesh out innovation. The scientifically proven effectiveness of behaviour modification programmes has already been discussed in this paper. It is namely programmes aimed at reducing problem behaviour and improving social and emotional development that have lasting and generalised effects. The effectiveness of education and intervention programmes for disadvantaged children remains problematical. They relate positively to programme linked testing and sometimes to aspects of a pupil's schooling such as resitting a class, secondary school type etc but have no transfer effects on academic performance and cognitive skills. In general positive effects on schooling are achieved through other programmes than behaviour modification ones. In our view the best chance of behaviour modification succeeding as an innovation is when it is used where it scores highest - in reducing behavioural problems and improving social and emotional development. The scientifically proven effectiveness in these areas has still not penetrated the education field properly. Thus dissemination is needed and then via the appropriate channels described earlier.

The workability of behaviour modification programmes in schools largely hinges on the amount of time teachers have to spend on them. As we have already mentioned, American findings show that using behaviour modification methods and techniques take up a lot of time. This will have to be taken into account, as well as the fact that positive rather than repressive techniques appeal more to the Dutch. If note is made of this, then information given during the dissemination phase could help polish up the tarnished image of behaviour modification among Dutch educationalists.

Each programme phase should also be accompanied by manuals for training teachers and for school advisors to avoid unnecessary repetition of ground already covered. These manuals should deal with the various innovation phases that make implementing reform easier and which have already been mentioned earlier. As far as we are aware support and in-service programmes are as yet unavailable. These resource materials too have a dissemination, adoption and implementation phase, for instance in the form of information gatherings and courses for school advisors, teacher training lecturers etc.

Institutes involved in studying exceptional children could attempt to develop concrete reforms based on behaviour modification and then assess (Paedological Institutes) their effects, particularly those related to reducing problem behaviour and stimulating social and emotional development. Such programmes are effective and there is a significant need for them (Van Lieshout, 1992; Hölscher, 1989; Maas, 1992 (the latter author points out that nearly all children with learning difficulties, also have social and emotional problems)). Appropriate training and in-service courses can be developed in conjunction with teacher training colleges and disseminated through an educational publisher. In this way behaviour modification can be successfully implemented in education.

Much of what has been put forward on implementing educational reforms is relatively easy for behaviour therapists. If they understand how the behaviour of individuals can be changed then they can also apply their science to implementing and disseminating their ideas and programmes. For this is simply nothing more than achieving behaviour changes among those involved in the education field. Simply developing the occasional programme pack, conference or article is not enough to change behaviour, as the therapists themselves must know. Hopefully this paper summarising research into educational reform has made this sufficiently clear.

REFERENCES

Anderson, T.K. and Kratochwill, T. (1988). Dissemination of behavioral procedures in the school. In: J.C., Witt, S.N. Elliott and F.M. Gresham. *Handbook of behavior therapy in education*. New York: Plenum.

Block, J.H., Efthim, H.E. and Burns, R.B. (1989). *Building effective mastery learning schools*. New York: Longman.

Bloom, B.S. (1976). *Human characteristics and school learning*. New York: McGraw Hill.

Braster, J.F.A. and Leune, J.M.G. (1986). *Composition and functioning of school governing bodies*. Rotterdam: Erasmus University.

Constandse, J.W. and Velzen, B.A.M. van (1983). *Child development and education programme*. Rotterdam: Education and Social Milieu project.

Constandse, J.W. and Magito, T.A.A.M. (ed.) (1981). *Problem behaviour in school*. Tilburg: Zwijsen.

Creemers, B.P.M. (1991). *Effective teaching*. The Hague: Institute for Educational Research, SVO.

Elliott, S.N. (1988). Acceptability of behavioral treatments in educational settings. In: J.C., Witt, S.N. Elliott and F.M. Gresham (eds) *Handbook of behavior therapy in education*. New York: Plenum.

Fraser, B.J., Walberg, H.J., Welch, W.W. and Hattie, J.A. (1987). Synthesis of Educational Productivity Research. *International Journal of Educational Research, 11*, 145-252.

Hölscher, M.C. (1989). *Social and emotional development of primary school pupils*. Zoetermeer: Ministry of Education and Science.

Holt, J.A. (1990). *Educational reform through structured systematic guidance (1): a literature study*. Rotterdam: Rotterdam School Advisory Service.

Horst, W.A. van der (1989). *Behavioural changes at school and in the family*. Rotterdam: Education and Social Milieu project.

Klaasman, R.R.P. (1989). *Implementing education programmes and academic performance*. Rotterdam: Education and Social Milieu project.

Kneedler, R.D. and Meese, R.L. (1988). Learning disabled children. In: J.C., Witt, S.N., Elliott and F.M. Gresham (eds) *Handbook of behavior therapy in education*. New York: Plenum.

Lieshout, C.F.M. van, (ed.) (1992). *Primary school children with social and emotional problems. Diagnosis and treatment*. Nijmegen: Catholic University.

Maas, C.J.M. (1992). *Problem pupils in primary education*. Amsterdam: Thesis Publishers.

Meijer, R.W.J. (1991). *Consultation for teachers*. Amsterdam: Free University.

Peters, T.A. (1989). Experiences with Education and Social Milieu compensatory education programmes. In: J.H. Slavenburg and T.A. Peters (ed.) *Education and Social Milieu project: a summing up*. Rotterdam: Rotterdam School Advisory Service.

Rotterdam School Advisory Service (1990). *Educational reform through structured systematic guidance (2): a strategy for systematic guidance*. Rotterdam: Rotterdam School Advisory Service.

Rutherford, R.B. and Nelson, C.M. (1988). Generalization and Maintenance of Treatment Effects: In: J.C., Witt, S.N. Elliott and Gresham F.M. (eds) *Handbook of behavior therapy in education*. New York: Plenum.

Scheerens, J. (1989). *What makes schools effective? Review and analyses of research results*. The Hague: Institute for Educational Research, SVO.

Slavenburg, J.H. (1986). *Compensatory and family intervention programmes*: The Hague: Foundation for Educational Research.

Slavenburg, J.H. (1989a). Results of compensatory and family intervention programmes in international literature. In: J.H. Slavenburg and T.A. Peters (ed.) *Education and Social Milieu project: a summing up*. Rotterdam: Rotterdam School Advisory Service.

Slavenburg, J.H. (1989b). Experiences with the dissemination strategy of Education and Social Milieu. In: J.H. Slavenburg and T.A. Peters (ed.) *Education and Social Milieu project: a summing up*. Rotterdam: Rotterdam School Advisory Service.

Slavenburg, J.H. (1989c). Implementation value, goal and transfer effectiveness of compensatory and intervention programmes. In: J.H. Slavenburg and T.A. Peters (ed.) *Education and Social Milieu project: a summing up*. Rotterdam: Rotterdam School Advisory Service.

Slavenburg, J.H. (1991a). Evaluation of compensatory education programmes in Rotterdam, the Netherlands. *International Journal of Educational Research, 15*, 21-43.

Slavenburg, J.H. (1991b). Mastering learning and academic performance. *The Individual and the Community, 43*, 300-302.

Slavenburg, J.H. (1992). Family intervention programmes in the Education and Social Milieu project. (To be published shortly.)

Slavenburg J.H. and Peters T.A. *Education and Social Milieu project: a summing up.* Rotterdam: Rotterdam School Advisory Service.

Snippe, J. (1991). *In-service training for teachers.* Groningen: Institute for Educational Research, Rion.

Stevens, L.M., Werkhoven, W. van, Goedhart, C.C., Sliepen, S.E. and Schaap-Hummel, I.J.T. (1990). *Harmonisation strategy. A practical guide for School Advisors.* Utrecht: State University Utrecht.

Stokking, K. (1989). Strategies for distributing information and materials in education. In: *Educational Lexicon 2nd edition.* Alphen aan den Rijn: Samsom.

Vandenberghe, R. (1989). Internal support. In: *Educational Lexicon 2nd edition.* Alphen aan den Rijn: Samsom.

Wallace, T. and Walberg, H.J. (1991). Parental Partnership for Learning. *International Journal of Educational Research, 15*, 131-145.

Werf, M.P.C. van der and Reezigt, G.J. (1983). *Developing a school curriculum in primary education.* Haren: Rion.

White, K.R., Taylor, J.T. and Moss, V.D. (1992). Does research support claims about the benefits of involving parents in early intervention programs? *Review of Educational Research, 62*, 91-125.

4

UNUSED OPPORTUNITIES FOR BEHAVIOUR THERAPY IN EDUCATION

Henck P. J. G. van Bilsen

Pedologisch Instituut
PO Box 8639
3009 AP Rotterdam
The Netherlands

The mention of 'education and behaviour therapy' in the title of this chapter refers to an uneasy attempt to draw together two otherwise quite separate work fields. Or at least that is the case in the Netherlands, where behaviour therapy, as a practical application of behaviourism, is largely used to practise (psycho)therapy. Thus, training, professional recognition and behaviour therapy itself is largely aimed at psychotherapeutic settings. In companies, schools, prisons etc its principles hardly exist. Dutch education as a whole is anything but contaminated by the knowledge of behaviour therapy. Its use is minimal. Very rarely it is used to solve an isolated behaviour problem of a pupil (see Engelen and Krab's summary in this compilation).

While it may seem that education and behaviour therapy have rarely made any overtures towards one another in the Netherlands, this book reports on a successful attempt to do just this. In Britain and the United States it is a different story. Here a branch of behaviourism *Applied Behavioural Analysis* (ABA) has had a major impact on education. This chapter attempts to introduce these two strange bedfellows to each other and to give an overview of how applied behavioural analysis has earned its reputation in education. The advantages of using a technology of change will become evident while at the same time the challenges facing education and behaviour therapy in the Netherlands are assessed.

What is applied behavioural analysis?

Applied behavioural analysis (ABA) is a systematic, performance-based, self-evaluating method for studying and changing socially important behaviour (Sulzer-Azaroff and Mayer, 1991). ABA can be regarded as systematically searching for knowledge gained in the laboratory in the less rigorously controlled setting of daily practice. It makes use of educational psychological insights in areas far removed from a therapy setting. It is used, among others, in companies, schools and hospitals.

Sulzer-Azaroff and Mayer (1991) mention other distinguishing aspects of ABA. Based on observable behavioural change, ABA is concerned with the interaction between people and their environment - the reason it is important for behaviour and environmental variables to be described as objectively and specifically as possible. Current applied research shows that reliable and objective descriptions of behaviour can be gained even under extremely difficult circumstances (Baer, Wolf and Risely, 1968).

Behavioral Approaches for Children and Adolescents, Edited by
H. P. J. G. van Bilsen et al., Plenum Press, New York, 1995

Analysis

Applied behavioural analysis uses methods of analysis which result in convincing, replicable and conceptually interesting demonstrations of how behavioural changes can be achieved. The procedures used have their basis in educational psychology and being able to replicate these is considered to be profoundly important. ABA has a technology for setting up replicable studies in a natural setting (Sulzer-Azaroff and Mayer (1986).

Socially Important

Applied behavioural analysis is aimed at appropriate behaviour in a particular setting. This can be related to:

- increasing the frequency of certain behavioural responses (i.e. using certain language more often, talking with other children more);
- learning new behaviour (i.e. asking to be praised more);
- maintaining a new learned behaviour pattern (i.e. enjoying mixing with children of another skin colour);
- generalising learned behaviour to other settings (i.e. learning to pay attention to teacher A and then doing the same thing by teacher B);
- controlling situations in which a certain behaviour occurs (i.e. teachers learn to control negative interactions with pupils during lessons;
- reducing the frequency of certain behaviour (i.e. pupils talking out of turn).

Context

Environmental variables on behaviour studied have been found to be increasingly important: the physical condition of those involved, the characteristics of the environment, preceding occurrences, occurrences happening simultaneously with the behaviour and so on are all seen as sustaining certain behaviour. All too often an intervention programme such as psychotherapy or compensatory education is introduced with undue attention for the setting in which behaviour modification is to take place. With ABA it is necessary to look at the broad framework to see whether unintentional negative effects such as interpersonal or environmental factors are likely to occur as the result of an apparently straightforward intervention (see Willems's summarising of disasters, 1974).

Accountability

Applied behavioural analysis does not look at people as if they are unresisting objects ripe for conditioning. In fact it is deemed important that those concerned are involved as much as possible in the modification programme (Van Houten et al, 1988). Applied behavioural analysis is concerned with accountability: the how, what and why of intervention. This responsibility is felt not only towards the subsidizers but in the first instance towards those for whom it is intended - children, teachers and parents.

Education and Applied Behavioural Analysis

Why should applied behavioural analysis have any significance for education? Education is meant to organise settings for children and young people in which they can expand their knowledge and skills. In other words, one aim of education is to organise changes in behaviour between children and young people. ABA is a technology which attempts to realise the systematic applying of scientifically proven principles of behavioural change in daily practice.

Distinguishing features of ABA tie in well with relevant aspects of education. Education in fact is aimed at increasing the frequency of certain behaviour (learning to talk), learning new behaviour (learning to read), generalising certain behaviour (adding up in class and later in the supermarket) etc. These are precisely the sort of changes ABA is aimed at and for which it has successful interventions as well as an explanatory technology.

Education is essentially an ecological and contextual process in which insight into the relationship between pupil attainment and the teaching/learning setting is vital. An increasing need is felt in education for clearly described, effective and practically replicable teaching methods. This is precisely what ABA is all about.

American Studies

In the *Journal of Applied Behavior Analysis* some 400 articles on applied behavioral analysis in education appeared between 1968 and 1987 (Sulzer-Azaroff et al, 1988). Sulzer-Azaroff divided these into several specific areas (this division is reproduced in this chapter):

1. Pre-school children
2. Learning language and social skills
3. Instruction and attainment
4. Classroom management
5. Behavioural problems
6. Fellow pupils as teachers
7. Teacher training.

This chapter presents a selection of more than forty studies (see appendix 1 for an overview), all of which conform to the requirement of being replicable, while the intervention and research procedures are clearly reported. The studies all took place under natural conditions. This has the advantage that the concern is with meaningful behaviour. The drawback is that studies largely concerned small groups (varying from N=1 to N=10) and that certain conditions may have played a role that were overlooked by the researchers.

Information on the Terminology Used

Applied Behavior analysis has developed its own terminology and this is inevitably used when describing the study data. Here is a short review of the terms used:

- *Reinforcement*: something pleasant follows a certain behaviour (a positive reward in the form of a pupil being complimented or the teacher withdrawing a difficult task for the pupils). The effect of reinforcement on behaviour is to strengthen or make it more probable in the future. Reinforcement can vary from encouraging nods and words ("You've done that very well") to tokens.
- *Pin-pointing*: the desired behaviour is clearly specified so that it is directly rewarded.
- *Time-on-task*: the time a child takes to complete a task.
- *Shaping*: Slowing working towards the desired behaviour by rewarding small steps in that direction.
- *Classroom management*: Using ABA techniques to organise lessons.
- *Intermittent*: a certain consequence occurs irregularly following certain behaviour.
- *Token*: something small such as a sticker given to children immediately they do something 'good', which can then be exchanged for real rewards.
- *Self-instruction*: children are taught to control their own thoughts so that this can then lead to a better control of their behaviour.

- *Feedback*: the giving of objective information on performance, whether or not weighed against a certain pre-agreed norm.
- *Contingent*: an emphatic time relationship between two occurrences. Contingent reinforcing means that reinforcement timely follows certain behaviour.
- *Response cost*: a certain behaviour costs something. Using positive reinforcement on the one hand and withdrawing already earned rewards on the other, an attempt is made to reduce the rate of inappropriate behaviour and increase the frequency of desired behaviour.

The following questions need to be addressed when assessing the significance of applied behavioral analysis in education:

a. Are ABA methods successful in 'improving' education?

b. Can these methods be translated into teaching skills?

c. Can these skills be taught to teachers?

d. Is it possible for teachers to apply these skills in practice?

e. Can the practical situation be organised in such a way that these skills can be used?

In each section the first three questions will be assessed, while questions d and e will be addressed at the end of this chapter.

APPLIED BEHAVIOURAL ANALYSIS AND YOUNG CHILDREN

What Are the Prominent Findings?

When infant teachers selectively apply social reinforcement, pupils learn to play in a more varied way (Goetz and Baer, 1973). A self-instruction programme to reduce hyperactivity in three boys was studied by Bornstein and Quevillon (1976). Changes brought about by the therapy were generalised towards the class. Task focused behaviour increased dramatically after self-instruction training was introduced and a follow up 22 weeks later showed the effects remained. Improved accuracy, increased time-on-task and more work completed were also achieved using another self-instruction programme, this time for impulsive children (Bryant and Budd, 1982).

Young children can also be taught to tap potential - but non-active - reinforcers in their own natural environment (Stokes, Fowler and Baer, 1978). In this study children were taught to encourage teachers to give feedback on the quality of their performance. By the study giving explicit attention to generalisation towards other adults, the children were taught how to draw on 'dormant' yet readily available reinforcers in the natural environment.

Conclusion

Applied behavioural analysis studies among young children shows that this appears to be promising for expanding play variation, increasing the frequency of playing cooperatively, task orientation, accuracy, extending time-on-task and increasing the availability of reinforcers. In all these areas selectively applying social reinforcement and self-instruction are used. By adding these two techniques to the scala of behaviour influencing options of teachers, a number of serious education problems among young children can be solved. The skill of applying selective social reinforcement under natural conditions can be learnt after intensive training (Sulzer-Azaroff and Mayer, 1986). Self-instruction methods have also been taught successfully to teachers (Russo, 1992).

Applied Behavioural Analysis and the Learning of Language and Social Skills

Teachers have used social reinforcement to increase the frequency of using play materials. Not only did this increase dramatically but interaction with other children also rose, while inappropriate behaviour such as acting in a babyish manner greatly diminished (Buell, 1968).

Social reinforcement by an adult contingent following cooperative play, appears to also increase the frequency of cooperative play (Hart et al, 1968).

Strengthening racial integration was tackled with 'Eating and drinking with a new friend', a programme which combined teachers' school rules and reinforcement of desired behaviour in the school canteen. This resulted in better racial integration both in the canteen as well as during free play (Hauserman, Walen and Behling, 1973).

Hart and Risely (1974 and 1975) studied whether it was possible to improve children's language skills with straightforward teaching and straightforward resources. The systematically dividing of material into small steps, which were then tested and reinforced, proved effective at improving language skills.

Language skills, racial integration, the use of play materials, social interaction with others, as well as cooperative play, are all positively affected by ABA techniques such as behaviour instructions, selective reinforcement and shaping. It is extremely interesting to discover that incorporating a few ABA techniques into straightforward teaching can produce positive effects. This means that ABA is not something that is something over and above other teacher tasks but can be integrated into the normal teaching day and be part of the teacher's natural way of working.

Applied Behavioural Analysis and Instruction and Attainment

Hopkins, Schutte and Garteon (1971) described how a different approach to planning the environment can influence children's writing. In this study, after children had finished their writing task they were allowed to spend the rest of the time in a play area, which positive effected both the quantity and quality of the writing. Essay writing was also studied by Brigham, Graubard and Stans (1972). They discovered that when selective reinforcement was used the total number of words, including different as well as new words, dramatically rose.

Ayllon and Roberts (1974) demonstrated that systematically reinforcing reading attainment by using tokens at the same time eliminated behavioural problems.

When positive consequences were attached to completing homework properly, such as being allowed to go and play, Harris and Sherman (1974) found the number of homework assignments completed increased as did the accuracy with which they were done.

In the study of Van Houten et al (1974), registration, direct feedback, making results 'public' and behaviour instructions to improve results led to double the total number of words used in pupils' essays, while the subjective quality of what was written also increased.

It is also possible to develop creative ability (operationalised as the number of responses, degree of fluency, different tenses used, number of words per answer, degree of detail, statistical infrequency of certain reply categories and originality) using instructions, reinforcement and exercises (Glover and Gary, 1976).

Dickerson and Creedon (1981) combined contingent reinforcement with attainment norms determined by the pupils themselves. They discovered that when pupils were allowed to set their own attainment norms, the learning attainment of these pupils was much better than in cases where the teacher decided this.

Smith, Schumaker, Schaeffer and Sherman (1982) studied the taking part in, and quality of, classroom discussion. To increase participation in classroom debate, the following techniques were adopted: establishing discussion rules (= behaviour instructions) and reinforcing participants contributions (teachers verbally paraphrased these or wrote them on the blackboard; contributions were recorded and used for assessment, while this assessment on taking part in classroom discussion was made public). A training in how to debate, combined with specifically recording and rewarding every discussion skill taught, led to an overall improvement in the standard of the discussions.

Conclusion

In education, academic achievement is extremely important. From the above, it is evident that behaviour instructions, contingent reinforcement, making 'public' achievement results, pupils establishing their own academic norms, tokens and rewarding can all be used to heighten learning performance in both a quantitative as well as a qualitative sense. ABA techniques positively effect learning to write, essay writing, reading, homework assignments, creative use of language and participating in classroom debate.

Hall, Lund and Jackson (1968) discovered that giving contingent attention to concentrated studying in class and ignoring non-concentrated studying behaviour positively effected the degree of concentrated studying among pupils.

O'Leary, Becker, Evans and Saudargas (1969) studied disruptive behaviour. They introduced several techniques consecutively to treat seven children (class rules, structured learning, rewarding desired behaviour and ignoring undesired behaviour and tokens). The most effective means of reducing disruptive behaviour was to combine all these techniques.

Another approach to reducing or preventing disruptive behaviour is the so-called Good Behavior Game (Barrish, Saunders and Wolf, 1969). A class was divided into two groups and any form of disruptive behaviour systematically and visibly recorded. Depending on the total number of disruptive behaviour points scored by each group, response cost was applied and a winning team proclaimed. The programme was judged positively by both pupils and teachers.

School interventions with cooperation from the home environment is also effective. Bailey, Wolf and Phillips (1970) found that teachers recording attainment in conjunction with parents reinforcing desired behaviour at home, positively effected classroom behaviour.

It has already been mentioned that pupils deciding attainment norms themselves positively effects learning attainment. Bolstad and Johnson (1972) report similar findings in a study of self-regulatory techniques to reduce disruptive behaviour in the classroom. When children are taught not only to observe their own disruptive behaviour but also - depending on the result - to reward themselves, this method is more effective then when the reward system is in a teacher's hands.

Alan Kazdin (1973) looked at the effects of social reinforcement in attentively following lessons. The interesting aspect of this study is that the effects on the trial group as well as on those children sitting close by were followed and it was found that levels of concentration increased in both groups. However, when non-attentive behaviour in the trial group was also reinforced, this positively effected the other children's attentive behaviour. Thus social reinforcement appears to be an antecedent stimulus for attentively following a lesson.

Kazdin and Klock (1973) studied the effects of teachers' non-verbal approval on pupils' attentive behaviour. Teachers smiling more frequently and patting pupils who were being attentive positively effected the degree of attentiveness.

Reinforcement through token programmes can reduce the frequency of rule breaking and non-task focused behaviour (Lawata and Bailey, 1974). Both a reward and a response cost system were effective. Drabman and Lahey (1974) used only teacher's feedback (a score between 1-10 given every 15 minutes to the child concerned) to modify a child's disruptive behaviour and found this to be an effective technique. This intervention also reduced disruptive behaviour in fellow pupils and made them respond more positively towards the child concerned. The teacher also responded more positively towards the child concerned. Foxx and Shapiro (1978) successfully used a time-out procedure to treat disruptive behaviour. The children were first treated with a system of reinforcement for good behaviour: they were each given a coloured ribbon and rewards for desired behaviour. When time out was introduced in the form of having a ribbon taken away, withholding of attention and participation in class activities for three minutes, disruptive behaviour dropped from 42 per cent to 6 per cent of the time.

Van Houten, Nau, MacKenzie-Keatin, Sameoto and Colavecchia (1982) studied the relatively unknown outcomes of a reprimand and found three factors that make this more effective in stopping inappropriate behaviour: non-verbal responses such as eye contact or grabbing the child, reprimanding the child close up and reprimanding pupil A effects nearby pupil B.

Pfifner, Rosén and O'Leary (1985) observed that when only a positive approach to classroom management is used in the form of social reinforcement and individual rewards, this can be effective in reducing the seriousness of behavioural problems, providing the teacher takes time for this, a variety of powerful rewards are available and the children already have the behaviour likely to occur in their behavioural repertoire.

Conclusion

Concentrated study, disruptive class behaviour, attentively following lessons and breaking rules can all be controlled using ABA techniques. Selectively paying attention to desired behaviour while ignoring undesired behaviour, positively effects not only the trial group but also others in the class. At the same time, teachers working together with parents regarding reinforcement, reinforcement in play form, reprimanding in a specific way as well as only using a positive approach are all effective in organising desired classroom behaviour.

Applied Behavioural Analysis and Behavioural Problems

Controlled token programmes are effective in reducing pupils' disruptive behaviour (Santogrossi, O'Leary, Romanck and Kaufman, 1973), though when this is replaced by a self-assessment system the positive effects disappear. Time-out is effective in reducing the frequency of disruptive behaviour (Clark, Rowbury and Baer, 1973) but is just as effective when used intermittently, rather than being used after every display of bad behaviour. Porterfield, Herbert-Jackson and Risley (1976) took up the challenge of tackling behavioural problems among toddlers. These were reduced in a playgroup of two-year-olds by a combination of stopping the disruptive behaviour, giving behavioural instructions and getting a child to observe the desired behaviour of the other children.

Russo and Koegel (1977) used a token programme - controlled by both the therapist and teacher - which modified an autistic pupil's behaviour to the extent that she was able to follow lessons satisfactorily in a normal infant school with 30 other children.

Another interesting study concerns a pupil who had problems with his teachers (Polirstok and Greer (1977). After the pupil was taught to use a more approving tone towards his teachers, the latter gained a more positive image and regarded him as less of a problem.

An intensive workshop on behavioural therapy techniques for entire members of school staff proved extremely effective in reducing vandalism (some 80 per cent less), increasing teachers' positive responses to pupils and improving task focused behaviour (Mayer, Butterworth, Nafpaktitis and Sulzer-Azaroff, 1983).

Conclusion

ABA techniques positively effect vandalism and disruptive behaviour, also among toddlers, as well as autistic-related behavioural problems. ABA training for school staff, problem pupils being taught how to reward their teachers more often, and token programmes, were all used to reduce behavioural problems.

Fellow Pupils as Teachers

Solomon and Wahler (1973) showed that disruptive behaviour is largely reinforced by the behaviour of fellow pupils and that by making 'therapists' of them through providing information, behaviour instructions and training, their behaviour changed and they had a positive effect on the disruptive behaviour. Another example of what fellow pupils can achieve (Trovato and Bucher) combined peer tutorship with a home reinforcement programme. This led to a progress in reading by 1.27 year over a 15 week period (=0.3 year). Greer and Polirstok (1982) studied the mutual effects of peer tutoring. Problem teenagers were used to teach younger children to read and taught how to respond positively to their pupils' task focused behaviour. in their turn, tutors' positive responses were rewarded with tokens. This had positive results for both pupils and tutors (more task focused behaviour and improved reading). Peer-group pressure, which is often seen as contributing to difficult to control problem behaviour, was put to positive good use by Smith and Fowler (1984) when they put fellow pupils in charge of a token system, which was successful in reducing disruptive and recalcitrant behaviour. Pupils were most consistent in handing out tokens when they too received feedback for their behaviour.

Conclusion

Peers can contribute positively to teaching. They can use token systems for fellow pupils to reduce behavioural problems, while peer tutors selectively rewarding can improve reading ability among young children. It seems possible to create a positive learning and environmental climate using ABA techniques. Indeed, if everyone concerned were deployed to reduce each other's problem behaviour we would arrive at a whole environment strategy (Favell, 1992).

Training Teachers in Applied Behavioural Analysis

Many studies have been reviewed in the aforementioned that show the effectiveness of ABA in education. Is it possible for teachers to learn such techniques as more often selectively rewarding desired behaviour, working with tokens, using fellow pupils as reinforcers, recording behaviour, giving feedback, or dividing desired behaviour into small, achievable learning goals?

Cossairt, Hall and Hopkins (1973) were successful in increasing the frequency with which teachers rewarded children by getting them to use a combination of behaviour instructions, feedback on performance and social reinforcement. Sherman and Cormier (1974) reversed the roles and trained pupils to be better pupils in order to influence teacher behaviour. The pupils succeeded in getting the teachers to pay more attention to their positive rather than their negative behaviour. In their study of the effects of a headteacher selectively rewarding pupils, Copeland, Brown and Hall (1974) found that when the head persistently praised absent children for their presence in their classroom, their presence increased. Also when children, who were performing badly, were allowed to visit the head and their achievements praised if they conformed to a certain pre-determined criteria, they then performed better in class. The head entering a class and praising pupils who were improving as well as the 'best' achievers also increased performance.

Koegel, Russo and Rincover (1977) attempted to develop reliable and valid criteria for measuring and training skills to teach autistic children. Twenty-five hours of training for teachers proved sufficient to give them the skills required. Autistic children's behaviour improved when teachers were trained while teachers were able to generalise their skills to other children with behavioural problems. Trained teachers can also convey their skills to other teachers, whose skills are just as effective as those originally trained by researchers: with either type of teacher, pupils' problem behaviour dramatically changed (Jones, Fremouw and Carples, 1977).

Conclusion

Teachers can be trained to be expert users of ABA and to incorporate its principles into their normal teaching. ABA is not something over and above other teaching skills and tasks, but an integral aspect of these.

Conclusions and Recommendations

From the aforementioned it is possible to look at and improve many aspects of teaching from an ABA perspective. At the same time we need to acknowledge that the various effective methods mentioned are not used in the Netherlands. Often we come across well-intended attempts to improve the quality of teaching by using elements from behaviourial therapy techniques, such as the familiar rewarding with gummed stickers etc, but the systematic application of any clearly prescribed methodology is rare. The rare occasion a teacher, encouraged by the school head, applies a tried and tested technique is largely directed at a pupil's severe problem behaviour. This is then something temporary and in addition to normal teaching and thus costs time and energy, which has a demotivating effect.

Lindsley (1992) gave several reasons why effective teaching tools are not used widely in the United States. "Effective educational methods are available. They have been available for a long time. They are mostly behavioural, structured, fast-paced and require a high proportion of regular daily practice." Yet, much energy is expended on thinking up and organising new research projects. Lindsley explains that we are searching for answers to questions for which we already had an answer a long time ago. A first possible reason is the funding pitfall. New educational developments can be made possible with extra funding. If funding is stopped, then, politically speaking, new developments also stop, otherwise why would anyone bother asking for funding if they can get along without extra grants? Seen this way, improvements financed with extra money will always remain the 'frills' and never replace existing conventions no matter how successful they are. A second obstacle is the preconception that learning must always be enjoyable and an 'all or nothing' phenomenon. Learning to change behaviour is particularly strenuous and sometimes painful. Many educationalists stick to views like this and are thus unable to see the point of structured exercises in new education techniques, recording pupil progress as a result of these new skills and applying them in the classroom under supervision. A third hurdle to implementing successful teaching techniques is our prejudice towards competition. In sport we find it normal to publicise our achievements worldwide, yet when it comes to education results or effectively applying educational tools we regard it as unethical. A further problem concerns the entertainment value of a number of ineffective educational techniques, such as the wonderful success of Sesame Street. It is fantastic entertainment but falls precisely in the trap regarding preconceptions about learning: learning is enjoyable, easy, and an all or nothing phenomenon. Then there is the obstacle that effective teaching is seldom rewarded. Lindsley sees only one answer to this for himself: to use his educational talent in industry. Does the same fate await the behavioural therapist or applied behaviour analyst in the Netherlands? The current situation appears to have all the elements for this. It is extremely unappealing for Dutch teachers to try to qualify in ABA skills - they hardly exist, there are no recognised courses and the teaching environment would respond adversely to them being introduced. The challenges for both education and behavioural therapy in the future should be aimed at preventing this fate.

What Can We Learn from This?

When behavioural therapy techniques are introduced these should be part of the standard teaching package. At the same time it must be made known that working with these techniques is no easy, playful and straightforward task.

From the foregoing, the following ABA techniques can become part of teachers' skills repertoire:

* clear and specific behaviour instructions;
* selective contingent reinforcement (social and tokens);

- shaping;
- self-instruction;
- public feedback;
- ecological reorganisation (in the school, classroom and home);
- pin-pointing;
- differential reinforcement of other behaviour (DRO);
- positive-negative ratio;
- punishment and time out;
- training people in ABA.

Applied Behavioural Analysis Training for Heads and Teachers

If education is to pick up on ABA then there has to be proper recognised training available for teachers. Moreover if teachers are to be able to apply these skills to their normal teaching then school heads must also be able to help implement them. Therefore, there should be:

- recognised ABA training for both heads and teachers;
- more awareness by the Association for Behavioural Therapy for the needs of education.

Until now the association has paid little attention to using ABA within the context of school learning. Without any exaggeration it may be said that effective and efficient education is the best prevention against psychosocial and social problems. An association which whole-heartedly embraces learning theory should not neglect precisely this sector. Paying more attention to the subject at conferences, special themed issues of the association's magazine as well as it keeping its doors open to heads and teachers could be first steps in the right direction;

- more interest in ABA from teachers themselves. Now in education it is only discussed in terms of helping serious behavioural disorders;
- well-planned introductory courses also for teacher training colleges, personal experiences of ABA in trade journals, workshops and conferences.

Developing a Shared Language for a Technology of Change

This is a petition for bringing closer together what seem to be until now two relatively strange bedfellows: education and behavioural therapy. It has been shown that ABA has much to offer education. As well as positively effecting many educationally relevant behaviours, it also offers something else which is essential: namely a shared language regarding a technology of influence. An ABA perspective can explain why certain interventions are effective and others are not. It enables the education field to go beyond an intuitive level by providing a scientific basis to that area of teaching often given too little attention: why something is effective. The following story may serve to illustrate this point. A research committee comprised of various education specialists, research workers and two behavioural therapists were discussing developing a new method for guiding teachers in particular classroom situations. The initial discussion was concerned with the general framework in which the teachers could apply their interventions. When the behavioural therapists began to start putting what had been said into concrete terms, they noticed that the specialists and research workers regarded the meeting as finished on the grounds that "A clear and general framework has been created and any qualified teacher would know what to do." In reply to the behavioural therapist's question to explain exactly what was supposed to happen and exactly how the interventions would be applied, the broad framework was continually given as a reply. ABA is not content with broad frameworks: precisely specifying procedures are necessary, even in education. Precise specifications, with a consistent and scientifically based explanation of why something works.

REFERENCES

Ayllon, T. & Roberts, M. (1974). Eliminating discipline problems by strengthening academic performance. *Journal of Applied Behavior Analysis*, 7, 771-76.

Bailey, J.S., Wolf, M.M. & Phillips, E.L. (1970). Home-based reinforcement and the modification of predelinquents' classroom behavior. *Journal of Applied Behavior Analysis*, 3, 233-233.

Barrish, H.H., Saunders, M. & Wolf, M.M. (1969). Good behavior game: Effects of individual contingencies for group consequences on disruptive behavior in a classroom. *Journal of Applied Behavior Analysis*, 2, 119-124.

Bierman, K.L. & Furman, W. (91984). The effects of social skills training and peer involvement on the social adjustment of pre-adolescents. *Child Development*, 55, 151-162.

Bilsen, H.P.J.G. van (1989). *Motivational Interviewing*. Paper gepresenteerd op het eerste Europese Congres van Psychologie, Juli 1989, Amsterdam.

Bolstad, O.D. & Johnson, S.M. (1972). Selfregulation in the modification of disruptive classroom behavior. *Journal of Applied Behavior Analysis*, 5, 443-454.

Bruin, I.J. de (1983). *Verwijzing Speciaal Onderwijs naar Jeugdhulpverlening*. Interne publicatie van het Pedologisch Instituut Rotterdam.

Cartlegde, G. & Milburn, J.F. (1986). *Teaching Social Skills to Children*. New York: Regano Press.

Clark, H.B., Rowbury, T. & Bear, A.M. (1973). Timeouts as a punishing stimulus in confinuous and intermittent schedules. *Journal of Applied Behavior Analysis*, 6, 443-455.

Copeland, R.E., Brown, R.E. & Hall, R.V. (1974). The effects of principal-implement techniques on the behavior of pupils. *Journal of Applied Behavior Analysis*, 7, 77-86.

Cossairt, A., Hall, R.V. & Hopkins, B.L. (1973). The effects of experimenter's instructions, feedback and praise on teacher praise and student attending behavior. *Journal of Applied Behavior Analysis*, 6, 89-100.

Drabman, R.S. & Lahey, B.B. (1974). Feedback in classroom behavior modification: Effects on the target and her classmates. *Journal of Applied Behavior Analysis*, 7, 591-598.

Favell, (1992). Persoonlijke mededeling,, Wereldconferentie Gedragstherapie, Australië.

Foxx, R.M. & Shapiro, S.T. (1978). The timeout ribbon: A nonexclusionary timeout procedure. *Journal of Applied Behavior Analysis*, 11, 125-136.

Greer, R.D. & Polirstok, S.R. (1982). Collateral gains and short-term maintenance in reading and on-task responses by innercity adolecents as a function of their use of social reinforcement while tutoring. *Journal of Applied Behavior Analysis*, 15, 123-139.

Hall, R.V., Lund D. & Jackson, D. (1968). Effects of teacher attention on study behavior. *Journal of Applied Behavior Analysis*, 1, 1-12.

Hoeben, S.M. & Lier, P.A. van (1992). *Bronnenboek sociaal-emotionele ontwikkeling*. 's-Hertogenbosch: Katholiek Pedagogisch Studiecentrum.

Hollin, C.R. & Trower, P. (1986). Applications across the life span. *Handbook of social skills training*, 1, Oxford: Pergamon Press.

Houten, R. van, Nau, P.A., MacKenzie-Keating, S.E., Sameoto, D. & Colavecchia,B. (1982). An analysis of some variables influencing the effectiveness of reprimands. *Journal of Applied Behavior Analysis*, 15, 65-83.

Jones, F.H., Fremouw, W. & Carples, S. (1977). Pyramid training of elementary school teachers to use a classroom management "skill package". *Journal of Applied Behavior Analysis*, 10, 239-253.

Jongbloed, M.H.B. & Gunning I.A.P.M. (1991). Gedrags- en emotionele problemen binnen enkele vormen van speciaal onderwijs. In H.J.P.G. van Bilsen & H.D. Swager (red.). *Speciaal; onderwijs & jeugdhulpverlening*. De Lier: Academisch Boeken Centrum.

Jonkers, J. (1991). *Programma sociale vaardigheden*. PI-school Rotterdam, interne publikatie.

Kazdin, A.E. & Klock, J. (1973). The effect of nonverbal teacher approval on student attentive behavior. *Journal of Applied Behavior Analysis*, 6, 643-654

Kazdin, A.E. (1973). The effect of vicarious reinforcement on attentive behavior in the classroom. *Journal of Applied Behavior Analysis*, 6, 71-78.

Koegel, R.L., Russo, D.C. & Rincover, A. (1977). Assessing and training teachers in the generalized use of behavior modification with autistic children. *Journal of Applied Beyhavior Analysis*, 10, 197-205.

Lahey, B.B. & Kazdin, A.S. (1977) (eds.). *Advances in Clinical Child Psychology*, 1. New York: Plenum.

Lieshout, C.F.M. van & Ferguson, T.J., Lier, P.A. van & Vierssen, D.J. van (1987). *Diepteproject Sociaal-emotionele Ontwikkeling*. Nijmegen: Katholieke Universiteit.

Lindsley, O.R. (1992). Why aren't effective teaching tools widely adopted? *Journal of Applied Behavior Analysis*, 25, 21-26.

Matson, J. & Ollendick, Th.H. (1988).*Enchanching Children's Social Skills. Assessment and Training*. New Yor: Pergamon Press.

Mayer, G.R., Butterworth, T., Nafpaktits, M. & Sulzer-Azaroff, B. (1983). Preventing school vandalism and improving descipline: A three-year study. *Journal of Applied Behavior Analysis*, 16, 355-369.

Minuchin, S., e.a. (9167). *Families of the Slums*. New York: Basic Books Inc.

Molen, H.T. van der & Zee, S.A.M. van der (1985). *Sociale redzaamheidprogramma's voor minderbegaafde jongeren*. Groningen: Rijksuniversiteit Groningen, vakgroep Persoonlijkheidspsychologie.

O'Leary, K.D., Becker, W.C., Evans, M.B. & Saudargas, R.A. (1968). A token reinforcement program in a public school: A replication and systematics analysis. *Journal of Applied Behavior Analysis*, 2, 3-13.

Petermann, F. & Petermann, U. (1988). *Training mit agressiven Kindern*. (Einzeltraining, Kindergruppen, Elternberatung). München-Weinheim: Psychologie Verlags Union.

Petermann, U. (1988). *Werken met sociaal angstige kinderen* (theorie en praktijk van de training). Nijmegen: Dekker & Van de Vegt.

Pfiffner, L.J., Rosén, L.A. & O'Leary, S.G. (1985). The efficacy of an all-positive approach to classroom management. *Journal of Applied Behavior Analysis*, 18, 257-261.

Polirstok, S.R. & Greer, R.D. (1977). Remidiation of mutually aversie interactions between a problem student and four teachers by training the student in reinforcement techniques. *Journal of Applied Behavior Analysis*, 10, 707-716.

Porterfield, J.K., Herbert-Jackson, E. & Risley, T.R. (1976). Contingent observation: An effective and acceptable procedure for reducing disruptive behavior of young children in a group setting. *Journal of Applied Behavior Analysis*, 9, 55-64.

Prochaska, J.O. & DiClemente, C.C. (1984). *The Transtheoretical Approach: Crossing Traditional Boundaries of Therapy*. Homewood, Illinois: Dow Jones-Irwin.

Ringrose, H.J. & Nijenhuis, E.H. (1986). *Bang zijn voor andere kinderen*. Groningen: Wolters-Noordhoff.

Russo, D.C. & Koegel, R.L. (1977). A method for integrating an autistic child into a normal public-school classroom. *Journal of Applied Behavior Analysis*, 10, 579-590.

Sanders-Woudstra, J.A.R. & Verhulst, F.C. (1987). Epidemiologisch-kinderpsychiatrische benadering van de ontwikkelingen in het speciaal onderwijs. In K. Doornbos & L.M. Stevens (red.). *De groei van het speciaal onderwijs. deel A. Analyse van historie en onderzoek*. 's-Gravenhage: Staatsuitgeverij.

Santogrossie, D.A., O'Lear, K.D., Romanczyk, R.G. & Kaufman, K.F. (1973). Selfevaluation by adolecents in a psychiatric hospital school token program. *Journal of Applied Behavior Analysis*, 6, 277-287.

Schuurman, C.M.A. (1991). Mogelijkheden en beperkingen van de stimulering van de sociaal emotionele ontwikkeling van kinderen in het speciaal onderwijs. In H.P.J.G. van Bilsen & H.D. Swager (red.). *Speciaal Onderwijs en Jeugdhulpverlening*. De Lier: Academisch Boeken Centrum.

Sherman, T.M. & Cormier, W.H. (1974). An investigation of the influence of studentbehavior on teacher behavior. *Journal of Applied Behavior Analysis*, 7, 11-21.

Smith, B.M., Schumaker, J.B., Schaeffer, J. & Sherman, J.A. (1982). Increasing partcipation and improving the quality of duscussions in seventh-grade social studies classes. *Journal of Applied Behavior Analysis*, 15, 97-110.

Smith, L.K.C. & Fowler, S.A. (1984). Positive peer pressure: The effects of peer monitoring on children's disruptive behavior. *Journal of Applied Behavior Analysis*, 17, 213-227.

Solomon, R.W. & Wahler, R.G. (1973). Peer reinforcement control of classroom problem behavior. *Journal of Applied Behavior Analysis*, 6, 49-56.

Trovato, J. & Bucher, B. (1980). Peer tutoring with or without homebased reinforcement, for reading remediation. *Journal of Applied Behavior Analysis*, 13, 129-141.

Wielkiewicz, R. (1986). *Behavior Management in the Schools*. New York: Pregmom.

Willems, E.P. (1974). Behavioral Technology and Behavioral Ecology. *Journal of Applied Behavior Analysis*, 7, 151-165.

5

COGNITIVE BEHAVIOR MODIFICATION OF ADHD

A Family System Approach

Harry van der Vlugt, Huub M. Pijnenburg, Paul M. A. Wels, and
Aly Koning

Stichting voor Pedologische Instituten
PO Box 10545
6500 MB Nijmegen
The Netherlands

INTRODUCTION

Children who suffer from the ADHD syndrome have problems regulating their behavior due to an imbalance between their excitatory and their inhibitory systems. Because of that they are unable to function optimally. In order to perform better the imbalance can be corrected by means of chemical treatment (medication) or by means of effort (behavior modification programs).

As a rule one might say, we try to medicate ADHD children as little as possible. This certainly holds true for the Stichting voor Paedologische Instituten (in the following: Pedological Institute in Nijmegen, the Netherlands (NPI). Consequently, over the past decade much emphasis has been placed upon behavior modification programs. Because our Pedological Institute is one of only three research institutes in the Netherlands with residential treatment facilities (the others are in Amsterdam and Oisterwijk), we are able to monitor a child's behavior 24 hours a day.

Initially we offered an individual cognitive behavior modification program to ADHD children in the form of daily 45 minute sessions. Although children responded favorably to these training sessions (they became more quiet and their attention span increased), the specific results of the individual training did not generalize to other situations, more specifically to the school or the residential group. In order to achieve such generalization we started instructing the teachers and residential group workers. In that way we were able to create a consistent and systematic therapeutic approach of ADHD throughout the day.

In spite of these efforts parents continued to comment that they did not experience any improvement or relief during the biweekly weekend home visits of their children. In response to these complaints we embarked upon the development of a parent training program. This program is an extension of the above mentioned cognitive behavior modification program as it is currently used at our institute.

Behavioral Approaches for Children and Adolescents, Edited by
H. P. J. G. van Bilsen et al., Plenum Press, New York, 1995

The implications of such an enterprise, the approach to pre- and post-testing, problems related to subject selection (parents and children), and monitoring such a program, and the implications for the Pedological Institute in terms of staff management, continuous education of the teachers and group workers are reviewed. Finally, suggestions for future treatment programs, including cost-efficiency aspects and specific organizational pitfalls are discussed.

ADHD Research at the Pedological Institute: A Historical Perspective

Because of its admission policy, the Nijmegen Pedological Institute has a relatively high percentage of ADHD children. All of these children have received previous outpatient treatment in their own residential areas. However, due to the complexity of their behavioral and learning problems treatment remained without success. As a result treatment in a highly specialized residential treatment centre was indicated.

Over the past decade we devoted considerable research efforts to diagnostic issues regarding ADHD. These efforts were aimed at trying to understand the underlying cause of this disorder. (Van der Vlugt and Feltzer, 1983; Brand and Van der Vlugt, 1986; Berndsen-Peeters and Van der Vlugt, 1986; Brand, Van der Vlugt and Oosterbaan, 1987; Brand and Van der Vlugt, 1989; Koning, Snijkers, Van der Vlugt, Pijnenburg and Wels, 1993a). This implies that we focused upon the ADHD children themselves, not their environment or their families. As a result we were quite successful in identifying those ADHD children who would benefit from medication. Most children (70%) responded favourably to our medication program and side-effects were marginal.

But what to do with the 30% that do not benefit from stimulant medication and what should we do for the children who suffer significant side effects from this medication? And even if medication is optimally effective, the environment still needs to know how to deal with an ADHD child who demonstrates medication-induced-improved behavior. An additional problem is that medication is not effective 24 hours a day. What to do in the late afternoon, or in the early evening, or in the early morning? What to do during the drug-free holidays? On top of all this it is also known that in the long run medication affects the overt behavioral symptoms, but does not improve the long-term treatment outcome for these children.

As in many other countries, in The Netherlands too the cry for behavior treatment programs has in recent years become louder. Also there still is a strong anti-medication movement in our country. As a result of these observations, as well as our growing interest in cognitive behavior therapy, we decided to direct our attention towards cognitive behavior modification programs as developed by Meichenbaum (1977), Kendall (1985) and Barkley (1990).

Meanwhile follow-up research has demonstrated that the initial combination of medication and behavioral therapy followed by a second stage of mere behavioral therapy is more successful than medication or behavioral therapy alone. It is suggested that the initially administered medication causes the child to be more open to behavioral therapy. As a result, the behavior program can be effective more quickly.

How did our research and development work with respect to treatment of ADHD evolve at the Pedological Institute? Initially, a special individual training program for ADHD children was developed, based upon the principles of cognitive behavior modification. This program consisted of twenty structured sessions. The trainer met with each child twice a week during school hours. This work was carried out in the mid-eighties (Dortmans and Prinssen, 1984; Alberts and Dam, 1985; Mostermans, 1987). The initial outcomes were disappointing. The children did quite well during the individual training sessions but failed to generalize what they had learned during the individual sessions to other contexts. So we trained the schoolteachers and the residential group workers and asked them to implement the training principles during the rest of the day. Despite this combined effort, the parents continued to voice complaints. They reported that during their biweekly-leaves and during the holidays, their children continued to show the same problem behavior. Often these complaints were not limited to typical ADHD features but also involved aggression, oppositional defiant behavior, underachievement in school, depression, lack of self-confidence, and problems with peer relationships. These are problems which in the long run can lead to even more serious problems such as dropping out of school, law violations, antisocial behavior, instable peer relationships, psychiatric disorders, divorce, unsuccessful job-records, traffic accidents later on (e.g. Lambeir, Bouman and Nolen, 1991).

Moreover, parents commented that they felt ill-informed and unable to create an optimal environment for their ADHD child at home. They reported feeling unable to explain to their neighbors what was wrong with their child.

Within the family situation this lack of insight or understanding can cause many additional problems such as a high amount of family stress induced by the ADHD related child rearing problems (Wels & Robbroeckx, 1991a). Wels goes as far as to state that hyperactivity might be considered a child rearing or family system problem of an interactional nature. Both the ADHD related behavioral problems of the child and the (in)abilities of the parents to cope serve as input for the clinical assessment of the problematic child rearing situation (Wels, 1992; Wels and Jansen, 1994).

Because of these complaints we decided to embark upon a project that would extend the program to include the parents in the cognitive behavior modification program. As yet very little is known about the effect of parent training programs (Barkley, 1990). This contrasts sharply with the hundreds of studies on the effect of stimulant medication. We were able to find only 16 studies (Koning et al., 1993a). Of these studies very few incorporated a parent training program into an overall treatment program. Surprisingly, all these programs had in common that they demonstrated some kind of improvement in the child's behavior. None of the studies however, provided information on selection criteria or procedures about which ADHD child in which family could benefit most from this kind of treatment.

When looking at these studies in detail, many inconsistencies and problems become apparent: there is no clear definition of the ADHD child involved, no information about training frequencies, no information about the exact nature of the training during the process, and many methodological problems. Many studies are based upon very small sample sizes and lack information about comorbidity, reliable base-line measurements and follow-up findings. In conclusion: there proved to be no standard approach we could follow.

This is not altogether surprising, when one contemplates the problems connected with clinical research. For instance those problems one can encounter when trying to assess the effect of a specific therapy. According to Rourke, Bakker, Fisk and Strang (1983) remediation can prove to be an exceptionally complex undertaking. The problems and questions are manyfold. Just to mention a few: how exactly does one determine the form of a treatment; how to study the effect of this specific treatment in a homogeneous group and how to evaluate the effectiveness of this specific treatment? Not to mention clinical-emotional aspects, for instance the collaboration and the motivation of the child, which are essential during such a project. Especially with ADHD children this is hard to achieve. Therefore we had to extend our initial 30 minute sessions to 45 minute sessions in order to have some time to create a constructive therapeutic climate first. Because in this study we trained children as well as their parents, a lot of therapeutic activities had to take place outside the institute. That is the major reason why we did not pay special attention to possible positive or negative changes in child behavior during this study. In a future study we hope (although perhaps the odds are against us) to be able to use two matched groups, allowing us to control for the variable "parent treatment." Furthermore one should realize that the end of this (parent training) project is imposed by our research design and not by the achievement of some preset goals. Although our program may be very successful in in terms of "curing" the ADHD symptoms, this does not necessarily mean that the child will be able to make the right decisions. So, given these problems, how are we supposed to measure the effectiveness of therapy?

In addition one should realize that the therapeutic needs of a child may change during the therapeutic process. This raises another question. Does one stick to the program for the sake of scientific evaluation or should one change the program in order to meet the changing needs of the individual child?

In view of these problems and deliberations we strongly believe that this kind of research should be done in a individual, step-by-step fashion, allowing us to offer the child a treatment program that keeps in touch with the individual needs of that child. Keeping this in mind we decided to train the parents to use the cognitive behavior modification program themselves. Assuming that the program was running quite well at the institute (we heard of no complaints), we developed an additional program for the parents. The underlying assumption here is that by including the parents we are able to create a supporting environment which offers optimal conditions for corroboration of the treatment results achieved within the institute. Therefore – as a new approach in measuring the effectiveness of the total family system approach - we included an instrument for the measurement of family- or child rearing stress (Wels and Robbroeckx, 1991a) into the present study design. This instrument enables assessment of possible changes in the parents' perspective on the ADHD related child rearing problems.

METHOD

Subjects and Selection Procedure

Based upon our previous experience we anticipated some problems in selecting ADHD children for this study. As mentioned earlier, due to the admission policy about 80% of the children that are accepted at the Pedological Institute demonstrate characteristics of ADHD to such an extent, that they meet the DSM IV criteria. So a multistage selection procedure was designed.

In order to include children in our study we *first* screened client records. These records contain information on a client's history, family background, psychological testing, neuro-psychological testing, school records and achievement testing, physical -, neurologi-cal - and psychiatric evaluation. This file based screening was carried out by the neuro-psy-chologist. Children below the age of seven and above the age of twelve were not selected. In order to be able to follow the program the child should have a minimum IQ of 75. Furthermore there should not be any indication of an evident neurological disorder such as epilepsy, head trauma, nor of a specific psychiatric disorder. The record of the child should also suggest a relatively stable home situation at present.

In a *second* screening stage the psychologist, responsible for the treatment all children in a residential group had to confirm the neuro-psychologist's opinion and make sure that, over the past year, ADHD was identified as one of the major problems of the child by the NPI residential treatment team.

During the *third* stage of our screening procedure the residential group workers and the teachers of the children at the institute's NPI school for special education were asked to rate the severity of the ADHD. The teachers also completed the Self Control Rating Scale (Kendall and Wilcox, 1979). Only the most severe ADHD children were selected. These

month:	1 (aug.)	8	9	10	11	12	14	15
phase:	pre	training	-----parents-----	----children----		post		
assessment data								
children		CBSK					CBSK	
parents			NVOS GTV GOO				NVOS GTV GOO Quest.	
teacher	TRF SCRS	SCRS CTRS			TRF SCRS CTRS	SCRS CTRS	SCRS CTRS	TRF
res.group workers	CBCL	SCRS CTRS			CBCL	SCRS CTRS	SCRS	CBCL
psychol.		NAP						NAP
trainer		-training observations- Video					Video	

CBCL/TRF = Achenbach's Child Behavior Checklist and Teacher Report Form, Dutch version (Verhulst, Koot, Akkerhuis & Veerman, 1990)
CBSK = Harter's Self Perception Profile for Children, Dutch version (Veerman, 1989)
CTRS = Conners' Teachers Rating Scale, Dutch version (Blöte & Curfs, 1986)
Quest. = Evaluation Questionnaire for Parent Training Program
GOO = Behavior Observation Scale for Parents (Dutch instrument) (Boorsma, 1990; in Gunning, 1992)
GTV = Sandoval Lambert & Sassone's Behavior and Temperament Survey, Dutch version (Korenromp & Verwaaijen, 1981)
NAP = Neuropsychological Assessment Procedure (Van der Vlugt, 1988)
NVOS = Nijmegen Child-Rearing Situation Questionnaire (Wels & Robbroeckx, 1991)
SCRS = Self Control Rating Scale (Kendall & Wilcox, 1979)
Video = Home video recordings of family activities (playing games, setting the table and having dinner)

Figure 1. Schematic overview of the design of the present study.

outcomes were double checked by the head of the school. Following this procedure 14 children and their families were selected for participation in our training program.

Finally the social worker, who collaborates with the family advised us about the feasibility of each family's participation in the program. The parents should have a level of cognitive development allowing them to follow our instructions. There should also be reasonable consensus between the parents about their joint child rearing practice, and none of the parents or the families should be engaged in any other form of parent therapy that might interfere with our program.

As a result of this final selection eight families were considered fit to enter the program. All these families were invited at the Institute and were informed about the program by the trainers. Six families agreed to participate.

Design

Figure 1 is a schematic rendering of the design of the present study. For a more extensive account the reader is referred to Koning, Pijnenburg, Snijkers, Van der Vlugt and Wels (1993a). The training programs for children and parents as well as those instruments not familiar to non-Dutch readers are elaborated upon in the following sections.

The Training Program for ADHD Children

The cognitive behavior modification program is based upon the original "Think Aloud" program of Camp and Bash (1981) and concentrates upon cognitive modelling and self-verbalisation. Throughout this program four basic questions are raised in order to promote children's systematic approach to solving problems.

1. What is my problem? or what am I supposed to do?
2. What is my plan? or how can I do it?
3. Am I using my plan?
4. How did I do?

The child has to answer the first two questions before beginning a task. While performing the task, question three is asked. Upon completing a task question four is raised.

The learning process of the program follows this structure:

1. the child observes how the model talks aloud to him/herself during the performance of a task;
2. the child performs the task while the adult verbalises the instructions;
3. the child performs the task while verbally instructing itself aloud;
4. the child performs the task while whispering instructions to itself;
5. the child performs the task while using inner speech.

The program was devised for use by special education/remedial teachers and therapists in a school setting, to be administered to individual children or small groups (up to four children). The program consists of 23 structured problem solving sessions, focusing on cognitive and interpersonal problems. The sessions are prepared as scripts to be followed by the teacher/therapist.

The Training Program for the Parents

Based upon the program we used for the child, and the parent training programs of Barkley (1981, 1987 and 1990), Braswell and Bloomquist (1991), Shure and Spivack (1978), Spivack and Shure (1974), and Spivack, Platt and Shure (1976), we developed an interven-

Introductory meeting:
> informing the parents about ADHD and the orientation and goals of the parent training program.

Session 1:
> informing the parents about the importance of the four basic questions how to reinforce and motivate a child by means of a reward system.

Session 2:
> familiarizing the parents with a five steps model for bringing children from vocalizing aloud to inner speech (modeling)

Session 3:
> teaching the child how to use the four questions (from session 1) and the five steps (from session 2) in interpersonal relationships

Session 4:
> as session 3, but with more emphasis on the evaluation of chosen strategies and self confirmation

Session 5:
> discussion of how to proceed after this training, how to anticipate future problems and how to bring about generalization of what children learn in the program to other situations.

Evaluation:
> after a six weeks summer holiday the parents discuss (among themselves and with the training staff) the benefits and problem they have encountered during and after the program.

Figure 2. Schematic overview of the objectives of the parent program training sessions.

tion program for parents in which the cognitive behavior modification techniques, put forward by Meichenbaum (1977) and Kendall and Finch (1979) take a central position.

In five sessions the program is presented to the individual families by the trainer who will also train the individual children. The parent program starts after the child has had at least 10 individual sessions. The two-weekly sessions with the parents take about two hours each. Preceding these five sessions, an introductory meeting with the trainer is scheduled for all participating parents. Likewise, at the end of the program an evaluative meeting for all participants is staged. The contents of the five home-sessions are described in detail in a training manual (Koning, Snijkers, Pijnenburg, Van der Vlugt and Wels, 1993b) designed in the course of our research project. The general outline of the parent-program is presented in figure 2.

Instruments

Assuming that the reader is familiar with most instruments used in this study (see Figure 1 for an overview) and for the sake of brevity, we will elaborate here only upon those instruments that non-Dutch readers are unlikely to be familiar with. For a comprehensive discussion of all instruments the reader is referred to Koning a.o., 1993a).

The *Nijmegen Child-rearing Situation Questionnaire* (NVOS: Nijmeegse Vragenlijst voor de Opvoedingssituatie, Wels and Robbroeckx, 1989; 1991a 1991b). The NVOS is a Dutch, Likert type questionnaire for parents and consists of four parts. Each part represents a different aspect of the parent's perspective on child rearing problems. The different parts are: (A) subjective family stress (46 items); (B) the evaluation of the child rearing situation (eight descriptions, one has to choose the best fitting); (C) the attributions regarding the actual child rearing situation (34 items) and (D) the expectation of help (36 items). The instrument was studied extensively (Wels & Robbroeckx, 1991b) and proved to be reliable and valid.

The *Behavior Observation Scale for Parents* (Boorsma, 1990, cited by Gunning), consisting of 15 items, was used as a supplementary questionnaire because of its focus on self control behavior.

The *Evaluation Questionnaire for Parents* was designed in the context of the present study to provide feedback on the following aspects: information prior to training; information offered during training; session features (length, frequency, timing and location); usefulness of techniques instructed during training; training structure and content.

The *Neuro-psychological Assessment Program* (Van der Vlugt, 1988) is a standardized screening procedure, consisting of a wide range of tests It is used to make an assessment of the following functions: intelligence, language, memory, attention and concentration, visual-constructive skills and fine motor skills.

RESULTS AND DISCUSSION

The major goal of this pilot study was to see if we could come up with an answer to the questions and concerns the parents continued to have, while their child was receiving a special treatment program at the Pedological Institute. In this respect the outcomes from the pre- and post test of the Nijmegen Child-rearing Situation Questionnaire are most informative. With respect to all aspects that were assessed, the parents' responses indicate a distinct improvement in the post-test situation as compared to the pretest. One should realize however that in the pretest situation the parents clearly indicated that rearing this child is particularly difficult because of the specific problems of the child and because of the fact that both parents have to put in a lot of effort. This is indicated by high initial scores on family stress, as assessed by means of the NVOS. It is also remarkable that the parents indicate that after the training their partner is much more involved. The training also results in a better mutual understanding between the partners. All parents also indicate that they do not feel "left alone" anymore. The need for external help was variable. Some parents indicate a need for extra counselling after six weeks with their child. As a result of the program the parents become more demanding of their children, which imposes a temporarily strain on the relationship.

During the plenary evaluation the parents indicate that the pace of the training program was too high: they would have been in favor of more sessions and also of more opportunities to practice with the program (instead of once every other week). They also would appreciate more extensive feedback on their homework. In our view, a combination of the present program and more extensive use of video hometraining techniques as proposed by Wels (1992) and Wels and Jansen (1994), may prove a valuable addition that can be instrumental in solving this problem.

With regard to the individual changes in behavior of the children the results are not clearcut. When looking at factors that can account for this finding, first of all we point to the fact that the training period was quite short (right after the training, the summer holidays started). Opportunities to implement the training consequences within the school system, or the residential group system were insufficient. We strongly believe that the "end of the year" effect (school trips, annual sports events and so on) may have influenced the behavior of the children.

Furthermore, clinical inspection of the neuro-psychological data suggests that some children performed suboptimally, because they were just starting to apply the rules they learned during the training. This implies that their "new behavior" is not yet acquired and internalized to such an extent that they could already actually benefit from it. Four months of training followed by two months outside the institute and the training program is not sufficient to shape the behavior to the amount we wished. More training, and especially more time to allow for a generalization within the school and the residential group setting is needed.

With regard to the parents, the outcomes are very favorable. All parents report that they are more capable of dealing with their child, and do not feel helpless anymore. They feel more confident about their child-rearing practices, and experience a closer collaboration. They are able to explain to their environment what is wrong and what is good about their child. In short they feel more competent and less frustrated. However, they also indicate that they would favor a longer period of training, allowing them more time to practice with the program. Within the present study they only had about 5 weekends to practice and then were left to their own devices for about two months in a row during the summer holidays.

In organizational/managerial terms a cognitive behavioral approach of ADHD in a residential setting has clearcut and quite profound consequences. First of all, in order to be able to run the individual cognitive behavioral modification program presented, here one must be able to invest about 45 minutes a day for each child. The basic individual training for a child spans 23 sessions, which means some 20 hours of individual training for each child in total. Furthermore, the program has implications for routine treatment practice within a residential setting such as the NPI: a child-in-training should be approached by the teachers and the residential group workers in a way that is in accordance with the principles underlying the ADHD training program. Because of the quick staff turn-over rate and the relatively high percentage of sick-leaves, it is all the more relevant to offer these staff members a basic training program at least once a year, consisting of two one-day sessions minimum. But this is not enough. Further investments are needed. In particular to enable training for social workers (also dealing with the parents), as well as continuous upgrading/training for the trainers carrying out the child and parent programs (in order to achieve maximum output and minimal coordination problems it is ideal to have one staff member deal with both children and parents). Treatment supervision and coordination hours must also be taken into account.

Considering these demands upon staff time, and consequently on institute budget, one should also be aware that such a program is only feasible for about 30% of the ADHD children undergoing treatment in a residential youth care setting. This estimate is based upon our clinical/project experiences. This still leaves us with 70% of the ADHD children, whose special needs have to be met adequately. The question we need to ask is: do we want to treat ADHD children by means of behavior modification without knowledge of the long term effects, do we prefer long term chemical treatment, or do we seek to combine both approaches? How convincing and valid are our scientific arguments for one approach and/or the other? At present the available literature does not provide us with clearcut answers. With the present (and future) limited funding in our field we should include this basic fact into our considerations: we know that chemical treatment has little or no positive influence upon long-term personality development. Because of that we argue to give a behavioral approach at least a fair chance.

As the situation stands today, the majority of Dutch children with ADHD do not receive appropriate treatment or guidance. In our view this is due primarily to the still widespread reluctance to offer long term medication to these children and the fact that we lack the financial means to realize a behavior modification approach for all ADHD children and their parents.

Given this situation, we have to develop and test even better approaches in the future. This project has shed some light on a combined child-family system approach and shows at least some improved features in terms of both set-up and results of the program. We have argued that in most cases parents of ADHD children show high levels of family stress, in combination with educational/pedagogical strain. Using a family system approach we were able to show expected and systematic changes in the perspective of parents as measured by a specially designed instrument for revealing changes in the parent's perspective on child rearing stress. Considering the pedagogical aim of this project, which is to support the parents in their daily task of raising their ADHD child, this is an important result. This result can be achieved by assisting the parents in creating optimal opportunities for their children's as well as their personal development, both of which are clearly at risk.

REFERENCES

Alberts, P. and Dam, M. (1985). *Eerst denken, dan doen. Een cognitief-gedragstherapeutisch trainingspro-gramma voor het individuele hyperactieve kind.* Doctoraalscriptie. Nijmegen: Instituut voor Orthopeda-gogiek en Paedologisch Instituut.

American Psychiatric Association (1994). *Diagnostic and Statistical Manual of Mental Disorders* (4th Ed.). Washington, DC: Author.

Barkley, R.A. (1981). *Hyperactive Children: A handbook for diagnosis and treatment.* New York: Guilford Press.

Barkley, R.A. (1987). *Defiant children: A clinician's manual for parent training.* New York: Guilford Press.

Barkley, R.A. (1990). *Attention Deficit Hyperactivity Disorder: A handbook for diagnosis and treatment.* New York: Guilford Press.

Berndsen-Peeters, J. and van der Vlugt, H. (1986). Development and application of a screening battery for the detection of hyperactive and learning disabled children. *Journal of Clinical and Experimental Neuro-psychology, 8,* 122.

Blöte, A.W. and Curfs, L.M.G. (1986). Het gebruik van de Conners Teacher Rating Scale in Nederland: Enige psychometrische gegevens. *Nederlands Tijdschrift voor de Psychologie, 41,* 226-236.

Brand, E. and van der Vlugt, H. (1986). Electrocardiac recording during a continuous performance task in hyperactive boys and two control groups. *Journal of Clinical and Experimental Neuro-psychology, 8,* 122.

Brand, E. and van der Vlugt, H. (1989) Activation: Base level and responsivity. A search for subtypes of ADDH children by means of electrocardiac, dermal, and respiratory measures. In: T. Sagvolden and T. Archer (Eds.), *Attention Deficit Disorder: Clinical and basic research.* Hillsdale: Lawrence Erlbaum Associ-ates.

Brand, E., van der Vlugt, H. and Oosterbaan, H. (1987) Electrocardiac recording during a simple reaction time task in hyperactive and normoactive children. *Journal of Clinical and Experimental Neuro-psychology, 9,* 276.

Braswell, L. and Bloomquist, M.L. (1991). *Cognitive behavioral therapy with ADHD children: child, family, and school interventions.* New York: Guilford Press.

Camp, B.W. and Bash, M.S. (1981). *Think aloud: Increasing social cognitive skills- A problem-solving program for children.* Champaign, Il. Research Press.

Dortmans, L. and Prinssen, D. (1984) *Luister naar jezelf. Een onderzoek naar de toepasbaarheid van een cognitief trainingsprogramma op impulsieve kinderen.* Doctoraalscriptie. Nijmegen: Instituut voor Orthopeda-gogiek.

Gunning, B. (1992). *A controlled trial of clonidine in hyperactive children.* Unpublished doctoral dissertation. Rotterdam: Erasmus University.

Kendall, P.C. (1985). *Cognitive-behavioral therapy for impulsive children.* Guilford University Press: New York.

Kendall, P.C. and Finch, A.J.Jr. (1979). Developing non-impulsive behavior in children: Cognitive-behavioral strategies for self-control. In: P.C. Kendall and S.D. Hollon (Eds.), *Cognitive-behavioral interventions: Theory, research and procedures* (pp. 37-80). New York: Academic Press.

Kendall, P.C. and Wilcox, L.E. (1979). Self-control in children: Development of a rating scale. *Journal of Consulting and Clinical Psychology, 47,* 1020-1029.

Koning, A., Pijnenburg, H., Snijkers, A., van der Vlugt, H. and Wels, P. (1993a) *Opvoedingsondersteuning voor ouders van kinderen met ADHD (Educational support for parents of ADHD children): Een oriënterend onderzoek naar de mogelijkheden voor toepassing van een gedragsmodificatieprogramma door ouders in de thuissituatie (An exploratory study into the possibilities for the use of a behavior modification program by parents in the home situation).* Nijmegen: Stichting voor Paedologische Instituten en Katholieke Universiteit.

Koning, A., Pijnenburg, H.M., Snijkers, A., Van der Vlugt, H. and Wels, P.M.A. (1993b). *Trainershandboek en ouderwerkboek voor het ADHD programma: Experimentele versie (Trainer manual and parents workbook for the ADHD training program: Experimental version).* Unpublished manuscript. Nijmegen: Stichting voor Paedologische Instituten.

Korenromp, G. and Verwaaijen, S. (1981). *Van minimal brain dysfunction naar hyperactiviteit: de ontwikkeling van een observatiecategorieënsysteem voor het meten van hyperactief gedrag.* Doctoraalscriptie. Nijmegen: Katholieke Universiteit en Paedologisch Instituut.

Lambeir, E.J., Bouman, N.H. and Nolen, W.A. (1991). Wat wordt er van hyperactieve kinderen? *Kind en Adolescent, 12,* 209-214.

Meichenbaum, D. (1977). *Cognitive behavior modification: An integrative approach.* New York: Plenum Press.

Mostermans, A. (1987). *Screening van hyperactieve kinderen. Onderzoek naar een screening-batterij en de validering van de Self-Control Rating Scale ter onderscheiding van hyperactieve en niet-hyperactieve kinderen.* Doctoraalscriptie. Instituut voor Orthopedagogiek en Paedologisch Instituut. Nijmegen.

Rourke, B.P., Bakker, D.J., Fisk, J.L. and Strang, J.D. (1983). *Child neuro-psychology: An introduction to theory, research and clinical practice.* New York: Guilford Press.

Shure , M.B. and Spivack, G., (1978). *Problem-solving techniques in childrearing.* San Francisco: Jossey-Bass Publishers.

Spivack, G., Platt, J.J. and Shure, M.B. (1976). *The problem-solving approach to adjustment: A guide to research and intervention.* San Francisco: Jossey-Bass Publishers.

Spivack, G. and Shure, M.B. (1974). *Social adjustment of young children: A cognitive approach to solving real-life problems.* San Francisco: Jossey-Bass Publishers.

Van der Vlugt, H. (1988). *Handleiding bij een neuropsychologisch testbatterij: Theorie en praktijk.* Unpublished manuscript. Tilburg: Brabant University, Neuro-psychology section.

Van der Vlugt, H. and Feltzer, M.J.A. (1983) Hyperactiviteit. In: J. de Wit, H. Bolle and J.M van Meel (red.), *Psychologen over het kind* (Vol. 7). Lisse: Swets & Zeitlinger.

Veerman, J.W. (1989). De Competentiebelevingsschaal voor Kinderen. Theoretische uitgangspunten en enkele onderzoeksgegevens. *Tijdschrift voor Orthopedagogiek, 28,* 286-301.

Verhulst, F.C., Koot, J.M., Akkerhuis, G.W. and Veerman, J.W. (1990). *Praktische handleiding voor de CBCL.* Assen: Van Gorcum.

Wels, P.M.A. and Robbroeckx, L.M.H. (1989). *Handleiding bij de Nijmeegse Vragenlijst voor de Opvoedingssituatie (NVOS, versie 3.2).* (Technical Report November 1989, ISBN 90 5085 015 4). Nijmegen: Instituut voor Orthopedagogiek.

Wels, P.M.A. and Robbroeckx, L.M.H. (1991a). Gezinsbelasting en hulpverlening aan gezinnen (I). Een model voor gezinsbelasting ten gevolge van een problematische opvoedingssituatie. *Tijdschrift voor Orthopedagogiek, 30,* 5-19.

Wels, P.M.A. and Robbroeckx, L.M.H. (1991b). Gezinsbelasting en hulpverlening aan gezinnen (II). De betrouwbaarheid en validiteit van de NVOS onderzocht. *Tijdschrift voor Orthopedagogiek, 30,* 63-79.

Wels, P.M.A. (1992). *Ondersteuning van ouders met hyperactieve kinderen met behulp van video-hometraining.* In: J.R.M. Gerris (Red.), *Opvoedings- en gezinsondersteuning. Gezinsonderzoek: Deel 6* (pp. 143-164). Amsterdam/Lisse: Swets & Zeitlinger.

Wels, P.M.A. and Jansen, R.J.A.H. (june 1994). *Video hometraining. A new family systems approach in supporting families with hyperactive children.* Paper submitted for inclusion in the book on the International Symposium on ADHD, 17-18 june 1994, Amsterdam.

6

COMPETENCY-BASED TREATMENT FOR ANTISOCIAL YOUTH

N. W. Slot

Pedologisch Instituut Amsterdam (VU)
PO Box 303
1115 ZG Duivendrecht
The Netherlands

INTRODUCTION

In 1968, Baer, Wolf and Risley published "Some Current Dimensions of Applied Behavior Analyses." This paper provided a framework for researchers and practitioners who propagated that the Skinnerian model for behavior change should be applied in order to solve problems of social importance. Applied Behavior Analysis (ABA) became a discipline for behaviorists working in fields as academic and vocational training, treatment of the developmentally disabled, treatment of behavioral problems but also in the fields of organizational management, traffic safety and environmental protection. Crime and delinquency have always been a major target of ABA. ABA principles have been the basis for the development of many intervention programs for adult and juvenile offenders.

One of the major contributions of ABA with respect to the treatment of juvenile delinquency has been the introduction of the *teaching-approach*. Instead of an emphasis on punishment which is the usual intervention in the juvenile justice system, or a focus on the diminishment of inappropriate behavior, which is a common approach in behavior therapy, the ABA programs for young delinquents emphasized the teaching of prosocial skills. A well know example is the Teaching Family Model: groups homes directed by couples - teaching parents - who live together with six to eight youths. Teaching parents were trained in the application of behavioral skill training. The model has been implemented on a broad scale (Braukmann and Wolf, 1987).

ABA and the Teaching Family Model served as an inspiration for researchers at the Paedologisch Instituut in Amsterdam/Duivendrecht. From 1974 onwards they have been working in the field of outpatient and residential treatment for young delinquents and their families. During the last twenty years a great number of programs within the field of juvenile justice and youth care and treatment have been developed and evaluated. During these decades their theoretical framework has been expanded. This paper describes their current model that can be characterized as a *behavioral competency-based approach* and summarizes the main projects that draw on this model. The paper concludes with a discussion

Behavioral Approaches for Children and Adolescents, Edited by
H. P. J. G. van Bilsen et al., Plenum Press, New York, 1995

focusing on the question how we may improve the effectiveness of treatment programs for juvenile offenders.

A BEHAVIORAL COMPETENCY-BASED APPROACH

The Lack of Criteria for Selecting Target Skills

The Teaching Family Model has been of great influence on the early programs developed at the Paedologisch Instituut. Skill-training was the focal part of these programs. The outpatient as well as residential training programs turned out to have promising results. (Bartels, Heiner, De Kruijff and Slot, 1977; Slot, 1984). However, the early programs lacked clear criteria for selecting target skills. According to Bartels (1986), the youths themselves often showed difficulties with respect to self observation and did not express explicit ideas about the skills they wanted to learn. In his opinion trainers or therapists had to rely on a functional analysis (1) of the delinquent behavior and their ability to choose target skills that were attractive to the youths.

The ABA literature in the seventies was not quite clear with respect to these criteria. The Teaching Family Handbook (Phillips, Phillips, Fixsen and Wolf, 1972) confined itself to a rule of thumb. The teaching parent was instructed to observe the inappropriate behavior of a youth and subsequently teach and reinforce an appropriate skill that would be incompatible with the inappropriate behavior. This 'new for old' procedure was good enough for teaching parents who lived together with a number of youths showing a wide array of inappropriate behaviors. In their case it would have been impossible to make a thorough functional analysis of each problem behavior occurring during the daily routine, in order to identify a target for teaching. Nevertheless this procedure seemed unsatisfactory. In the first place there was the risk for overlooking a youths previous learning history. A second disadvantage pertains to the fact that it was the inappropriate behavior that triggered a teaching interaction. This could easily result in overlooking skill deficiencies that do not cause problem behaviors per se, but still represent a developmental risk.

In order to find a criterium for the choice of target skills, Slot (1988) suggested a developmental approach in addition to an approach focusing on the problem behavior. He suggested a competence model rather then a skill-deficiency model. This model as it is used nowadays will be described in the next section.

What Is Competence?

According to Masten (1993): competence is "a pattern of effective performance in the environment, evaluated from the perspective of salient developmental tasks in the context of the late 20th century US-society."

Instead of 'US-society' one may choose for a perspective from another society, culture or subculture. The definition clearly indicates that competence should be considered as time- and situation specific. By introducing the concept of salient developmental tasks, Masten brings in a developmental approach.

The concept of developmental tasks has received attention through the work of Erikson (1950, 1968). Erikson conceptualized eight stages of development. Each stage can be characterized by a certain theme, or task that the child or adolescent has to solve. Eriksons thematic approach to the concept of developmental tasks leads to more general descriptions as "autonomy versus shame and doubt" which he considered a major theme during early childhood. In adolescence the major theme is the "formation of an identity versus identity diffusion." Other authors have attempted to provide more concrete and behavioral descriptions of developmental tasks. Havighurst (1952, 1973) for example, defined 10 developmental tasks for adolescence. Partly he drew back on the work of Erikson, but he also paid attention to the consequences of biological maturation and the societal expectations that change as maturation proceeds. Diekstra (1992) suggests that modern youth is faced with new developmental tasks, for example the task to handle free time and consumption goods in a responsible way. Thus the number of developmental tasks and the way these tasks are defined may differ. The central idea of developmental tasks is that adequate fulfilment of these tasks is a condition for further development.

Slot (1994) gives a description of seven adolescent developmental tasks based on two sorts of research: the study of Compass, Davis en Forsythe (1985) who asked high school and college students what they considered to be the most important issues in their daily life, and the studies of Le Blanc en Fréchette (1989), and Jagers (1992) on the correlates and development of antisocial behavior among youths. These seven tasks are:

(1) The acquirement of a new position within the changing relationships in the family.
(2) Bearing responsibility for personal health and appearance.
(3) The use of free time.
(4) The integration of sexuality in one's personality.
(5) Academic or vocational achievement.
(6) Making and keeping contacts with peers and friends.
(7) Responding to authority.

Competence according to Masten (1993) and Slot (1994), can be conceptualized as an equilibrium between tasks and skills. A competent fulfilment of a developmental task and all subtasks that are part of it, requires a sufficient repertoire of task related skills.

The equilibrium between tasks and skills can be disturbed through stress.

Stress refers to the occurrence of stressors: events that - objectively speaking - are harmful, frightful, painful or dangerous, also to somebody's subjective interpretation of events (cf. De Wit, Van der Veer and Slot, 1995).

According to Rutter (1979) the occurrence of one or two stressors does not cause a problem for a person. It is the cumulation of several stressors that may endanger somebody's functioning.

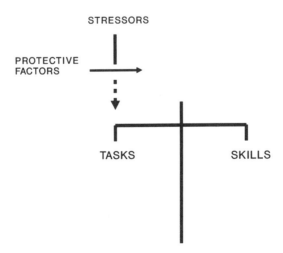

Figure 1. Social competence as a balance between tasks and skills the influence of stressors and protective factors.

Developmental tasks are harder to fulfil when the individual is faced with stress. The task of acquiring a new position within the family relations for example will be difficult when one or both parents have psychiatric problems. Accumulation of stress is common in families with delinquent youths (Junger-Tas, Junger, Barendse-Hoornweg and M. Sampiemon, 1983). There is also evidence that delinquent youths more often experience stress as a result of a misunderstanding of social situations of an ambiguous nature. The study of Freedman, Rosenthal, Donahoe, Schlundt and McFall, (1978) shows that delinquent boys, in contrast to non delinquents, tend to interpret expressions and gestures of other people in these situations as hostile or dangerous.

Research shows that certain traits of a person or some specific aspects in the environment may shield an individual against the harmful influence of stressors (Garmezy, 1987). Examples of these so called *protective factors* in children and adolescents are: intelligence, a warm and accepting climate in the family circle, an encouraging school, supportive family members and peers, a group of friends etcetera.

Assessment

Assessment in competency-based treatment programs for delinquent adolescents has different levels.

The first level is a *functional analysis* of the delinquent and/or antisocial behavior. This analysis focuses on the functional relations between the different aspects of the problem behavior and environmental variables (cf, Brinkman, 1974; Burger, 1994). A functional analysis seeks to determine how the problem behavior has been learned and maintained by means of positive and negative reinforcement, and prosocial behavior has been discouraged through punishment.

The second level is an *analysis of competence*. The analysis focuses on the following questions:

(a) Is the youth engaging in the developmental tasks that are typical for his or her life period and culture? If not, which environmental variables are related to the avoidance of developmental tasks?
(b) Has the youth sufficient skills for mastering the different tasks? What are his or her strengths? Which skills are lacking?
(c) Is the youth being confronted with stress? Which stressors are involved? Is the stress caused by a subjective interpretation of the events?
(d) Are there any protective factors within the youth, or in his or her environment?

The analysis of competence may reveal skill deficiencies and stress and is therefore in that respect it is problem oriented. But it also seeks to identify existing skills, strengths and protective factors. In that way it is growth oriented.

The third level is an *analysis of outcome*. This sort of analysis is needed in order to demonstrate the effectiveness of an intervention. Outcome measures can be applied on an individual as well as a group level.

In the orthodox ABA tradition, assessment should focus strictly on direct naturalistic observation and recording. This view is not widely supported anymore. Standardized tests, formal diagnoses, and observations through significant informants may be used in addition to direct behavioral observation.

Interventions

Promoting competence can be achieved through different approaches: (a) skill training and, (b) alleviation of tasks and the introduction of new tasks, (c) stress reduction and (d) activation of protective factors.

(A) Skill Training. Skill training techniques can be categorized in four categories: positive feedback, instruction, modelling and practising.

- Positive feedback can be used to reinforce existing skills and to foster an appropriate use of skills that are already in the repertoire of a youth or a family. It should be noticed that competence promotion and skill training does not always imply the building of new skills. Firstly, families, children and adolescents often are more capable in solving their problems than a therapist is inclined to believe. Their problem is not a skill deficiency but a lack of confidence in their own possibilities. Positive feedback may serve as a tool for 'empowerment': the encouragement to rely on one's own resources (Kinney, Haapala and Booth, 1991). The second reason pertains to the fact that many adolescents tend to experiment with different behavior patterns. In some situations they may come up with a reaction to some demand that is more appropriate compared to their usual behavior. In that case immediate positive feedback may be used in order to "freeze" the new skill.

Positive feedback is one of the most important tools for teaching skills because it can be used numerous times during the day. Although the use of positive feedback may seem simple, it's application proves to be difficult. This technique not only requires the ability to observe on a behavioral level, but also awareness of the level at which the youth functions and which behaviors need positive attention. Moreover, some therapists or staff-members find it difficult to give their opinion straight away on the behavior of a youth.

Positive feedback can be administered orally and through gestures, but also through written communication or tangible rewards. Token systems are based on a combination of oral feedback with conditioned reinforcers (points, tokens) which can be exchanged for back-up reinforcers (rewards).

- Instruction either describes the different components of a skill or clarifies the conditions during which a particular skill is required. The latter function of instruction is called discrimination training: the youth learns to discriminate between stimuli indicating that a certain behavior will have positive consequences and stimuli indicating that a behavior will be punished. A staff-member in a group home for example, might explain that it may be right to argue with friends, but that a submissive reaction could be more appropriate if one has been stopped by a police officer.
- Modelling is the demonstration of a skill. This technique can be used in different ways. Some skill training programs use videotaped model behaviors. In residential care, staff-members often act as a model. They show the residents not only concrete skills like the use of the dishwasher, but also more complicated social skills like responding to criticism.
- Practising means that the youth actually performs a skill under supervision of the therapist or staff-member. Practising can be done in vivo or during role play.

These four categories of skill training are cumulative: each category requires the application of the foregoing category. Practising for example is most effective when the skill that has to be practised has been demonstrated through modelling, while modelling requires clear instructions. Positive feedback is indispensable: the fact that a youth responds to instruction and modelling and participates in practising should be rewarded, but also the performance of the target skill.

(B) Alleviation of Tasks and Introduction of New Tasks. Competence can be conceptualized as a balance between tasks and skills. Skill training is not the only alternative for creating a balance between skills and tasks. Tasks may also be the target for interventions. Task alleviation is required when a youth or a family is facing one or more tasks that are too

difficult to fulfil. For example, living independently can be too difficult for a youth who has never learned any independent living skills. A placement in a supervised living project could be a realistic intervention in this case: the balance between skills and tasks has been artificially restored and provides an opportunity for skill training. This example also illustrates that alleviation of tasks is usually a temporary measure. As soon as the youth has learned sufficient skills, the original task should be reinstalled.

The introduction of new tasks is required when youths are underexposed with regard to developmental tasks. Some youths may avoid particular tasks, while others are not confronted with certain tasks because they live in an isolated or underprivileged environment.

(C) Stress Reduction. Stress impedes the fulfilment of tasks, consequently stress reduction may contribute to competence. Sometimes it may be possible to remove one or more stressors. The living conditions for a child which is being sexually molested by the father, for example, will probably ameliorate with the leaving of the perpetrator. In other cases reduction of stress can be achieved through interventions that enable the youth to deal with stress in a better way. Children and adolescents with a post traumatic stress syndrome, for example, may benefit from individual cognitive behavioral therapy or from group sessions together with other victims (Yule, 1992).

(D) Activation of Protective Factors. The effects of stress can also be mitigated through protective factors. In some cases the beneficial influence of protective factors can be strengthened. For example, a youth can be encouraged to intensify the contacts with friends or family members. The activation of protective factors needs special attention in residential treatment since placement in an institution often implies the weakening of the ties with friends and family members.

Results of Competency-Based Treatment

The treatment programs for young delinquents and their families that have been developed at the Paedologisch Instituut draw on the principles of the above mentioned model. It should be noted, however, that these principles have been elaborated during the years. The results of these treatment programs have been described in detail by Bartels (1986), Slot and Jagers, (1986; 1991) and Slot, Jagers en Beumer (1986). The main results can be summarized as follows.

Outpatient Individual Social Skill Training for young male delinquents has been evaluated by Bartels (1986). Follow-up data showed a recidivism rate of 24% for the treatment group and 66% in the control group. Residential competency-based treatment has been evaluated in several studies. In one study competency-based treatment had been introduced in one cottage -out of six- in a correctional institution. Follow-up research indicated improvement in several domains of daily life functioning in the youths from the control cottages. However, these effects had been surpassed on a significant level by the results of the youths from the experimental cottage who performed very well in the domain of work and school, relationships in the family, contacts with friends and recidivism. This result was overshadowed by the fact that the correctional institute had decided to end the competency-based program before the outcome data had been collected. This decision was made because of difficulties on a organizational and personal level between staff-members in the experimental cottage and other staff-members in the institute (Slot, 1988).

The Teaching Family Model has been replicated in the Netherlands. A follow-up study based on data of 50 former residents of the "Kursushuis" (The Dutch name for this program) showed significant improvements in all domains of daily life functioning with one exception: alcohol consumption. The recidivism rates can be summarized as follows. From 17 residents who were non delinquent when they entered the program, 76% refrained from offending during their stay in "kursushuis" as well as during the nine month follow-up period. From a group of 33 residents who were delinquents when entering the program, 61% showed no offenses in their record at the moment of the follow-up (Slot, Jagers and Dangel, 1992).

The programs at the Paedologisch Instituut came to the attention of the Dutch Juvenile Justice Authorities. This resulted in the implementation of two competency-based programs in the Juvenile Justice System. Both programs are so-called "alternative sanctions." The Individual Social Skill Training developed by Bartels, has become a widely used alternative sanction which judges pass on youths, who are beyond the first offending level but are not yet involved in a criminal career. More than 200 social workers have been trained at the Paedologisch Instituut in order to apply this training. Another alternative sanction initiated at the Paedologisch Instituut is a competency-based day program of three months. This sanction is passed on youths committing crimes as burglary, car theft, robbery and assault. Van der Laan and Essers (1990) found positive follow-up results: youths who had successfully ended the program showed less recidivism compared to the youths on the same level of offending who had received a traditional penitentiary sentence. Drop outs from the program showed the same level of recidivism as those with a traditional sanction. This program has been replicated in several places.

A new approach in promoting competence has been developed in the COACHING project. This program used non professionals who had been hired via newspapers, radio stations, churches and other community resources. These persons - COACHES - were trained to guide and supervise youths who were under supervision of the juvenile judge. This project differed from the usual projects by volunteers with respect to supervision and consultation for COACHES. Each volunteer discussed the progress of his or her pupil every two weeks by telephone with the project leader at the Paedologisch Instituut. In addition there was a "hot line" for COACHES in case of problems or urgent questions, and face to face contacts between the COACH and the project leader every two months. A comparison of youths who had been in contact with a COACH with youths who had been supervised by a probation officer, showed better results for the former in two domains: peer contacts and behavior problems (Beljaars and Berger, 1988).

A recent development is the replication of the Homebuilders model for families in crises who are facing the outplacement of one or more children. The original Homebuilders model has been developed by practitioners and researchers working in the tradition of ABA (Kinney, Haapala and Booth, 1991). In the US it has proven to be an effective intervention for families in crises (ibid). The first results show that the Dutch version of Homebuilders is effective with respect to the main goal: keeping the child in the family (Spanjaard and Berger, 1994; De Kemp, Veerman, Ten Brink, 1994).

All the mentioned projects have had a considerable spin off in terms of program development in Dutch youth services in the field of outpatient and residential treatment, day treatment, forensic youth psychiatry, treatment for deaf adolescents with conduct disorders, treatment for developmentally disordered youths and the field of juvenile justice.

How do these results compare to other research on the treatment of antisocial behavior? The review of the literature suggests that the training of concrete behavioral and cognitive skills is the most promising approach (Bartollas, 1985; Van Gageldonk and Bartels, 1990; Kazdin, 1987; Rutter and Giller, 1983; Tolan and Loeber, 1993). This general conclusion supports the viability of a competency-based approach. Kazdin and Tolan and Loeber also mention the positive results of interventions focusing on the improvement of parental skills.

Some reviewers however express serious doubts about the impact of treatment programs for young delinquents. The fact that several programs do have good outcomes does not mean that juvenile delinquency can be easily treated. Evidence for long lasting effects is still lacking.

Kazdin (1993) concludes that considerable progress has been made during the last decade in the field of child and adolescent therapy, including the programs for juvenile offenders. But he also warns for too much optimism. The study of Weisz and Weiss (1993) for example shows that effective programs usually have been set up in experimental situations under supervision of researchers safeguarding program integrity. The effects of treatment programs under routine conditions are usually less positive or zero.

Thus the data support both a pessimistic and an optimistic view. This is also true for the outcomes of the projects at the Paedologisch Instituut. On the one hand there are positive results and recognition of practitioners, but on the other hand there are the numbers of youths who do not improve, the concerns about long term outcomes and the difficulties pertaining to the maintenance of program quality.

DIRECTIONS FOR FUTURE RESEARCH AND TREATMENT

One of the contributions of Applied Behavior Analysis to the treatment of antisocial and delinquent youths has been the introduction of a skill teaching approach. During the last decade numerous programs based upon this principle have been developed, however the problem of juvenile crime has not diminished. What are the possibilities for reducing antisocial behavior in youths?

One direction has been propagated by Wolf, Braukmann and Ramp (1987), who are representatives of ABA from the early hour. They suggest that a focus on short term treatment in order to "cure" delinquency might be an unrealistic goal once a youth has developed persistent serious delinquent behavior. They compare a condition that is composed of multiple antisocial and dysfunctional behaviors with a condition as mental retardation, and call for a low intensive, long term support for youths with this condition. The above mentioned COACHING model could be a viable approach in providing such a support.

The fact that persistent serious delinquent behavior is extremely resistant to change, points to a second direction: prevention. The possibilities for prevention have been augmented because of the advances in criminology during the last decade. Longitudinal research has resulted in reasonably valid predictors of antisocial behavior (Loeber, in press). The research on the development of antisocial behavior shows that problematic behavior patterns unfold along different pathways. (Loeber and Hay, 1994). A youths position on one or more pathways provides an indication of the risk for serious delinquency. Although it might become more easy to target youths at risk for developing delinquent behavior, few adequately documented prevention programs are available (Tolan and Loeber, 1993). According to Yoshikawa (1994) effective prevention programs include two components: family support and education (teaching of skills).

A third direction pertains to the quality of treatment programs. The conclusion of Weisz and Weiss (1993) that routine treatment in youth care services has no or very limited success is a reason for great concern. Researchers at the Paedologisch Instituut have been confronted with a variety of difficulties during the implementation of treatment programs in the field of youth care. Demands on an organizational or economic level often interfere with the requirements for treatment. Procedures that have proven to be effective in promoting competence in youths, may also be applied for increasing professional skills in staff. Research methodology for the assessment of program outcome could also be applied for establishing quality control.

Generally speaking, it is not the developing of new treatment techniques that should have high priority on the agenda for future research, but a better use and timing of existing treatment methodology.

NOTES

(1) A functional analysis seeks to identify environmental variables that are related to the learning or the maintenance of inappropriate or problem behavior.

REFERENCES

Baer, D.M., Wolf, M.M. and Risley, T.R. (1968), Some current dimension of applied behavior analysis. *Journal of Applied Behavior Analysis, 1.* 91-97.

Bartels, A.A.J. (1986). *Sociale-vaardigheidstraining voor probleemjongeren.* [Social skills training for delinquent youths]. Lisse: Swets and Zeitlinger.

Bartels, A.A.J., Heiner, J., Kruijff, G. de, and Slot, N.W. (1977). *Effecten van ambulante gedragstherapie aan 'delinquente' adolescenten* (EAGDA). Amsterdam: Paedologisch Instituut.

Bartollas, C. (1985). *Juvenile Delinquency.* New York: John Wiley.

Beljaars, I.C.M., Berger, M.A. (1988). The coaching project: *Training by non-professionals for youths with poor community living skills.* In: P.M.G. Emmelkamp, W.T.A.M. Everaerd, F. Kraaimaat and M.J.M. van Son (Red.). Advances in theory and practice in behaviour therapy. Lisse: Swets en Zeitlinger.

Brinkman, W. (1978). *Het gedragstherapeutisch proces.* In: J.W.G. Orlemans, W. Brinkman, W.P. Haaijman and E.J. Zwaan (Red.). Handboek voor gedragstherapie; afl.1. Deventer: Van Loghum Slaterus.

Burger, A.W. (1994). *Functie-analyse van neurotisch gedrag, een handleiding voor gedragstherapeuten.* Amsterdam: Van Rossum.

Compas, B.E., Davis, G.E. and Forsythe, C.J. (1985). Characteristics of life events during adolescence. *American journal of Community Psychology, 13,* 677-691.

Diekstra, R.F.W. (1992). *De adolescentie: biologische, psychologische en sociale aspecten.* In: R.F.W. Diekstra, (Red.) met: J.L. van den Brande, P.G. Heymans, G.A. Kohnstamm, N. van Oudenhoven and P.R.J. Simons. Jeugd in ontwikkeling. Wetenschappelijke inzichten en overheidsbeleid. Den Haag: Wetenschappelijke Raad voor het Regeringsbeleid/SDU.

Erikson, E.H. (1950). *Childhood and society.* Norton. New York

Erikson, E.H. (1968). *Identity, youth and crisis.* Norton, New York

Freedman, B.J., Rosenthal, L., Donahoe, C.P., Schlundt, D.G. and R.M. McFall R.M. (1978). A Social-Behavioral Analysis of Skill Deficits in Delinquent an Nondelinquent Adolescent Boys. *Journal of Consulting and Clinical Psychology. Vol. 46, No. 6,* 1448-1462.

Gageldonk, A. van and Bartels, A.A.J. (1990). *Evaluatie onderzoek op het terrein van de hulpverlening.* Leiden: Centrum Onderzoek Jeugdhulpverlening. Rijksuniversiteit.

Garmezy, N. (1987). Stress-resistente kinderen: op zoek naar protectieve factoren. In: H. Groenendaal, R. Meijer, J.W. Veerman and J. de Wit (Red.). *Protectieve factoren in de ontwikkeling van kinderen en adolescenten. 17 - 40.* Lisse: Swets & Zeitlinger.

Havighurst, R.J. (1952). *Developmental tasks and education.* New York: D McKay

Havighurst, R.J. (1973). History of Developmental Psychology: Socialization and Personality Development through the Life- Span. In: P.B. Baltes and K.W. Schaie. (Red.) *Life-Span Developmental Psychology: Personality and Socialization.* (3-24). New York: Academic press.

Jagers, J.D. (1992). *Sociale Competentie: een model met implicaties voor hulpverlening.* Amsterdam/Duivendrecht: Paedologisch Instituut, afdeling GT-Projecten.

Junger-Tas, J., Junger, M., Barendse-Hoornweg, E. and Sampiemon., M. (1983). *Jeugddelinquentie, achtergronden justitiële reactie.* 's-Gravenhage: Staatsuitgeverij.

Kazdin, A.E. (1987). Treatment of antisocial behavior in children: current status and and future directions. *Psychological Bulletin, 102,* 187-203.

Kazdin, A.E. (1993). *Psychotherapy for Children and Adolescents. Current Progress and Future Research Directions. American psychologist Vol 48, No 6,* 644-657

Kemp, R. de, Veerman, J.W. and ten Brink, L.T. (1994), *Onderzoeksgegevens Families First Derde Kwartaal 1994.* Duivendrecht: Paedologisch Instituut.

Kinney, J., Haapala, D. and Booth, C. (1991). *Keeping Families Together: The Homebuiders Model*. New York: Aldine DeGruyter.

Laan, P.H. van der and Essers, A.A.M. (1990). *De Kwartaalkursus en recidive*. *WODC reeks Onderzoek en Beleid nr. 99*. Arnhem: Gouda Quint.

Le Blanc, M. and Fréchette, M. (1989). *Male Criminal Activity from Childhood Trough Youth: Multilevel and Developmental Perspectives*. New York: Springer-Verlag.

Loeber, R. (In press). *Which boys will become worse? Early Predictors of the onset of Conduct Disorder in a six-year longitudinal study*.

Loeber, R. and Hay, D.F. (1994). Developmental Approaches to Aggression and Conduct Problems. In: M. Rutter and D.F. Hay (Eds.) *Development Through Life. A Handbook for Clinicians. 488-516*. Oxford: Blackwell.

Masten, A.S. (1993). *Competence over time. Paper presented at the 60th Anniversary meeting of the Society for Research in Child Development*. 25-28 maart

Phillips, E.L., Phillips, E.A., Fixsen, D.L. and Wolf, M.M. (1972). The Teaching *Family Handbook*. (2nd ed., 1974). Lawrence, Kansas: University of Kansas, Dep. of Human Development.

Rutter, M. and H. Giller. (1983). *Juvenile Delinquency, Trends and Perspectives*. Harmondsworth: Pinguin Books.

Rutter, M. (1979). *Protective factors in children's responses to stress and disadvantage*. In: M. Kent and J.E. Rolf (Eds.), Primary prevention of psychopathology. Vol. 3. Social competence in children. New Hampshire: University Press of New England.

Slot, N.W., (1984), *Achievement place in the Netherlands: first results of a community-based program for problem youths*. Paper presented at the 14th annual Congress of the European Association for Behavior Therapy, Brussels, september 1984.

Slot, N.W. (1988). *Residentiële hulp voor jongeren met antisociaal gedrag* [Residential treatment for antisocial youths]. Lisse: Swets and Zeitlinger.

Slot, N.W. (1994), *Competentie-gerichte behandelingsprogramma's voor jongeren met gedragsstoornissen. Gedragstherapie, 27, 3*, 233-249.

Slot, N.W. and Jagers, J.D. (1986). *De GT-projecten; twaalf jaar onderzoek naar de effectiviteit van ambulante en residentiële vormen van hulpverlening voor 'probleemjongeren'. Kind en Adolescent. Jrg. 7, No. 3*, 192 - 204.

Slot, N.W. and Jagers, J.D. (1991). Sociale competentie en antisociaal gedrag. Een transactioneel model. In: J. de Wit, N.W. Slot, H.M.P. van Leeuwen and M. Meerum Terwogt (Red.). *Paedologie in de jaren negentig*. Amersfoort: Acco.

Slot, N.W., Jagers, J.D. and Beumer, M.H. (1992). *Tien jaar Kursushuis: ervaringen en follow-up gegevens. Kind en Adolescent. 13 (2)*. 86-96.

Slot, N.W. Jagers, J.D. and Dangel, R.F. (1992), *Cross-cultural Replication and Evaluation of the Teaching Family Model of Community-based residential treatment. Behavioral Residential Treatment, 5*, 341-354.

Spanjaard, H. and Berger, M.A. (1994). Families First. Hulp aan gezinnen ter voorkoming van uithuisplaatsing van kinderen. *Jeugd en samenleving. 24, 12*, 720-729.

Tolan, P.H. and Loeber, R. (1993). Antisocial Behavior. In: P.H. Tolan & B.J. Cohler (Red.) *Handbook of Clinical Research and Practice with Adolescents. 307 - 333*. New York: Wiley

Weisz, J.R. and Weiss, B. (1993). *Effects of Psychotherapy with children and adolescents*. Newbury Park: Sage.

Wit, J. de, Veer, G. van der and Slot, N.W. (1995). *Psychologie van de adolescentie*. Nijkerk: Intro.

Wolf, M.M., Braukmann, C.J. and Ramp, K.A. (1987). *Serious delinquent behavior as part of a significantly handicapping condition: cures and supportive environments. Journal of Applied Behaviour Analysis, 20, 4 347 - 359*.

Yoshikawa, H. (1994). Prevention of Cumulative Protection: Effects of Early Family Support and Education on Chronic Delinquency and its Risks. *Psychological Bulletin, Vol. 115. No1, 28-54*.

Yule, W. (1993). Risico-factoren en protectieve eigenschappen bij post-traumatische stress-stoornissen in de kindertijd. In: S.M.J. van Hekken, N.W. Slot, J. Stolk & J.W. Veerman (Red.) *Pedologie tussen wetenschap en praktijk. 204-211*. Utrecht: De Tijdstroom.

7

BEHAVIOUR THERAPY WITH LEARNING PROBLEMS

Chris Struiksma

Pedologisch Instituut
PO Box 8639
3009 AP Rotterdam
The Netherlands

It is often heard nowadays that behavioural problems are increasing in mainstream and special education. This increase not only relates to the number of pupils with problems, but also to the intensity and seriousness of these (Council for Youth Policy, 1990). Epidemiological research by Verhulst & Akkerhuis (1986) and a study by Jongbloed and Gunning (1991) both show that behavioural and emotional problems frequently occur among children in primary and special schools. Though no comparative study has been made over several years to conclude there has been an increase in these problems (Sanders-Woudstra and Verhulst, 1987), nevertheless an increase, particularly in behavioural problems, has been experienced (Doornbos and Stevens, 1988).

Behavioural and learning problems often go hand in hand. In his literature review, Gunning (1992) mentions percentages between 40 and 80 per cent for various combinations of hyperactivity, behavioural and learning disorders. Children with behavioural problems are often referred to Child Guidance Clinics. Therapists from these clinics provide treatment for these children for instance in the form of individual or group therapy. This chapter focuses on the possibilities of applying the principles and techniques of behaviour therapy *within* schools in dealing with situations where both learning and behavioural problems occur. This can be referred to as mediation therapy, with the teacher acting as co-therapist or mediator.

The Relationship Between Learning and Behavioural Problems

The educational world commonly distinguishes between so-called primary and secondary behavioural problems (Dumont, 1976). Behavioural problems are seen as secondary when analysis of a pupil's developmental history shows that the child had difficulty learning from the beginning of form 1 and that the behavioural problems began later, especially - in the beginning - during those lessons in subjects where he/she had most problems, usually reading. The behavioural problems are then seen as a reaction to the failure of a pupil to learn.

Where the behavioural problems are considered to be secondary, treatment is focused on learning problems. The pupil is expected to react positively to remedial treatment and

Behavioral Approaches for Children and Adolescents, Edited by
H. P. J. G. van Bilsen et al., Plenum Press, New York, 1995

once learning has been re-established, the behaviour problems are expected to subside by their own accord.

If analysis of a pupil's developmental history shows that behavioural problems were already present in infant school, or even earlier, and then escalated over the years, then there is no hesitation that the behavioural problems are primary ones. These are then seen as causing the learning problems, which are then termed 'secondary.'

Once a verdict of 'primary behavioural problems' has been pronounced, referral to some form of professional help may follow. After referral, the professionals do not usually take into account the learning problems in their diagnosis and treatment, as this is seen as the school's responsibility. Thus the learning difficulties are lost sight of and didactic help is no longer a point of discussion.

> Peter is nine years old and has serious behavioural problems, both at school and home: hyperactivity, aggression, fits of crying, stubbornness, inattention, unwillingness to go to bed, bad eater, poor work attitude and unmotivated.
>   Peter was already a difficult child in his playgroup and in infant school behavioural problems were already mentioned: hyperactivity, being quickly upset and unable to play well, which all became worse over the years. Learning was already a problem from the very beginning of form 1.

When assessing pupils, teachers, school-heads and even therapists make a too strict division between learning and behavioural problems and the distinction between primary and secondary behavioural problems is insufficient. Usually there is not just one primary problematic development but several different ones (Verheij and Van Doorn, 1991).

Hawton, Salkovskis, Kirk and Clark (1989) recommend that when analysing a problem, a persons 'functioning' should be systematically examined for four separate response systems: behavioural, cognitive, affective and physiological. They stress the invalidity of considering psychological problems as single syndromes and reject, with reference to Lazarus, the mechanistic notions concerning the relation between diagnosis and treatment, which typifies medical science and which is sometimes referred to as the 'medical model' (see De Wit and Tak, 1988).

Haynes and O'Brien (1990) refer to this issue as the discrepancy between structural and functional analysis. A structural analysis is based on the assumption of a causal relationship. The manner in which the typical child with learning and behavioural disabilities (known in the Netherlands as LOM pupils) and the typical child with extreme behavioural disorders (known as ZMOK pupils) are diagnosed, is an example of a structural analysis. However there are many behavioural problems in a special LOM school and these are seldom conveniently limited to difficult learning situations. In a ZMOK school on the other hand, learning problems are the rule rather than the exception. Analysis is in fact mainly complex, various factors overlap and pupils show features of both LOM and ZMOK categories. Rather than the one simply causing the other, disruptive behaviour and learning problems only seem to 'co-vary', but can be related to each other in a functional way.

A second, important element of Hawton et al's argument is that the four response systems are only loosely coupled systems. In the first instance, this means in behaviour therapeutic practice that the nature of the relationship between the various response systems is not fixed, but has to be decided with each client. Secondly, that simple causal relationships are more the exception than the rule, so that improvement in one area, such as behavioural problems, does not automatically result in improvement in the other (learning difficulties, for instance). Finally there is the implication that treatments cannot be standard prescriptions but should take into account the various problem areas and the nature of the relationship between them.

> Problems in the way Peter functioned were described, restricted to what took place in school. We did however systematically check the four, aforementioned response systems. Behavioural problems at school related to not listening, leaving his place, quarrelling (rudeness and fighting), being

constantly distracted, not getting on with work and never completing tasks on time. In cognitive terms, tests showed that Peter was at least two years behind with reading and spelling, though his overall development was satisfactory. From various talks with Peter, it was obvious there were signs of feelings of failure. During assessment Peter was cooperative enough but extremely tense. When given a reading task, this provoked a fear reaction in him.

In behaviour therapy terms it is possible to make a functional analysis here, analysing the factors that trigger problem behaviour and those factors that reinforce it. The departure points of Hawton et al imply that when making a functional analysis of each problem, in theory each of the four response systems should be considered to prevent problems being interpreted one-sidedly. With learning problems this avoids the role which behavioural problems may play from being overlooked, while with behavioural problems it prevents the problems with basic school skills not being included in the analysis.

When a pupil has learning difficulties, learning situations will imply failure for the pupil and will have a negative connotation. Should the pupil chance to display certain disruptive behaviour such as talking, falling off a chair or letting a pen drop on the floor, than some form of sanction follows, like having to stand in the corridor. This sanction is obviously intended as a (positive) punishment, but unintentionally it acts as a (negative) reinforcement: the pupil escapes the negative learning situation. Thus in this way the pupil learns to avoid learning situations by using disruptive behaviour. Initially, the stimuli that trigger this disruptive behaviour will be sharply defined, for instance by having to read aloud, but via stimulus generalisation this quickly and easily extends to other learning situations and even possibly to everything associated with school.

The above situation refers to operant learning. Analysis will be obvious. It is the typical 'LOM story': behavioural problems gradually develop *after* learning difficulties appear. The analysis does not hold true therefore when behavioural problems were already obviously present.

Eelen (1988) has shown that the persistence of problem behaviour is often better explained when analysis is not restricted to an operant paradigm, but elements are looked for in which classical conditioning plays a role.

New, unexpected stimuli from the environment are followed by a set of responses that Pavlov has already identified as the orientation reflex (Luria, 1973). This is a good example of a cluster of behaviours in which an unconditional ('innate') component is present. It concerns reactions which together create a state of readiness in the body. There are huge individual differences in the degree of heightened arousal with which people respond to new stimuli. Also huge differences in arousal levels are possible. Examples of behavioural components of heightened arousal are: hyperactivity, suddenly stopping with what one is doing and a tendency to notice only the salient aspects of a situation and no longer the more subtle ones (Douglas, 1980).

Children who quickly, frequently and predominantly respond with heightened arousal run an extreme risk of developing problem behaviour (Barkley, 1981). Responses from the pedagogic environment to this, can easily result in disruptive behaviour escalating. Children who quickly responded with a highly heightened arousal level were earlier labelled as children with minimal brain dysfunction. Nowadays they are referred to as children with Attention Deficit and Hyperactivity Disorder.

Disruptive behaviour appears by chance within the framework for typical secondary behavioural problems, but among children like Peter this had already been crystallised within his behavioural repertoire. The very first experience of learning failure that came along led to heightened arousal which triggered disruptive behaviour. The connecting of a learning situations to problem behaviour is so immediate and happens so forcefully that it does not need to be learnt by trial and error. Already existing behavioural problems can, on the basis of learning experiences, thus acquire the function as an avoidance responses. What is essential in this, is that the existence of behavioural problems at a young age do not in themselves indicate the absence of learning problems. Particularly the demands at the beginning of form 1 with regard to listening and sitting still are much higher than those made at infant school. Even these sort of simple situations are already a source of tension. Children who quickly respond with highly heightened arousal will then miss important moments of teaching instruction. The chance that children such as Peter quickly experience a sense of failure with learning is therefore extremely great. If such a development is allowed time then the increasingly lost ground in learning ensures that Peter and his teacher become trapped in a vicious circle of failure, tension and problem behaviour. Eventually, the question of whether there are indications here of 'real' (i.e. non-secondary) learning problems can no longer be answered, but is also irrelevant with respect to treatment.

If this analysis is a correct one, what will be the effect of a direct approach towards behavioural problems at school, for instance by using a reward system? The non-displaying of disruptive behaviour is sometimes rewarded, but it means at the same time a confrontation with the negative 'learning situation' stimulus. This creates tension and tension leads again to problem behaviour. The relation between tension and disruptive behaviour exists for years and is firmly established. Displaying disruptive behaviour will again result in punishment. This is again a negative stimulus, which once more creates tension and tension again creates disruptive behaviour, etc. The paradoxical situation then exists that after a possible positive effect in the extremely short term, the intervention in fact results in the behaviour problems increasing. We see that it is impossible for pupils to give up disruptive behaviour in school if there is no learning achievement.

Does this mean that treatment outside the school situation is called for? Within a secure out-of-school therapeutic situation it is possible for the pupil to give up his or her disruptive behaviour when this is followed by reward. The pupil then learns there are more pleasurable ways of interacting with others than those he or she displays. In the classroom, however, dropping disruptive behaviour is still linked to extremely negative consequences: i.e. being confronted with learning situations that result in failure. This could explain why sometimes good progress is made in therapy sessions but little of this unfortunately is noticed in a school setting.

From the school's perspective, in all cases where pupils fall behind with their learning there is the duty to create teaching situations where they can again achieve success. The existence of behavioural problems is no reason not to, because when success is again achieved in learning, the aforementioned vicious circle is broken. It is interesting that more evidence appears to exist for improved learning attainment favourably affecting behavioural problems (Ferritor, Buckhold, Hamblin and Smith, 1972) than the other way round (Ayllon and Roberts, 1974). Learning situations should be created in such a way that they obviously and emphatically take behavioural problems into account. Behavioural therapeutic principles and techniques can be used by the teacher or remedial teacher and a behaviour therapist can also assist here.

Organising a Working Relationship and Method of Treatment

An analysis of Peter's reading problems and a treatment strategy included the following aspects:

Peter has an end-of-form 1 reading level. He reads by spelling out the letters but has difficulties in tasks dealing with the phonemic structure of words, necessary for reading through decoding, and he lacks automation of these functions. In general he has a poor memory for language material.

Regarding his reading, the idea is to unlearn Peter's exaggerated decoding approach to reading and expand his word recognition skills through the method of 'talking books'. Elements of Peter's individualised educational plan are: every week Peter will be given a book and a tape which has to be practised twice daily, or ten times a week. With his remedial teacher he practises so-called word families, while at home he reads a pre-arranged amount of text every day. In order to practise his reading technique, each piece of text is read three times, one after the other.

Children like Peter are being spoken of in broad terms for years: a young boy with disruptive behaviour, a poor work attitude and unmotivated. A young boy who is seen as such by his environment will almost certainly have to hear remarks, subtle or otherwise, to this effect. What sort of self-image or self-esteem will such a pupil have who knows he is disruptive, works badly and is unmotivated?

ENCOURAGING MOTIVATION

How can Peter be persuaded to increase his efforts in a field that gives him trouble and where he has a history of experiencing failure, while at the same time being pressured by others to work on this? What can behaviour therapy offer when it comes to providing a form of treatment aimed at alleviating the learning problems of pupils who are disruptive and unmotivated? Kanfer and Schefft (1988) distinguish several phases in the therapeutic process. Van Bilsen (1991) incorporated these within the model for the stages of change of Prochaska and DiClemente (1984) with respect to forms of supplementary help in schools. He concentrates on the importance of being *motivated to change*. This can only take place when the client (pupil) is sufficiently aware of the problem, is sufficiently concerned about it, has sufficient self-esteem to make the effort and enough confidence in his or her ability to achieve results (feeling of competence). It is evident that motivation is no precondition here for change, but the result of a professional approach on the part of the professional treating the client.

The following steps within the motivation process will be explained:

- eliciting: creating a willingness to change
- information: analysing the problem in behavioural terms
- negotiation: negotiating learning objectives and methods
- treatment: beginning the treatment and retaining the motivation, recording and assessing progress and bringing about generalisation.

Eliciting: Creating a Willingness to Change

This phase is concerned with eliciting self-motivated statements from the pupil which reveal an awareness of the problem, concern and a sense of competence or self-esteem. This involves various interview techniques such as selective active listening, concretisation and positively restructuring.

We spoke to Peter about how he rated his reading ability. Would he be able to improve on this? Would it cost him a lot of effort? Could he make that effort? What would it mean to him if he were to improve? What would he be able to do, what he could not do now? By verbalising all of this, the general learning objective became an attractive one ("I can read the film subtitles on television and be able to talk about them next day."). Self-motivating statements such as this are encouraged and then rewarded with extra attention. The work relationship is also defined: "So you would really like to learn to read properly and you think you would be able to do this if we work on it together."

Information: Analysing the Problem in Behavioural Terms

The pupil is told in detail about the precise nature of his/her problem, in terms which are as concrete as possible and which focus on what is wrong and how it can be improved, rather than then being judgemental or moralising. As a result, the pupil is taken seriously and develops a sense of self-esteem. The exact nature of the problem is discussed in behavioural terms which Peter can understand.

> You can already read well by spelling the words. You make very few mistakes. The next step is to look and say the word. There are special exercises for this and it is important to practise these regularly. In the end you will be able to look at the words and say them automatically.

Negotiating Learning Objectives and Methods

It has been shown that children achieve more when they have a say in deciding their own learning objectives (Dickerson and Creedon, 1981). The pupil feels he has some influence on the situation and this helps to give him a feeling of competence.

> We draw up an agreement with Peter in which we acknowledge that reading has priority for the time being and that we should first do something about it. The nature of his problem is explained to him and we discuss the exercises in a way he can understand - reading with the help of a tape - and which will help him to achieve success. The treatment is given in a one-to-one situation. The method is tried out and together we conclude that it works all right.

The point then comes when the exercises have to be done independently as these are only effective when practised between the remedial lessons on a daily basis. This of course has to be negotiated first.

> How many times does Peter think he can do the exercises without anyone else helping him? The point here is that a realistic objective has to be agreed. One complaint against Peter is his lack of motivation, so it would be particularly demotivating for him to fail immediately at the start of his treatment. One can better set a lower target that can easily be surpassed than a higher one that is never going to be achieved. It was agreed that the exercises would be done four times a week.
>
> Other aspects of the treatment also needed to be precisely agreed and where necessary negotiated: the exercise method, the practise times, whether at school or also at home, should the teacher remind Peter to exercise or not, the circumstances, etc. Everything that was agreed was put in writing on an appointment card. On the reverse of this a tally was to be kept of each exercise Peter completed. Peter then told his teacher what had been agreed and it had already been decided beforehand that no matter what he told his teacher, he/she would respond in a neutral/agreeing manner.

Treatment: Beginning the Treatment, Retaining the Motivation, Recording and Assessing Progress and Creating Generalisation

Treatment begins with a plan that is realistic and has an extremely good chance of succeeding, after which new, secondary goals can be added. In this way the cycle of inducing or eliciting, informing, negotiating and treating can be variously repeated.

> The first week Peter did the exercises exactly four times and the frequency was then renegotiated. Peter wanted to stick to this number and the remedial teacher did not react by saying something like "What a shame, I'd really hoped you'd agree to an extra one," or "What a clever boy if you could just manage six." Instead, the appropriate response was worded positively. "You think that if you agree to four times again next week, you'll be able to achieve that. I think you're looking at the right way." In the third week, Peter goes for practising six times a week and the following week, ten. The exercises are agreed between Peter and his remedial teacher and sometimes he is allowed to tell his teacher what he has agreed with his remedial teacher.

Telling someone what you have decided to do makes it easier to do something for yourself than when it is forced on you. The golden rule is to create successful experiences which the pupil can ascribe to his/her own efforts. Here it is important to provide regular and systematic feedback on progress.

> It is important for Peter that the number of words he can read without first spelling them is increased. If this does not improve at the beginning, then we only pay attention to the number of correctly read words, so long as there is visible progress. With every reading exercise there is a

short test, such as a row of ten words, which is done before and after the exercise. The results of the test are set out in chart form and discussed with Peter. Good results are presented in an exaggerated form to him. Much attention is given to the fact that if he practises in the manner agreed, this immediately leads to better results.

Generalisation does not happen automatically, but needs to be created. Signs need to be looked out for, so that from these it can be inferred that the right moment for this has occurred. Where necessary, this can also be preceded by phases of inducement, information and negotiation.

A few weeks after the start of Peter's individual treatment, his teacher noticed the first signs of change in him in class, especially regarding his work attitude. It was agreed that the teacher should mention to Peter that his work was going much better, that he could see he was practising for longer periods and that he was pleased about this. At this point the teacher is again involved with Peter's reading. Only now is it agreed that Peter should read daily from his own reading book. The way in which he should do this is practised beforehand. It is also evident to Peter that this way works: a passage is read three times over and he asks the teacher the difficult words.

The amount of text read can be put in chart form again and if practising reading independently proves too difficult, it can be rewarded afterwards with something pleasant. For instance, being allowed to take home the chart with all the teacher's written positive comments, etc.

Peter now hears totally different remarks from the important people around him. No longer that he is disruptive, works poorly and is unmotivated, but that he works well, does his best and is making tangible progress. It goes without saying that this positively influences his motivation, self-image and own sense of worth.

In conclusion, I am not contending here that teachers and remedial teachers are generally failing to apply these sort of principles. I simply wish to draw attention to the possibilities when devising learning situations of working systematically with aspects such as these. Fostering motivation and increasing self-esteem can also be approached in a planned way.

Careful analysis of pupil behaviour in various situations combined with an analysis of the developmental history can lead to the hypothesis that behavioural problems act as an escape route from too difficult learning situations. Even where the behavioural problems already existed before the learning problems, this can still be the case.

REFERENCES

Ayllon, T. and Roberts, M. (1974). Eliminating discipline problems by strengthening academic performance. *Journal of applied behavior analysis, 7*, 71-76.

Barkley, R.A. (1981). *Hyperactive children. A handbook for diagnosis and treatment.* New York: The Guilford Press.

Bilsen, H.P.J.G. van (1991). Grenzen verleggen: jeugdhulpverlening met de school als basis. In: H.P.J.G. Bilsen, van and H.D. Swager, (red.). *Speciaal onderwijs and jeugdhulpverlening.* De Lier: Academisch Boeken Centrum.

Council for Youth Policy (1990). *Zorg-en-de-school. Een advies over de samenhang tussen regulier en speciaal onderwijs en de (jeugd)hulpverlening.* Rijswijk: Ministerie van Welzijn, Volksgezondheid en Cultuur.

Dickerson, E.A. and Creedon, C.F. (1981). Self-selection of standards by children: the relative effectiveness of pupil-selected and teacher-selected standards of performance. *Journal of applied behavior analysis, 14*, 425-433.

Doornbos, K. and Stevens, L.M. (1988). *De groei van het speciaal onderwijs. Deel B: Beeldvorming over beleid en praktijk.* 's-Gravenhage: SDU uitgeverij.

Douglas, V.I. (1980). Higher mental processes in hyperactive children. In: R.M. Knights and D.J. Bakker, (Eds.). *Treatment of hyperactive and learning disordered children.* Baltimore: University Park Press.

Dumont, J.J. (1976). *Leerstoornissen deel 1. Theorie en model.* Rotterdam: Lemniscaat.

Eelen, P. (1988). Leerpsychologie en gedragstherapie. In: *Handboek voor gedragstherapie.* F.3-1 - F.3-122. Deventer: Van Loghum Slaterus.

Ferritor, D.E., Buckhold, D. Hamblin, R.L. and Smith, L. (1972). The noneffects of contingent reinforcement for attending behavior on work accomplished. *Journal of applied behavior analysis, 5*, 7-17.

Gunning, W.B. (1992). *A controlled trial of clondine in hyperkinetic children*. Rotterdam: Universiteitsdrukkerij Erasmus Universiteit.

Hawton, K., Salkovskis, P.M., Kirk, J. and Clark, D.M. (1989). The development and principles of cognitive-behavioural treatments. In: K., Hawton, P.M., Salkovskis, J., Kirk and D.M., Clark (Eds.). *Cognitive behaviour therapy for psychiatric problems. A practical guide*. Oxford: Oxford University Press.

Haynes, S.N. and O'Brien, W.H. (1990). Functional analysis in behavior therapy. *Clinical Psychology Review, 12*, 649-668.

Jongbloed, M.H.B. and Gunning, I.A.P.M. (1991). Gedrags- en emotionele problemen binnen enkele vormen van speciaal onderwijs. In: H.P.J.G. Bilsen, van and H.D. Swager, (red.). *Speciaal onderwijs & jeugdhulpverlening*. De Lier: Academisch Boeken Centrum..

Kanfer, F.H. and Schefft, B.K. (1988). *Guiding the process of therapeutic change*. Illinois: Research Press.

Luria, A.R. (1973). *The working brain. An introduction to neuropsychology*. London: The penguin press.

Prochaska, J.O. and DiClemente, C.C. (1984). *The transtheoretical approach: crossing traditional boundaries of therapy*. Homewood, Illinois: Dow Jones-Irwin.

Sanders-Woudstra, J.A.R. and Verhulst, F.C. (1987). Epidemiologisch-kinderpsychiatrische benadering van de ontwikkelingen in het speciaal onderwijs. In: K. Doornbos and L.M. Stevens, (red.). *De groei van het speciaal onderwijs. Deel A: Analyse van historie en onderzoek*. 's-Gravenhage: Staatsuitgeverij.

Verhey, F. and Doorn, E.C. van (1991). Een integratief werkmodel voor emotioneel-sociale en leerproblemen. In: A.M.L. Collot d'Escury-Koenigs, T.J. Engelen-Snaterse and L. Tijhuis, (red.). *Gelukkig op school?* Amsterdam: Swets and Zeitlinger.

Verhulst, F.C. and Akkerhuis, G.W. (1986). Mental health in Dutch children: (III) behavioral-emotional problems reported by teachers of children aged 4-12. *Acta psychiatrica Scandinavica, suppl. 330, 74*.

Wit, J. de and Tak, J.A. (1988). Theoretische achtergronden van klinische diagnostiek. In: T., Kievit, J., Wit, de, J.H.A., Groenendaal and J.A. Tak, (red.). *Psychodiagnostiek voor de hulpverlening aan kinderen*. Amersfoort: Acco.

8

TREATING CHILDREN WHO LACK SOCIAL SKILLS IN A PEDOLOGICAL INSTITUTE SCHOOL

Ria Swager

Pedologisch Instituut
PO Box 8639
3009 AP Rotterdam
The Netherlands

Social skills are increasingly important for children. From the time they enter nursery school they are confronted with a range of social situations. A lack of social skills, which can lead for instance to shyness and aggressive behaviour, is often seen as an indicator of diverse problems later in life, such as addiction and dropping out of school. Ringrose and Nijenhuis (1986) have reviewed a large number of studies which show a correlation between the level of functioning socially as a child and adaptability in the long term. In the studies they describe, the prognosis is unfavourable for both extremely withdrawn as well as aggressive children. Thus the timely treating of a lack of social skills is something that is highly desirable.

Children who lack social skills are more often found in special schools than in normal education (Van der Molen and Van der Zee, 1985, Sanders-Woudstra and Verhulst, 1987). Jongbloed and Gunning (1991) found that among the special schools they studied in Rotterdam, including the school attached to the Pedological Institute (PI school) as well as schools for learning and behavioural disabilities (LOM schools) and extreme learning and behaviour disabilities (ZMOK), there was a high percentage of children with serious emotional and behavioural problems.

This study's data is in keeping with our own clinical impression. Special education is flooded as it were with children with behavioural problems and a serious lack of social skills. Also at the PI school we have been confronted with these problems in recent years and the interventions described below are an attempt to alleviate the lack of social skills among children at the school.

DEFINING THE CONCEPT

Social skills consist of two components: behaviour and cognitions (Wielkie-wicz, 1986). A socially skilled person is someone who has found the right balance between adapting to his/her environment - doing what others expect - and positively influencing this

Behavioral Approaches for Children and Adolescents, Edited by
H. P. J. G. van Bilsen et al., Plenum Press, New York, 1995

environment so that the wishes of the individual are taken into account - the environment does what the individual wants - (van Lieshout, Ferguson, Van Lier and Van Vierssen, 1987). This balance is missing in a person lacking social skills (Lahey and Kazdin, 1977; Bierman and Furman, 1984).

Petermann (1988) made a distinction among children lacking social skills between withdrawn, shy ones, on the one hand, and disruptive, aggressive children, on the other. Children who belong to the more withdrawn group include those

- incapable of standing up for their needs, wishes and desires in interpersonal contacts (behaviour);
- who continually doubt themselves (cognitions).

Disruptive, aggressive children are characterised by

- serious behavioural problems such as frequently shouting, starting a row for little or no reason and ignoring the rights of others. The expressed aggression is both verbal and physical (behaviour);
- incorrectly assessing the behaviour and intentions of others;
- a cognitive style distinguished by a lack of inhibiting cognitions.

Kendall (1988) refers to the cognitive processes as either "cognitive distortions " (shy, nervous children) or "cognitive deficiencies" (aggressive children).

Among a large group of children in special education we see an accumulation of various problems: learning disabilities, difficult family circumstances as well as emotional and behavioural problems. The families of children in special education lacking social skills are organised in such a way that this deficiency is partly reinforced by the way individual family members treat each other (Kendall, 1983; De Bruin, 1983; Minuchin et al; 1967). These families are distinguished by a lack of appropriate social skill models, a lack of a "natural" rewarding of social skills behaviour and a rigid structure regarding the roles of family members.

A Shortage of Social Skills Training for Special Education Pupils

Reports on treating socially unskilled children between 7 and 13 using cognitive/behavioural therapeutic programmes show varying degrees of success (Matson and Ollendick, 1988; Petermann and Petermann, 1988). These programmes have limited success among children with several problems. This is attributed to the fact that they are only effective in one specific field - that of the child. They are also seen as being too intensive. For children with multiple problems, such as the group in special education, there are no behavioural therapeutic programmes available (Van der Molen and Van der Zee, 1985; Hollin and Trower, 1986; Petermann, 1988; Cartledge and Milburn, 1986).

Petermann and Petermann emphasise the need for more integrated treatment aimed at three appropriate areas: the child, school and family. Treating special education pupils who lack social skills should include the following elements:

- restructuring the immediate environment: not only treating the child but active interventions in school and family;
- giving special attention to strengthening the willingness for change on the part of both parents and child;
- treatment should be immediately rewarding for the children and include much repetition;
- emphasis on "doing" rather than "talking."

The School Attached to the Paedological Institute (PI School)

The PI school is used for observing and treating children. Children who attend our school are those who have many problems which other forms of special education are unable to tackle as yet. Most of the children have serious emotional and behavioural problems, including a lack of social skills. The Youth Welfare sector of the Paedological Institute is also closely involved in observing and treating these children.

In recent years the school and Youth Welfare have jointly developed two strategies for treating a lack of social skills. The "Social Skills in the Class" programme is a curriculum intervention and consists of lessons in social skills in a classroom setting, while "Group Therapy in Social Skills is an external training intervention in which children are trained intensively in social skills."

CURRICULUM INTERVENTION: SOCIAL SKILLS IN THE CLASSROOM

The acquiring of social skills is a hidden component of the school curriculum (Cartledge and Milburn, 1986). Similar to the parents, the class teacher is an important and influential figure in a child's life and acts as a role model for social skills behaviour. He influences, consciously or subconsciously, a child's social behaviour through a process of reinforcement. In their turn, children also influence their teacher. Children who have positive social behaviour (seeking the teacher's help, smiling at him/her and listening to instructions) for instance receive more attention from the teacher and achieve more than children who do not display this type of behaviour (Cartledge and Milburn, 1986).

The "Social Skills for Children between 6 and 13" programme, developed by Jonkers (1991), is a curriculum intervention at an interpersonal level (Schuurman, 1991). The programme comprises 25, 30 minute lessons and concentrates on stimulating social skills and social cognitions.

The lessons are given in the classroom by a special teacher attached to the school. The children call her the Sova Miss (from an abbreviation of the Dutch programme's title). The training group coincides with the class group and is incorporated into the teaching. Hoeben and Van Lier (1992) refer to the advantage of this approach in that it makes the training more "real" for the pupils and makes generalisation easier.

Lessons for the 6 to 10 age group follow a set pattern. A topic is introduced by means of a five-minute role play and then practised for 10 minutes by the entire group under the supervision of the class teacher and the Sova Miss. The group is then divided into smaller groups and practises for a further 10 minutes. The lesson finishes with a group discussion on the newly acquired skill (five minutes).

Some examples of how topics for the lessons are presented:

- When introducing the topic "Saying something nice" , the teacher explains that it is sometimes difficult to say something nice about oneself. Most children find it namely much easier to say what they cannot do or what they do not like about themselves. The teacher then gets each child in turn to say something nice about their appearance, followed by another turn in which they mention something they are good in. The teacher prompts a child who cannot think of anything. The group is then divided into two and the children continue the exercise, completing sentences such as "I can..." or I'm pleased that I can... Outside the lesson, the teacher looks out for competent behaviour among the children and rewards it.

- The topic "Recognising feelings" is introduced by the teacher with the help of so-called "smile" figures on the blackboard depicting anger, fear, happiness and sadness. The children are then asked how they can recognise how someone else is feeling. The teacher then makes several statements to the children for them to guess how she/he is feeling.

During lessons much attention is given to concrete problems that arise among the children in the classroom or school playground, such as being teased or having something taken from them. These problems form the starting point for discussion and role play. Alternative solutions are proposed and the skills needed are practised within the group.

In the higher age group a topic is chosen together with the pupils which then lasts for some two months. The children for instance may work on a video on social skills or create group games together.

Behavioural therapy techniques are also used. The teacher prompts the children and helps them exhibit social skills behaviour. Alternative solutions for conflict situations are also touched on: the teacher thinks along with the children in finding creative solutions. Sample situations are created (modelling) and appropriate behaviour for the child is taught in small steps (shaping). Desired behaviour is immediately rewarded - sometimes via a points system - while undesired behaviour is ignored or time-out is applied.

TRAINING INTERVENTION: GROUP THERAPY IN SOCIAL SKILLS

For certain children curriculum intervention, as described above, is not enough. Their lack of social skills is so great and their cognitions so disturbed that they need intensive training outside the classroom.

The cognitive and behavioural therapeutic treatment programme of the PI in Rotterdam is based, among others, on a model of change described by American psychologists Prochaska and DiClemente (1984). Using this as a basis, certain motivation techniques were developed (Van Bilsen, 1989) such as:

- selective active listening: indications of motivation such as feelings of self-esteem, concern and competence were rewarded;
- positive labelling or restructuring: something positive is made out of something negative.

This technique was used to heighten the willingness of parents, teachers and children to change. It consists of interventions related to three areas:

- group therapy: the child
- family guidance: the family
- teacher guidance: teaching situation.

GROUP THERAPY

Group therapy takes place in one of the therapy rooms of the Youth Welfare department. A training group comprises six children and two trainers who meet every week for 75 minutes.

Therapy consists of three phases: motivation, "doing" and integration. During the motivation phase the therapists create a work relationship with the children. They make only low demands and try to stimulate feelings of self-esteem and competence. Gradually the therapists make greater demands while making sure the children still notch up achievements. During this phase several skills are again practised such as waiting your turn, listening to others, taking the initiative in making contact, non-verbal behaviour (posture, voice level, eye contact), identification, expressing feelings and looking at one's own behaviour. In the "doing" phase some eight topics are dealt with such as:

- "How do I ask that?" (Asking someone something)
- "What shall we do?" (Negotiating with another child)
- "Yes, I did that." (Responding to criticism and admitting your wrong)
- "They're teasing me." (How to respond to bullying and teasing).

Each topic takes up two consecutive sessions. First the topic is explored and practised via role play, while the second time the topic is also explored and much attention given to homework which is played out in the group.

In the integration phase the practise material is repeated according to the specific weaknesses of the children during so-called booster sessions.

During group therapy we use a points system which acts as a motivation and reinforcement tool. During the session the children earn points for appropriate behaviour, such as taking part in role play, and these are noted on the blackboard.

The children can also loose points (response cost), for instance for disruptive behaviour. At the end of the session the points earned are exchanged for small tokens in the "shop."

PARENTAL GUIDANCE

Parental guidance makes use of the following techniques: selective active listening, structuring and concretisation, restructuring and provocation. This means that unmotivated parents are able to take part in the treatment. Prior to treating the child and parents we analyse what stage of change the parents are still in.

Maintaining contact with parents is extremely important. For instance, when a child is suddenly absent, the parents are immediately contacted. Occasionally it happens that parents are absolutely unable or unwilling to take part in parental guidance. They are then informed by short, friendly letter of their child's progress.

During parental guidance the parents are told in detail about the training: its content, their child's progress and the possibility of also rewarding their child's desired behaviour at home. In this way we try to make parents better role models for social skills behaviour and to get them to reward this in a natural way. The videos of the group sessions are an important, almost indispensable asset for this as they are extremely motivating for parents. They see their child achieving success, they experience their child differently and also discover ways themselves of rewarding appropriate social behaviour.

TEACHER GUIDANCE

When guiding teachers there are a number of points to consider. Teachers need to be informed about the training: the type of behaviour concerned and the stages involved. We discuss the functional analysis of the child including an insight into his/her behaviour, consequences of such behaviour, what precedes such behaviour and how it is influenced. Videos of the training are shown, among others, to demonstrate techniques. Therapist and class teacher together plan a course of treatment for in the classroom that ties in with that used in the child's group therapy and for parental guidance.

THE CASE HISTORY OF HARRY

Harry is 10 years old and has been attending the PI school for a year. Before that he attended a Medical Infant Nursery and a special school. He is an only child and his parents have been divorced for many years. He lives with his mother and sees his father sporadically. Mother and son are more like partners than a divorced parent and child. Mother has little say over her son and her social contacts are limited. Harry is teased a lot by the neighbourhood so that he hardly goes out.

Despite a higher cognitive potential, Harry's academic progress is at a severely mentally retarded level. The most important learning problem is his lack of motivation. He needs to be constantly encouraged and easily drops everything.

On a social level, Harry has serious behaviour shortcomings - and too many of them. He has no idea how to make friendly contact with other children (he pushes and kicks if he wants something from someone else), cannot stand up to teasing and prefers to play with children much young than himself. He sometimes has angry outbursts (if he does not get his own way) and teases other children. Harry is rejected by his classmates because of his problem behaviour.

A positive aspect is that Harry loves sport and does competitive swimming, although he is sometimes in conflict with his trainer and other children due to his clumsy social behaviour.

During the social skills lessons in the class, Harry has great difficulty contributing. He often refuses to take part in the group assignment (making a video), distracts other children and hangs around by himself. His teacher has the feeling he has little hold over him and in connection with approaching secondary school believes it is important for Harry to have intensive social skills training.

During the intake phase, it emerges that Harry is weighed down by his own social isolation. He feels extremely incompetent and has the sense that everything he does is always wrong. He does not expect much can be done about this (helpless behaviour). Diagnosed according to the stages of change of Prochaska and DiClemente (1984), Harry is in the stage of reflection: he recognises there are problems but fears he is incapable of bringing about the necessary changes. His mother, too, is in the same phase. She is concerned for him but is prepared to help him to change.

Before the training starts we draw up the following objectives:

(1) For Harry: learning to make friends with other children in a more positive way; defending himself against bullying and teasing; being able to give and receive compliments; standing up to criticism and solving his own conflicts.
(2) For mother: heightening her feeling of self-esteem and competence in order to tackle her son's problems and re-establishing the authoritative mother-son relationship.
(3) For the classroom: stimulating the skills learned.

Harry enthusiastically began his training and learnt the basic skills very quickly. However, when we practised the more complex skills, he did not want to know. He did not do his homework anymore and tried to disrupt the group. By giving him choices ("You can take part, but only if you want to yourself."), making specific agreements with him, providing much more positive feedback, giving directed behaviour instructions and allowing him to act as model for the other children, very slowly a synchronisation of response and effect occurred. Harry began to have the feeling he could exercise some influence on his environment. He renewed his participation in role play and began doing his housework again. The points system in particular increasingly encouraged Harry to take part in group activities. He gladly saved for the more expensive presents and in discussions with his mother we tentatively explored ways in which she could influence Harry's behaviour.

Mother made a number of agreements with her son regarding several of his disruptive tendencies. Because these agreements worked and mother could see the advantages (better atmosphere in the house, she and her son more relaxed), we were able to suggest a number of options with regard to partly re-establishing the authoritative relationship with him.

Mother also did a number of activities without Harry which she enjoyed doing. Talks with Harry's teacher centred on ways of systematically influencing his behaviour. By giving him choices, positive feedback, focusing on his sporting achievements (hero of the sports day) and rewarding appropriate social behaviour, Harry adjusted better to the school routine and the recalcitrant behaviour diminished.

At the end of the training, Harry's teacher noted an increased interaction with other children, even though it was still not really with children of his own age. Harry was able to stand up more to being teased and he also teased considerably less. His position in the class changed in a positive sense and he found a special friend in another class. Harry also went camping for the first time with the school and he drew attention with his sports achievements. He is increasingly proud about these. Mother is satisfied with Harry's behaviour.

He now dares to play outside more and is able to defend himself against teasing. His mother is proud of him and Harry is particularly glad that he is no longer teased by the neighbourhood. He still finds it difficult to get along properly with other children, but can now solve a number of situations for himself. He proudly tells how he resolved a conflict during swimming lessons, for instance. He is also happy that he now plays more outside and has a special friend.

CONCLUSION

Both the curriculum and training interventions are, in our clinical experience, effective in tackling a lack of social skills.

The lessons have a positive effect within a classroom setting. Problem interactions can be discussed in behavioural terms and this makes them better understood by the children and better able to be influenced. Parents and teachers also noted generalisation to other situations: clubs, sports activities and school camp.

The training intervention also positively affects the child, the family and the class. Training motivates the child and the family to tackle other problems. The training also provides us with diagnostic information by giving us a better insight into the problems of child and family. After a mainly hesitant start, teachers and parents are enthusiastic co-therapists. In particular, video images of the children's achievements are a powerful motivating force.

In the coming years we hope to develop this "package" further and eventually make it available to colleagues in youth care work and school guidance.

REFERENCES

Bierman, K.L. & Furman, W. (1984). The effects of social skills training and peer involvement on the social adjustment of pre-adolescents. *Child Development*, 55, 15-162.

Bilsen, H.P.J.G. van (1989). *Motivational Interviewing*. paper gepresenteerd op het eerste Europese Congres van psychologie, Juli 1989, Amsterdam.

Bruin, I.J. de (1983). *Verwijzingen Speciaal Onderwijs naar Jeugdhulpverlening*. Interne publicatie van het Pedologisch Instituut Rotterdam.

Cartledge, G & Milburn, J.F. (1986). *Teaching Social Skills to Children*. New York: Regano Press.

Hoeben, S.M. & Lier, P.A. van (1992). *Bronnenboek sociaal-emotionele ontwikkeling*. 's-Hertogenbosch: Katholiek Pedagogisch Studiecentrum.

Hollin, C.R. & Trower, P. (1986). Applications across the life span. *Handbook of social skills training*. 1, Oxford: Pergamon Press.

Jongbloed, M.H.B. & Gunning, I.A.M.P. (1991). Gedrags- en emotionele problemen binnen enkele vormen van speciaal onderwijs. In H.P.J.G. van Bilsen & H.D. Swager (red.). *Speciaal Onderwijs & Jeugdhulpverlening*. De Lier: Academisch Boeken Centrum.

Jonkers, J. (1991). *Programma sociale vaardigheden*. PI-school Rotterdam, interne publikatie.

Lahey, B.B. & Kadzin, A.S. (1977) (eds.). *Advances in Clinical Child Psychology*, 1. New York: Plenum.

Lieshout, C.F.M. van, Ferguson, T.J., Lier, P.A. van & Vierssen, D.J. van (1987). *Diepteproject Sociaal-emotionele Ontwikkeling*. Nijmegen: Katholieke Universiteit.

Matson, J & Ollendick, Th. H. (1988). *Enhancing Children's Social Skills. Assessment and Training*. New York: Pergamon Press.

Minuchin, S., e.a. (1967). *Families of the Slums*. New York: Basic Books Inc.

Molen, H.T. van der & Zee, S.A.M. van der (1985). *Sociale redzaamheidprogrammma's voor minderbegaafde jongeren*. Groningen: Rijksuniversiteit Groningen, vakgroep Persoonlijkheidspsychologie.

Petermann, F & Petermann, U. (1988). *Training mit agressiven Kindern*. (Einzeltraining, Kindergruppen, Elternberatung). München-Weinheim: Psycholgie Verlags Union.

Petermann, U. (1988). *Werken met sociaal angstige kinderen* (theorie en praktijk van de training). Nijmegen: Dekker & Van de Vegt

Prochaska, J.O. & DiClemente, C.C. (1984). *The Transtheoretical Approach: Crossing Traditional Boundaries of Theapy*. Homewood, Illinois: Dow Jones-Irwin.

Ringrose, H.J. & Nijenhuis, E.H. (1986). *Bang zijn voor andere kinderen*. Groningen: Wolters-Noordhoff.

Sanders-Woudstra, J.A.R. & Verhulst, F.C. (1987). Epidemiologisch-kinderpsychiatrische benadering van de ontwikkelingen in het speciaal onderwijs. In K. Doornbos & L.M. Stevens (red.). *De groei van het speciaal onderwijs. Deel A: Analyse van historie en onderzoek*. 's-Gravenhage: Staatsuitgeverij.

Schuurman, C.A.M. (1991). Mogelijkheden en beperkingen van de stimulering van de sociaal emotionele ontwikkeling van kinderen in het speciaal onderwijs. In H.J.P.G. van Bilsen & H.D. Swager (red.). *Speciaal Onderwijs en Jeugdhulpverlening*. De Lier: Academisch Boeken Centrum.

Wielkiewicz, R. (1986). *Behavior Management in the Schools*. New York: Pergamom.

9

STOP THINK DO

Improving Social and Learning Skills for Children in Clinics and Schools

Lindy Petersen

Child and Family Psychology
266 Melbourne Street
North Adelaide
South Australia 5006

ABSTRACT

STOP THINK DO was developed in a clinic as a group social skills training program for children and adolescents, referred with social-behavioural problems. It also involves the child's critical social supports including parents, teachers and peers to ensure transfer and maintenance of skills in the real world.

The program is a cognitive-behavioural-motivational approach to social skills training which is both didactic and experiential. The STOP THINK DO method of social problem solving is the core of the program, following the traffic light symbol, a simple cue for learning the process for children and adults alike.

Through liaison with educationalists, the clinical treatment program has been adapted with a preventive focus for use in school classrooms, incorporating a social skills training curriculum and a teacher training program. Research described in the paper indicates the utility of the program to enhance social competence in children in clinic and school settings.

The STOP THINK DO method is also useful as a framework for motivating learning in any child, including those with attention deficits, learning disabilities or gifted under-achievement. In essence, the application of the STOP THINK DO model in either a social or learning context attempts to de-emotionalise these areas, and empower the child with cognitive and behavioural skills with motivation to change through peer and adult support.

Development of Stop Think Do Program

The STOP THINK DO social skills training mehtod was developed as a group treatment over 15 years by the author and colleagues at the Adelaide Children's Hospital. The program aims to develop social skills and pro-social attitudes in children and thereby, facilitate more positive social relationships with family members, teachers and peers. The program is offered to children who are socially isolated, lacking in confidence, withdrawn, immature, or impulsive, boisterous, physically or verbally aggressive. About 6 to 8 children

Behavioral Approaches for Children and Adolescents, Edited by
H. P. J. G. van Bilsen et al., Plenum Press, New York, 1995

attend each group with 1 or 2 leaders trained in group counselling skills. The children are divided roughly into age ranges of 6-9, 10-12 and 13-15 years. The program runs for about 7-10 weeks with parents participating in a concurrent training program to transfer skills to the home situation. The children's teachers are also invited to 1 or 2 training sessions throughout the term of the group to reinforce skills in the school (Petersen and Gannoni, 1991; Petersen, 1992).

The positive feedback from teachers involved in the clinic program prompted its adaptation as a social competence building and behaviour management strategy for regular school classrooms (Petersen and Gannoni, 1992). The development of the classroom curriculum programs represent a shift of focus from a therapeutic, treatment emphasis to a more preventative role in school classrooms where reasonably functional children or "at risk" children are taught social skills to encourage positive social development, thereby protecting them from social rejection or neglect.

Theoretical Frame: Cognitive-Behavioural-Motivational-Broad Based

A definition of social skills by Ladd and Mize (1983) reflects the main emphases of the STOP THINK DO program. Social skills refer to the "ability to organise cognitions and behaviours into an integrated course of action directed toward culturally acceptable social or interpersonal goals" (p127).

This definition defines the critical elements in social development which the program aims to train in children, namely

1. **cognitive** skills such as knowledge and comprehension of appropriate social behaviours and strategies, social problem solving and decision making skills.
2. **behavioural** skills, verbal and non-verbal, such as careful looking and listening, approach behaviours and play styles, conversational skills, gesture and facial expression, assertive behaviours.
3. pro-social **motivation** and attitudes which provide the impetus for skills training.

These social skills and attitudes are indicators of social competence and affect the development of social relationships.

Research (e.g. Kazdin et al, 1987) plus clinical experience also indicates another critical variable in social skills training.

4. a **broad base** which involves significant social supports usually parents, peers and teachers in the training program in order to transfer skills to the real world and to maintain them over time. Moreover, in the STOP THINK DO context, behaviour management is considered a social skill for adults who also need to develop cognitive and behavioural skills, plus the motivation to relate positively and effectively with children, and their adult peers.

The major psychological approaches incorporated in the program are the Behavioural and Cognitive Problem Solving methods which are based on sound theory and research. In the combined approach, children are taught how to think about, evaluate and choose solutions to their social problems before they initiate behaviour. This problem solving method was pioneered by Spivack and Shure (1974). Behavioural techniques are concurrently used to model, role play and reinforce alternative strategies in social situations, together with instruction in discreet social behaviours (e.g. initiating conversations, approaching peers, saying 'no'). The program also emphasizes democratic conflict resolution and purposeful, responsible choice in social interactions.

However, cognitive and behavioural skills will not be acquired unless people are socially interested and motivated, and want to improve their interpersonal relationships.

Accordingly, the training program focuses on the identification and achievement of prosocial goals for the individuals involved. The motivation for goal achievement and skills acquisition comes largely from positive feedback which further promotes self confidence and self esteem when social goals are achieved.

The role of peers in the social skills training program is critical, whether it be in the classroom or small group intensive program. Correspondingly, the role of group leader is not only to teach specific social skills, but also to develop a social support group. Thus, STOP THINK DO is a didactic and experiential approach, since skills are taught through positive relating experiences which motivate children and adults to learn them.

The theoretical framework for the parent and teacher training programs mirrors the cognitive-behavioural-motivational framework of the children's program. Essentially, for parents and teachers, the program incorporates a democratic behaviour management/counselling program along the lines of STEP (Dinkmeyer and McKay, 1976) into the STOP THINK DO framework. Concepts like I-messages, reflective listening and logical consequences are steps at STOP or THINK or DO.

Moreover, research (e.g. Hymel et al, 1990) and experience indicates that the expectancies and perceptions of the child's usual peer group are very resistant to change, and may actually extinguish positive gains made by individuals receiving social skills training. Accordingly, attempts are made to involve class peers in training, by encouraging their teachers to use the STOP THINK DO method in the classroom and optimally, conduct classroom programs which parallel the treatment program. Class peers then act as social supports, anticipating and reinforcing positive changes in each other, including target children.

Essentially, the classroom program aims to improve the social competency of all students as a preventive strategy. It may however, be necessary for children who have identified social-behavioural problems or high risk students to be withdrawn from classrooms for extra skills training and group support in liaison with classroom teachers and optimally, their parents. Thus, the STOP THINK DO program adapts to a treatment or prevention role in the school setting.

The STOP THINK DO package therefore represents the confluence of theory, research and practice in social psychology, plus a practical interface between developmental, systems and community psychology.

STOP THINK DO Method: Core of the Program

This method of social skills training and behaviour management focuses primarily on the development of communication, problem solving and behavioural skills, and the building of self confidence and social interest. These skills and attitudes are developed in children, parents and teachers through repeated practice in the STOP THINK DO steps, optimally in a supportive group situation. Children learn to use this method when they are having problems with their peers. Parents and teachers learn the same method for managing children's problem behaviour, and also for helping children deal more effectively with peers and siblings. Thus, the adults act as models of appropriate social behaviour and also as social skills trainers for the children.

A traffic light symbol reminds people of the steps to follow.

The red light cues them to STOP before they react impulsively, and to work out what is actually happening, how those involved are feeling and what they want to happen. This is the hardest stop of all for children and adults alike. The yellow light cues people to THINK about what they could do to solve the problem, and the likely consequences of those possibilites.

The emphasis is on learning **how** to think, not **what** to think.

The green light cues people to choose the solution with the best consequences, and DO it. If it does not work, they go back to STOP and THINK again about what to DO!

Essentially, the method stresses communication skills including looking and listening, feeling recognition and expression at STOP; cognitive problem solving and consequential thinking wkills at THINK; decision making and behavioural skills at DO; with the motivation for skills acquisition coming from feedback from peers and primary socialisers. Children with social-behavioural problems are considered to be 'stuck' at one of these stages. For example, impulsive or aggressive children may be stuck at DO - the keep doing, without much stopping and thinking. Shy, withdrawn children tend to be stuck at STOP, or maybe THINK - they rarely get to DO. The program aims to develop the skills and the motivation in children (and adults) to complete the process in their social interactions by repeated practice in a safe, supportive environment.

The STOP THINK DO steps for behaviour management and social skills training are summarized in Figure 1 and are also available on a training video, STOP THINK DO in Practice.

Research

Independent research (Andary, 1990) evaluated the effectiveness of the STOP THINK DO program for improving the social behaviour of 25 children aged between 7 and 11 years, referred to the Adelaide children's Hospital clinic for treatment.

The results of the study indicated a significant reduction in social-behavioural problems on scales rated by teachers, parents and children themselves at 3 month follow up. Moreover, there was also a reduction in **clinically** significant problems reported by parents and teachers on a standardized behaviour checklist. A very high degree of parent and teacher satisfaciton with the program was also reported.

Andary concluded that the program is "a comprehensive package which addresses most of the major issues which the literature reports as being optimal for the acquisition and maintenance of social skills development in children. These factors include a cognitive-behavioural training model, with a didactic and experiential approach, a peer group setting and the inclusion of parents and teachers, with an impetus towards classroom training" (p 24).

Beck and Horne (1992) reported on the effectiveness of the STOP THINK DO program in a special school setting. This study involved 85 students with mild-moderate intellectual disability, the majority of secondary school age and many with poor socialization skills and some emotional disturbance. The school required a remedial program for children who have social-behavioural-emotional difficulties and also as a preventive strategy helping all students to cope with their feelings, particularly anger and frustration in non aggressive ways, preparing them for wider social and vocational success.

The STOP THINK DO program was chosen because it provides a long term, incremental approach to the development of communication, conflict resolution and decision making skills and positive social relationships, suitable for children with intellectual delay. It also offers the simplicity of the traffic light theme as a cue for learning. In addition, the program may be taught by classroom teachers and the single, step by step process applied universally.

The program was implemented across the whole school in 1991, with parents and teachers receiving training prior to and during the program, and children trained in groups of 8 for 3 sessions per week. Significant gains were reported by students, parents and teachers particularly in terms of students developing a broader range of social skills, being less likely to get upset by teasing, more likely to keep friends, less likely to act without thinking and less likely to fight with others including siblings at home.

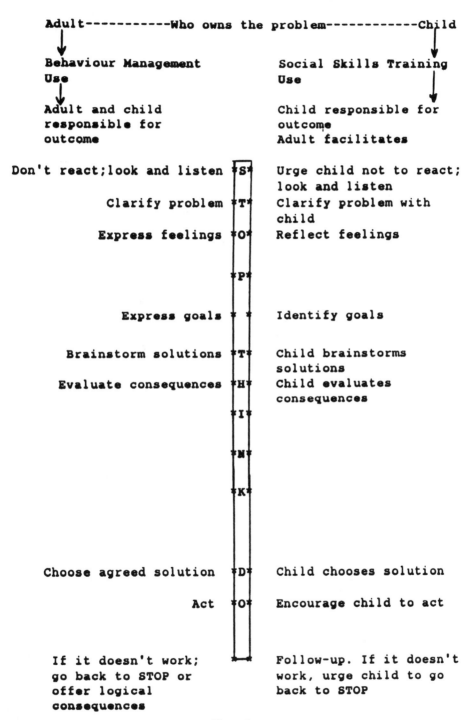

Adult-----------Who owns the problem------------Child

Behaviour Management   Social Skills Training
Use   Use

Adult and child   Child responsible for
responsible for   outcome
outcome   Adult facilitates

Don't react;look and listen *S*   Urge child not to react;
                                        look and listen
             Clarify problem *T*   Clarify problem with
                                        child
            Express feelings *O*   Reflect feelings

                              P

               Express goals * *   Identify goals

        Brainstorm solutions *T*   Child brainstorms
                                        solutions
       Evaluate consequences *H*   Child evaluates
                                        consequences

                              I

                              N

                              K

        Choose agreed solution *D*   Child chooses solution

                         Act *O*   Encourage child to act

If it doesn't work;   * *   Follow-up. If it doesn't
go back to STOP or   work, urge child to go
offer logical   back to STOP
consequences

Figure 1.

The authors conclude that 'the STOP THINK DO program has grown in popularity both as a preventative program in regular schools, as a remedial program in special classes for the emotionally disturbed, and a program for small groups run by specialist teacher(s). It has been shown to skill both teachers and students and if parents are involved, to raise their awareness of their child's social strengths and weaknesses, and to assist in improving such skills. On a practical level, it provides useful sequential lesson plans to develop pro-social motivation and behaviour in our students.'

A study by Nimmo (1993) also investigated the adequacy of the STOP THINK DO program for enhancing the social competence of socially inept children in primary school settings. The study involved 96 children aged 7 to 11 years in 3 groups; a control group receiving no training in the program, a withdrawal treatment group removed from the classroom for training with their parents also involved, and an in-class teatment group whose classroom peers were also exposed to the program.

The results indicated that children in both treatment groups made significant gains in social competence and peer acceptability from the 10 week program. Children, teachers and parents noted changes in terms of making and keeping friends, coping with teasing, controlling aggression, being less attention seeking, and being less shy. From sociometric data, class peers rated children in the treatment groups as more accepted by peers and also reported mroe friendships between peers and participants.

Moreover, equal benefits were derived from the program on a withdrawal basis with parent involvement and an in-class basis with peer support. Teachers are able to implement the program in both settings. Another outcome of the study was a further significant improvement in social competence and peer acceptability in the treatment groups at 3 month review. In addition, evidence for generalization across settings was obtained when parents reported significant improvements in socially appropriate behaviour in the home.

Nimmo (personal communication) reports that teachers generally enjoy the inservice training and implementing the program in schools, and that their own skills are enhanced considerably. A whole school inservicing, including ancilliary staff is most useful to promote consistency. The traffic light symbol has proved useful around the school as well as the classroom.

Adaptability for Treatment and Prevention of Relating Problems

In the clinic, the program has been adapted for individual or group therapy with preschoolers, children, adolescents and adults, since the only pre-requisite is some under-standing of the language. The program may be applied through interpreters to multi-cultural groups; signed for people with hearing problems; modified to allow for more repetition and structured cueing for younger children, slow learners, language disordered people, or others with special needs; extended for older adolescents to include skills involved in sexual and employment relations, independence issues and stress management; applied as the frame-work for family counselling; and used as a model for case management and administrative decision making.

As a treatment program, STOP THINK DO emphasizes problem solving and dicision making as the strategy for coping with life's stressors. Using this strategy, people are empowered through self-awareness and self-control, social awareness and social skills training. Confidence, self-esteem, independence, maturity, responsibility, respect - all the ethereal personal and social qualities for which we strive in ourselves and our children - grow through the recognition of how "I feel", the realization that "I can", the actualization that "I do", and the feedback that "You do O.K.."

Moreover, the STOP THINK DO problem solving and decision making process has face validity as a strategy for primary prevention. Similar longstanding school based programs in the United States which aim to promote social competency in children through training in the social competency in children through training in the social problem solving process have yielded successful outcomes in terms of improved behavioural adjustment and ability to cope with stressors like transition to middle school, substance abuse, peer pressure and conflict, teacher relations and the organizational requirements of school life. More positive self-concepts and increased sensitivity to the feelings of others are also reported outcomes (Elias and Weissberg, 1990).

These preventive programs are curriculum based (e.g. Elias and Clabby, 1989; Weissberg et al, 1988). A curriculum focus implies greater commitment to the value of the core problem solving process, and the need for prerequisite, high quality teacher training. It ensures a structured and consistent approach to the teaching and practice of concepts and skills in a formal lesson format, which may then be reinforced throughout the school day. It also precipitates a common problem solving language to use within the classroom, the schoolyard, the staffroom, the home, and between school and home.

The problem solving model need not be confined to the social skills curriculum. The same model may be applied to more academic curriculum areas. The empowerment offered to students by this process is further enhanced when they work in groups (e.g. Balson, 1983). The psychodynamics of the cooperative learning group generated from shared reinforcement contingencies, responsibilities of group membership, group goal setting and achievement and regular feedback may be readily harnessed to provide the impetus for learning academic or interpersonal skills alike.

Treatment of Learning, Concentrating, Achieving Problems

The STOP THINK DO model may be adapted to motivate learning in children individually (Petersen, in publication). The method provides a framework into which any learning program may be fitted, regardless of its purpose or content. It can be the frame for a remedial program for children with learning difficulties, a concentration and behaviour control plan for children with attention deficits, an extension program for bright underachievers, or a maths, writing, sport or whatever program for any child. The aim is to encourage children to want to change and achieve.

The method takes account of the basic principles of motivation namely, that people learn what interests them and what they consider of value to them. The way to make learning interesting and valuable is to involve the learners in choosing, planning and actively committing themselves to it. As a consequence, they feel some degree of power and control in the learning situation, and are more likely to feel some responsibility to follow through with their commitment. When they set and achieve goals, their self-esteem and confidence is enhanced, providing impetus or motivation for further goal achievement and sustained learning. They are emotionally, cognitively and behaviourally committed to their own progress.

Whether the aim is the achievement of social-relating or learning goals, motivation grows by the same process. It proceeds from the recognition that 'I understand' the problem, the realiation that 'I can' find answers, the actualization that 'I do' try solutions, and the feedback from others that 'You do O.K.'. This is the STOP THINK DO process.

Applying STOP THINK DO to Motivate Learning

To begin the process of change, children need to understand the nature of their difficulties or relative weaknesses. The STOP stage involves supplying children with factual information about their strengths and weaknesses which may come from formal assessments or subjective observations. All children have areas of relative strength and weakness, and these are clarified for them. Their feelings about these aspects and their goals for change are also discussed at a level of sophistication suitable for the age of the child. At the THINK stage, children are encouraged to consider many solutions for their learning, concentration or underachievement problems in the light of the likely consequences of the suggested strategies. Possible solutions might include involvement in specific remedial, or extension programs, changing schools, medication, modifying physical environment, classroom concentration and memory plans or any idea which occurs to the people involved. At the DO stage, the child chooses 1 or 2 'tricks' from the list of suggestions and a plan of action is initiated and regularly monitored. Plans may be drawn up using traffic light stickers (red, yellow and green circles), with children choosing the words to describe their goals and plans. They are encouraged to recognise that, if the plan doesn't work, other 'tricks' will be tried until success is achieved. Parents, teachers and even peers may be involved as co-workers in the planning and implementation process.

In essence, the STOP THINK DO method can improve both the quality of social relationships for children and the quality of their learning achievements by de-emotionalizing their difficulties in either area and empowering them with cognitive and behavioural skills plus the motivation to use them from supportive feedback. This is achieved by teaching children to insert some 'thinking' in between "feeling" and "behaving", to understand their difficulties and commit themselves to change in all life's arenas, to reach their fullest potential for learning and happy living.

REFERENCES

Andary, L. (1990). *An Evaluation of the Adelaide Children's Hospital's Cognitive-Behavioural Social Skills program.* Unpublished M. Psych thesis, Flinders University of S.A.

Balson, M. (1993). *"Understanding Classroom Behaviour"* (3rd Edition). Hawthorn, Victoria: Australian Council for Educational Research.

Beck, J. and Horne, D. (1992). *"A whole school implementation of the Stop Think Do! social skills training program at Minerva Special school".* In: B. willis and J. Izard (Eds). "Student Behaviour Problems: Directions, Perspectives and Expectations". Hawthorn, Victoria: australian council for Educational Research.

Dinkmeyer, D. and McKay, G.D. (1976). *"Systematic Training for Effective Parenting".* Minnesota: AGS.

Elias, M. and Clabby, J. (1989). *"Social Skills and Social Decision Making Skills for the Elementary Grades: A Curriculum guide for educators and other school-based professionals".* Rockville, MD: Aspen.

Elias, M.J. and Weissberg, R.p. (1990). *School-based social competence promotion as a primary prevention strategy: A tale of two projects.* In: R.P., Lorian, (Ed) "Protecting the Children: Strategies for Optimising Emotional and Behavioural Development". New York: Haworth.

Hymel, S., Wagner, E. and Butler, L.J. (1990). In: S. Asher and J. Coie (Eds). *"Peer Rejection in Childhood".* New York: Cambridge University Press.

Kazdin, A.E., Esveldt-Dawson, K., French, N.H. and Unis, A.S. (1987). Effects of parent management training and problem solving skills training combined in the treatment of antisocial child behaviour. *"Journal of American Academy child and Adolescent Psychiatry",* 26, 3, 416-424.

Ladd, G.W. and Mize, J. (1983). A cognitive social learning model of social skill training. *"Psychological Review",* 90, 2, 127-157.

Nimmo, J. (1993). *Social Competence: A pilot study of a cognitive-behavioural social skills program with comparisons of outcomes for in-class and withdrawal groups.* Unpublished Master Ed thesis, Queensland University.

Petersen, L. and Gannoni, A.F. (1991). *("Manual for Social Skills Training in Young People with Parent and Teacher programs").* Hawthorn, Victoria: Australian Council for Educational Research.

Petersen, L. and Gannoni, A.F., (1992). *"Teachers".* Manual for Training Social Skills while Managing Student Behaviour". Hawthorn, Victoria: Australian Council for Educational Research.

Petersen, L. (1992). *"Stop and Think Parenting".* Hawthorn, Victoria: Australian council for Educational Research.

Petersen, L. *"Stop and Think Learning: Motivation for children with learning disabilities, attention deficit and gifted underachievement"*. In: publication.

Spivack, G. and Shure, M.B. (1974). *"Social Adjustment of Young Children: A cognitive Approach to Solving Real-Life Problems"*. San Francisco: Jossey-Bass.

STOP THINK DO in Practice (1991). *Video. Adelaide Children's Hospital Educational Resource Centre,* North Adelaide, South Australia.

Weissberg, R.P., Caplan, M.Z. and Bennetto, L. (1988). *"The Yale-New Haven Social Problem-Solving (SPS). Program for Young Adolescents"*. New Haven, CT: Yale University.

10

COGNITIVE AND BEHAVIORAL TREATMENT OF CHILDHOOD DEPRESSION

Kevin D. Stark and Anne Smith

University of Texas at Austin
Department of Educational Psychology
Austin, Texas 78712-1296

Historically there has been much debate about the existence and nature of depressive disorders during childhood. During the 1980s a consensus emerged within the literature that depressive disorders exist and that they are expressed in much the same fashion as adult variants with some developmental differences. Depressive disorders during childhood appear to be more common and of longer duration than previously thought. Onset of a depressive disorder during childhood is a risk factor for later episodes and impacts all areas of the youngster's psychosocial functioning, the youngster's family system, the parent-childs dyads, and has potentially life-threatening consequences. Perhaps due to a recognition of the seriousness of the disorder and the growing number of youths affected by it, research in the area has mushroomed over the past 15 years. Numerous advances have been made in our understanding of the nature of the disorder, its impact on the youngster and his or her family, its course, common cooccuring disturbances, and how to assess it. However, issues surrounding the treatment of depressed children have been sorely neglected and few developmentally sensitive treatment models have been proposed.

To develop an effective intervention for depressed youths an attempt was made to identify etiologic variables and disturbances that are associated with the disorder, and then an intervention package was developed to address each of the disturbances. The chapter begins with a review of the disturbances in cognition, behavior, and the family environment and then a treatment model is proposed.

COGNITIVE, BEHAVIORAL, AND FAMILIAL DISTURBANCES

Overview

The study of depressive disorders during childhood has often used as its starting point, or guiding principles, existing research with adults who are depressed. In many ways this has proven fruitful as it has allowed investigators to conduct research with children that is parallel to research that has demonstrated explanatory utility with adults. Much of this research with adults has been theoretically driven or designed to evaluate portions of a model.

Behavioral Approaches for Children and Adolescents, Edited by
H. P. J. G. van Bilsen et al., Plenum Press, New York, 1995

These adult models have also served as guides to the study of depressive disorders during childhood, and the accompanying treatment models have been employed with depressed children.

Contemporary theories of *adult* depression conceptualize it as the "final common pathway" (Akiskal and McKinney, 1975) for the reciprocal influence of cognitive, behavioral, contextual/interpersonal and biochemical factors (Bedrosian, 1989; Hammen, 1991). The fit of this multifactorial approach seems promising for childhood variants of depressive disorders as well, and has direct implications for the development and implementation of effective interventions for depressed youths. In the following sections we briefly review research that evaluates the relationship between cognitive, behavioral, and familial variables and depressive disorders during childhood. The objective of the review is to identify empirically derived disturbances in the functioning of youngsters who are depressed. In a later section, intervention strategies designed to address these disturbances are discussed.

Cognitive Variables and Depression during Childhood

The major cognitive theories of depression are stress-diathesis models in which the cognitive disturbance represents the diathesis and negative life events represent the stress. The cognitive disturbance moderates the effects of stress on depressive symptoms. In other words, cognitive variables are assumed to interact with negative life events to produce depression. In Beck's model (e.g. Beck, 1967), the cognitive disturbance stems from maladaptive schemata which are hypothesized to be latent variables that are activated by related negative events. Once activated, the schemata filter and guide the processing of information in a negatively distorted fashion which leads to information processing errors and a plethora of intrusive and believable (to the individual) negative cognitions. These cognitions produce the depressive symptoms. In a similar vein, a depressogenic attributional style is assumed to mediate the impact of negative life events and depressive symptoms. In the learned helplessness/hopelessness model (Abramson, Seligman and Teasdale, 1978; Abramson, Metalsky and Alloy, 1988), the individual who is prone to the development of depression is assumed to have a trait-like tendency to attribute the cause of negative events to internal, stable and global causes and positive events to external, unstable and specific causes. Attributional style is hypothesized to be a stable variable that serves as a filter for processing information.

Given the similarities in the symptom pictures of depression from childhood through adulthood, it has become common practice to apply the adult models, including the cognitive models to the study of depression during childhood. However, this also assumes that the cognitive functioning of children, adolescents, and adults is similar. In other words, that there are no developmental differences in the cognitive variables that are relevant to these models. Results of relevant research are mixed, with some investigators finding the cognitive functioning of youths and adults to be remarkably similar (Gotlib, Lewinsohn, Seeley, Rohde and Redner, 1993; Moilanen, 1993; Prieto, Cole and Tageson, 1992) while others have found developmental differences (Garber, Weiss and Shanley, 1993; Rholes, Blackwell, Jordan and Walters, 1980). Based on a review of research from developmental psychology, Garber (1992) concludes that children begin to be able to make negative self-evaluations around 8 years old, and it is at this age that their sense of self, future, and causality develop. Similarly, it appears as though children experience hopelessness and helplessness similar to adults between the age of 8 to 10 (Rholes, et al., 1980). Overall, this research suggests that children have the cognitive ability to experience depression in a fashion consistent with the major cognitive models by the age of eight. While the cognitive functioning of depressed children may be similar in form and content to that of adults, due to the very fact that children are still developing, the cognitive disturbances may not be structuralized or as entrenched as they are in adults. Consistent with this hypothesis, Cole and Turner (1993) found that a mediational model rather than an moderational model (Baron and Kenny, 1986) was a more accurate depiction of the relationship between stressful events, cognitive disturbances, and depression in youths. More specifically, cognitive errors and attributional style completely mediated the effect of negative competency feedback on depressive symptoms. The relationship between positive and negative life events and depressive symptoms was partially mediated by the cognitive variables. Life events had a direct effect on depressive symptoms, and an indirect effect on depressive symptoms through attributional style and cognitive errors. Thus, cognitive disturbances were associated with depression and these disturbances may reflect, or be related to, negative life events.

Cognitive Theory of Depression. The applicability of a number of the major tenets of Beck's model (e.g. Beck, 1967) have been evaluated for depressed children. Central to his model of depressive disorders is the notion that depressed individuals experience a negative bias in their thoughts about the self, the world, and the future which is referred to as the depressive cognitive triad. An association has been found between each component of the depressive cognitive triad and severity of depressive symptoms in children. Depressed children have lower self-esteem (e.g. Reynolds, Anderson and Bartell, 1985) and perceived competence (e.g. Asarnow and Bates, 1988; Asarnow, Carlson and Guthrie, 1987; Blechman, McEnroe, Carella and Audette, 1986), feel more hopeless about their future (e.g. Benfield, Palmer, Pfefferbaum and Stowe, 1988; Kazdin, Rodgers and Colbus, 1986) and experience more negative thoughts about their lives in general (e.g. the automatic thoughts studies). Kaslow, Stark, Printz, Livingston and Tsai (1992) developed a measure for assessing the cognitive triad in children and results of their study indicated that depressed children report a more negative view of self, world, and future than anxious and control children. In addition, the children's views of the self, world, and future differentiated youngsters with depressive disorders from those with anxiety disorders or no disturbance at all.

The self-schema is considered to be comprised of the individual's most central rules for life which are those about the self ("I am inadequate, unlovable, and unacceptable")
and it is believed that the self-schema guides information processing. The self-schema is presumed to facilitate encoding, storage, and retrieval of negative self-relevant information and may account for such symptoms as selective attention to, and personalization of, salient negative events. Support for the existence of a self-schema which facilitates the processing of self-relevant information has been found using an incidental recall depth of processing task. While Beck hypothesizes that a negative self-schema guides the information processing of depressed individuals, support for this contention with depressed youths has been mixed with some investigators reporting that depressed individuals, unlike their nondisturbed peers, do not possess a positive self-schema (Jaenicke, Hammen, Zupan, Hiroto, Gordon, Adrian and Burge, 1987; Hammen and Zupan, 1984), while others have found evidence of a stronger negative self-schema among the depressed youngsters (Zupan, Hammen and Jaenicke, 1987). Recognizing that reaction time (efficiency and consolidation), recall (encoding and availability), and recognition (accessibility of stored information) measures may assess different aspects of information processing, Prieto and colleagues (Prieto, et al., 1992) used all three measures to evaluate the schematic functioning of psychiatric patients who reported depressive symptoms relative to those who didn't. The self-schemes of nonclinic nondepressed and clinic nondepressed youngsters were positive and much stronger than their negative self-schemes. In contrast, clinic youngsters who reported elevated depressive symptoms possessed more of a balance of positive and negative self-schemes. The authors concluded that the self-schema seems to affect the acquisition of new positive and or negative information much more than it affected retrieval. Thus, it appears to guide selective attention, encoding, and retrieval.

According to cognitive theory, the negative self-schema and other maladaptive schemata are maintained through, and give rise to, errors in information processing which result in the depressed individual exhibiting a negatively biased distortion in active information processing. Support for this theoretical contention has been reported for youngsters who self-report depressive symptoms (Haley, Fine, Marriage, Moretti and Freeman, 1985; Leitenberg, Yost and Carrol-Wilson, 1986). This stands in contrast to some early research with depressed youngsters where the investigators reported that children who reported elevated levels of depressive symptoms experienced a deficit in information processing (Schwartz, Friedman, Lindsay and Narrol, 1982). Results of a series of three investigations were consistent and indicated that depressed youngsters suffered from a distortion in self-evaluative information processing and did not suffer from a deficit in active information processing (Kendall, Stark and Adam, 1990). These errors in information processing along with the activation of dysfunctional schemata are hypothesized to shape the content of the cognitions of a depressed individual. Beck (1976) hypothesizes that each emotional disorder is characterized by a unique disturbance in cognition. This is referred to as the cognitive specificity hypothesis. With respect to depressive disorders, Beck (1967) hypothesizes that the cognitions centre around a theme of loss. Support for the cognitive specificity hypothesis has been found, although the relationship between specific cognitions and depression and other disorders may be more complex than initially hypothesized (Ambrose and Rholes, 1993; Garber, et al., 1993; Gotlib, et al., 1993; Laurent and Stark, 1993).

Learned Helplessness/Hopelessness Model. As noted above, the central premise of the learned helplessness/hopelessness model of depression is that stress will interact with a stable negative attributional style (moderational affect) to produce depression in some individuals. Results of early studies that evaluated the reformulated model of learned helplessness depression while mixed, were generally encouraging as children who self-reported symptoms of depression also reported a more depressogenic attributional style. More specifically, they self-reported internal, stable, and global attributions for negative events and external, unstable and specific attributions for positive events. Although the results for the positive events were not as strong (Asarnow and Bates, 1988; Kaslow, Rehm and Siegel, 1984; Seligman, Peterson, Kaslow, Tannenbaum, Alloy and Abramson, 1984). Recent research also provides support for the basic tenets of the model (Cole and Turner, 1993; Garber, et al., 1993; Tems, Stewart, Skinner, Hughes and Emslie, 1993). Although results of a recent study suggest that a negative attributional style may not be specific to depressive disorders but may be nonspecific to psychopathology in general.

A number of investigators have attempted to conduct a more complete evaluation of the attributional model of depression by looking at the interaction of stress and attributional style as they predict depressive symptoms (Cole and Turner, 1993; Dixon and Ahrens, 1992; Hammen, Adrian and Hiroto, 1988; Nolen-Hoeksema, Girgus and Seligman, 1986). While the results have varied, this may be due to the populations studied and the form of stress that was evaluated. Nolen-Hoeksema and her colleagues (1986) followed school children over a year to evaluate the interactive effects of stress and attributional style on depressive symptoms. Major life events, attributional style and depressive symptoms were assessed five times producing four intervals. Results indicated that attributional style alone predicted change in depressive symptoms during two intervals, the stress attributional style interaction significantly increased the predictive power of depression scores. Secondary analyses revealed that the effect of stress on depression was greatest for those who had a negative attributional style. In a study that included children of depressed parents, the interaction effect of stress (major life events) and attributional style failed to predict depression 8,4 months later (Hammen, et al., 1988).

Development of Depressive Cognitive Style. Results of the investigations discussed above indicate that the cognitive variables are highly related to depression. The question becomes, how do these disturbances in cognition develop and how are they maintained? Beck (Beck, Rush, Shaw and Emery, 1979) as well as others (e.g. Freeman, 1986) hypothesize that depressive schemata are formed through early learning experiences, especially those within the family. Cole and Turner (1993) believe that repeated exposure to negative life events, stressors, or specific forms of pathogenic feedback to the child lead to the internalization of negative cognitions and the eventual development of dysfunctional schemata. In addition, they note that at certain developmental periods youngsters actively seek information from daily experiences and from their peers about their own competencies which they use to construct their sense of self. Young (1991) hypothesizes that maladaptive schemata could be the result of inadequate parenting or ongoing aversive experiences within the family milieu such as repeated criticism or rejection. From the social learning perspective (Bandura, 1977), it also is possible that cognitive disturbances could be learned vicariously through parental modelling. Similarly, Stark, Schmidt, Joiner and Lux (in press b) hypothesized that a youngster's sense of self, world, and future could represent the internalization of messages, verbal and nonverbal, that he or she receives from interactions with parents. A study was conducted to evaluate the relationship between a negative view of the self, the world, and future (depressive cognitive triad) and parentally communicated maladaptive messages and parental modelling of a depressogenic style of thinking (Stark, et al., in press b) were evaluated. Results indicated that children's cognitive triad ratings were highly predictive of the severity of their level of depressive symptoms. Given this relationship, we tried to identify which parental variables were predictive of the children's cognitive triad. Partial support was found for a social learning perspective as mother's cognitive triad ratings were significantly related to their children's cognitive triad ratings. Results also indicated that perceived parental messages predicted the children's level of depression, and consistent with our hypotheses, perceived parental messages communicated to the children about the self, the world, and the future are strongly predictive of the children's sense of self, world and future. Furthermore, the mediation analyses indicated that the effects of parental messages on the children's depression were completely, not partially, mediated by the child's view of self, world, and future. Perceived parental messages about the self, world, and future are predictive of the children's depression, but only as a function of their association with the children's sense of self, world, and future. Goodness of fit tests supported the model which predicted that perceived parental messages predicted the children's cognitive triad which would predict the children's level of depression. To rule out the competing hypothesis that the depression was causing the depressive cognitions which were leading to the perception of negative parental messages, we ran additional mediational analyses to test this hypothesis. Results of these analyses were not supportive of this competing model. Overall, preliminary support was found for two mechanisms that were hypothesized to be instrumental in the development of a depressogenic style of thinking.

Implications and Treatment Issues. Overall, there is strong support for an association between disturbances in cognitive functioning and depressive disorders during childhood. Furthermore, the disturbances appear to be parallel to those reported in the adult literature. Thus, suggesting that cognitive therapy might be useful for depressed children. However, in order to effectively intervene, it is necessary to identify and understand developmental differences in cognitive processing between children and adults. A consensus is appearing that indicates that children's cognitive processes are adequately developed for experiencing depressive disorders by the age of eight. However, it is not known whether the cognitions assume different forms at different ages. Some investigators find the same two broad categories of cognitions, expectations and attributions, in youths and adults (Gotlib, et al., 1993), while others have not found this (Garber, et al., 1993). In a similar vein, it is not known whether new issues arise as the youngster develops. For example, Garber et al. (1993) reported an increase in egocentrism with age which could be a vulnerability factor. These youngsters are at increased risk for personalizing negative events and undefined events. This suggests that an objective of treatment would be to help them become less self-focused. If additional developmental risk factors exist and they can be identified, they may guide the nature and direction of intervention. Another developmental consideration is the degree to which the stress diathesis models of depression are appropriate for children. Unlike adults, disturbances in cognitive processes serve a mediational rather than moderational role in depressive disorders in children (Cole and Turner, 1993). Stressful events and negative competency feedback affect cognition which then affects depressive symptoms. Cole and Turner (1993) suggest that this mediational relationship may be due to the cognitive disturbances not having been in existence for long enough that they have become structuralized. If this is true, does it mean that these disturbances in children are more amenable to change, or does it mean that if you intervene at this critical developmental period that the intervention should be directed toward the environmental disturbances that are leading to the dysfunctional cognitions? If so, than when the environmental disturbance is altered in a healthy way, will changes in cognition naturally follow? At least, these findings point to the importance of evaluating the primary contexts within which the child lives and they point to the importance of devising interventions for these environmental stressors. Thus, unlike cognitive therapy with adults, the individual is not the primary and sole source of intervention. Rather, interventions directed toward the environment and significant others in the environment are equally important.

As noted above, stressful events impact cognition and they have a direct relationship to depression. It appears as though stressful events, perhaps daily hassles more than major life events (Dixon and Ahrens, 1992), have a direct impact on a youngster and lead to emotional distress, and with prolonged exposure a depressive disorder eventually develops. These findings suggest that recurrent negative events lead to the perception that the world is a distressing place, life is full of pain, and that it will always be this way. These results suggest that it is critical to intervene in the youngster's environment to eliminate or reduce the sources of stress. However, it is not clear whether the most effective way to do this is to actually alter the environment or to enhance the youngster's coping skills for dealing with the distressing events, or both. If the hassles are of an interpersonal nature, then the intervention may be directed at the youngster's social skills or interpersonal environment. If the intervention is directed at the environment, then the youngster's teachers or other school personnel will need to be involved in the intervention.

A self-schema appears to guide the information processing of children. Among depressed youths, relative to nondepressed youths, their self-schema is less positive (Hammen and Zupan, 1984; Jaenicke, et al., 1987; Zupan, et al., 1987). Furthermore, this less positive self-schema affects the acquisition of new positive and negative information through selective attention, encoding and retrieval of information (Prieto, et al., 1992). These results suggest that a goal of treatment is enhancement of the youngster's sense of self. A common strategy for altering this disturbance is to have the children self-monitor positive events (Stark, et al., 1987). However, this may not have the desired effect and it may be especially difficult to accomplish since the existing self-schema will be guiding information processing in a fashion that prevents the acquisition of schema-inconsistent information. Thus, positive information is likely to be overlooked. It may be necessary to train significant others within the child's daily environment to help the youngster with the self-monitoring and with processing the outcome on at least a daily basis. Depressed youths have a tendency to negatively distort self-evaluative information (Kendall, et al., 1990) which further inhibits the individual's chances to acquire positive self-relevant information. Once again it may be necessary for school personnel and parents to become involved in the treatment process. While research indicates that depressed youths distort information processing, the specific errors have yet to be identified. Thus, the specific nature of the intervention is not yet clear. It is very likely that each youngster will possess a unique pattern of information processing errors and thus require a unique set of intervention strategies. Once again, no research has been directed toward the elucidation of the most effective strategies for altering information processing errors in children.

Research (Stark, et al., in press b) and theory (Beck, et al., 1979; Young, 1991) suggest that the cognitive disturbance may develop as a result of negative messages the youngster receives from his or her parents (Stark, et al., in press b), stressful events and negative competency feedback (Cole and Turner, 1993). Further research is needed to identify the mechanism for this. This once again highlights the importance of intervene with the child's family and school. Both environments could be the source of negative messages, stressful events, and negative competency feedback.

While children might have cognitive disturbances that are similar to those of adults, and they may have the cognitive ability to reflect on these disturbances, do they have the same metacognitive ability as adults to be able to accurately identify, reflect upon, evaluate, and counter maladaptive cognitions? What is the best way to do this? Through traditional cognitive therapy procedures such as what's the evidence and alternative interpretation, or are behavioral experiments the preferred mode for producing meaningful change? Does the mix of cognitive, behavioral, and environmental interventions change with developmental level? Obviously, numerous questions remain about the most effective way to treat depressed youths.

Behavioral Variables and Depression during Childhood

Empirical/Theoretical Rationale. Social skills deficits have been hypothesized to be a primary casual variable in the development of depression through the resulting loss of social reinforcement and disruption of close interpersonal relationships (Lewinsohn, 1975). According to Lewinsohn, deficits in social skills lead to a reduction in the amount of response contingent positive reinforcement that the individual receives. Furthermore, it has been posited that depressed individuals elicit a corresponding pattern of rejection in others that reinforces the depression (Coyne, 1976). In other words, a vicious cycle is established where poor social skills lead to interpersonal rejection which produces depression and social withdrawal. Depressive symptoms are aversive to others which leads to further interpersonal rejection which exacerbates the depression. Given the "magnitude and severity" of problems associated with deficits in social skills, Matson and Ollendick (1988) concluded that social skills deficits should be considered a major part of the underlying etiology of emotional, personality, and adjustment problems of children. In addition, these authors state that efforts at improving social skills deficits may have very beneficial preventative effects.

Research suggests that depressed youths experience interpersonal difficulties. Depressed children are less popular (Jacobson, Lahey and Strauss, 1983; Lefkowitz and Tesiny, 1985; Strauss, Forehand, Frame and Smith, 1984), and are less liked (Blechman, et al., 1986; Faust, Baum and Forehand, 1985; Peterson, Mullins and Ridley-Johnson, 1985) or rejected by peers (Kennedy, Spence and Hensley, 1989). Perhaps this is sensed by depressed youths and accounts for findings that indicate that depressed youngsters engage in less social interaction (Kazdin, Esveldt-Dawson, Sherick and Colbus, 1985). Consistent with Coyne's hypothesis, depressed children elicit negative reactions from adults (Mullins, Peterson, Wonderlick and Reaven, 1986) and peers (Kennedy, et al., 1989). Social skills deficits (Kennedy, et al., 1989; Matson, Rotatori and Helsel, 1983) as well as disturbances in social cognition (Sacco and Graves, 1984) may contribute to these interpersonal difficulties. Based on an integrative cognitive-behavioral model, it is believed that if a social skills disturbance exists, it stems form a lack of social skills knowledge and/or a performance deficit that is the result of cognitions and physiological arousal that interfere with enactment of appropriate social behavior (Stark, Linn, MacGuire and Kaslow, in press a).

Results of one of our own investigations (Stark, et al., in press a) suggest that the social skills disturbance associated with depression may not be as straight forward as previously thought. Based on teachers' and children's ratings, depressed children with and without a comorbid anxiety disorder were described as exhibiting significantly fewer appropriate social skills relative to their nondepressed classmates. According to the children's self-ratings, depressed and comorbid depressed anxious children experienced social skills disturbances with the comorbid group experiencing the most and most severe disturbances. The social behaviors of children with a depressive disorder were characterized by an angry, jealous, and withdrawn style of interacting with others. Comorbid depressed and anxious children displayed additional inappropriate aggressive behaviors. Bell-Dolan, Reaven and Peterson (1993) reported similar disturbances in social behavior as they found a relationship between severity of depressive symptoms and aggressive behavior, negative support seeking, and social withdrawal. Negative social behaviors may be the most robust predictor of depressive symptoms from the social domain (Bell-Dolan, et al., 1993).

The social skills deficits may not be due to a lack of social skills knowledge. In the author's study, the disturbed children knew what was appropriate and inappropriate social behavior, but they did not enact appropriate behaviors. Relative to non-disturbed controls, children with a depressive disorder reported experiencing significantly more negative and significantly fewer positive cognitions in social situations (Stark, et al., 1993 a) and a disortion in their evaluations of their social competence (Bell-Dolan, et al., 1993). They also reported experiencing more aversive physical arousal in social situations (Stark, et al., 1993 a). As noted below, these results have implications for designing effective social skills interventions for depressed youths.

Implications and Treatment Issues. Depressed children have interpersonal difficulties which lead to them being less popular (Jacobsen, et al., 1983), less liked (Blechman, et al., 1986), and rejected (Kennedy, et al., 1989). They appear to experience a deficit in social skills which is characterized by an angry and withdrawn style of interaction. Research suggests that depressed youths know how to behave in a socially appropriate fashion, but don't. This appears to be due to a cognitive disturbance and to the experience of aversive physical arousal in social situations (Stark, et al., 1993 a). Are the physical arousal and negative cognitions a reflection of a mood disturbance (anger) which is causing the angry and withdrawn behavior? While it appears as though social skills training may be an important component in a treatment for depressed youths, Kazdin's (1989) and Matson's (1989) belief that social skills training is an effective treatment for depressed children has not yet been empirically evaluated. It would appear as though a social skills intervention should include components that are directed at the cognitive, possible mood, and physical disturbances. Thus, cognitive restructuring, relaxation training, and other procedures designed to improve mood may have to be incorporated into the social skills training. Once again, parents and teachers may have to be included in the intervention. They can provide the youngster with encouragement for enactment of appropriate social behaviors through a reward program and they can provide the youngster with objective feedback about the youngster's social interactions. Thus, countering any distortions.

Family Variables and Depression during Childhood

There is compelling evidence to support a link between a genetic vulnerability and depressive disorders during childhood (Clarkin, Hass and Glick, 1988). In addition, it is generally recognized that the family plays an influential role in the psychological and psycho-social adjustment of children. Evidence from clinical observations and research indicates that many depressed youngsters come from disturbed families (for reviews see Burdach and Borduin, 1986; Stark and Brookman, 1992). Early reports provided evidence for the existence of disturbances within the families of depressed youths, but they did not identify the specific nature of the disturbances. For example, Kaslow and colleagues (1984) reported greater general dysfunction among the families of children who had elevated scores on the Children's Depression Inventory (CDI; Kovacs, 1981), relative to normal controls. Asarnow and colleagues (1987) also reported disturbances in the perceived family environments of depressed children, but these disturbances were nonspecific to psychopathology. Additional research and clinical observations have identified a number of possible disturbances within the families of depressed youths. The families of depressed youths are characterized by greater chaos, abuse and neglect (Kashani, Ray and Carlson, 1984), conflict (Forehand, Brody, Slotkin, Fauber, McCombs and Long, 1988), a critical, punitive and belittling or shaming parenting style (e.g. Arieti and Bemporad, 1980; Poznanski and Zrull, 1970), communication difficulties (Puig-Antich, Lukens, Davies, Goetz, Brennan-Quattrock and Todak, 1985), lower activity level (Puig-Antich, et al., 1985), structural disturbances (Grossman, Poznanski and Banegas, 1983), and when affection is expressed, it is contingent upon behavior that is consistent with parental expectations (Grossman, et al., 1983). In addition, the tone of the mother-child, and to a somewhat lesser extent the father-child relationship, was characterized as cold, hostile, tense, and at times rejecting (Puig-Antich, et al., 1985). In one of our own studies, an attempt was made to evaluate mothers' and depressed children's perceptions of their family milieu using a measure that assessed a breadth of characteristics of family functioning (Stark, Humphrey, Crook an Lewis, 1990). Results of the investigation of the family milieu indicate that there appears to be a unique pattern of disturbances in the families of depressed, anxious, and comorbid depressed anxious children. Based on the children's perceptions, two significant discriminant functions were identified that explained approximately 90% of the accounted for between group variance in their ratings of depression and anxiety. The first discriminant function reflected how tightly knit, supportive, and free of conflict the family was. The second function reflected how sociable, concerned with morality and religion, enmeshed, conflict free, nonsupportive, and autocratic the family was. Based on maternal figures' perceptions, one significant discriminant function emerged which explained approximately 62% of the accounted for between group variance in the children's depression and anxiety scores. This function reflected how satisfied mothers were with their family, how involved the family was in recreational activities, and how autocratic the parent(s) were in their decision making. The diagnostic groups of the children could be accurately predicted based on the children's and parents' discriminant functions.

Implications and Treatment Issues. Depressed youngsters appear to be placed at risk for the development of a depressive disorder by a genetic diathesis (Clarkin, et al., 1988). This diathesis may be triggered by stressors within the youngster's family environment including elevated levels of conflict (Forehand, et al., 1988), critical and punitive parents (Arieti and Bemporad, 1980), decreased involvement in social and recreational activities, low levels of support, and limited involvement of the children in decisions made within the family (Stark, et al., 1990). From existing research it is not evident to what extent these environmental disturbances precede the child's depressive disorder and to what extent they result from the depressive disorder. The sources of conflict have not been identified. It is possible that the conflict is between the marital partners, a parent and the depressed child, the depressed child and siblings, or some other combination of family members. While clinical observations indicate that parents of depressed youngster use critical and punitive parenting techniques, research has yet to validate this observation and to elucidate the specific behavior. The failure of the family to participate in pleasant activities may stem from a variety of factors; perhaps even the conflict and punitive parenting tactics. Regardless, it is apparent that a family intervention component is necessary. This intervention should be directed toward reducing conflict which may involve the entire family or it may include the treatment of a depressed parent.

Integrated Model

As noted in previous sections, there is empirical support for the association of cognitive, behavioral, and family variables with depression during childhood. Most of the existing research evaluates the association between one of these domains to depression. A minimum of research has explored the possible concurrent and relative contribution of these variables to depression in children. A study was designed to identify which cognitive, behavioral, and family variables, from among those associated with the predominant models of depression, would differentiate depressed from anxious and normal control children (Stark, Humphrey, Laurent, Livingston and Christopher, 1993), Results indicated that a combination of seven variables from the cognitive, behavioral and family domains contributed more to the differentiation of the diagnostic groups than the variables from any single domain. Two significant discriminant functions were identified which accounted for 91% of the between group variability and could be used to accurately predict the diagnostic group membership of 71% of the children. The first variable to enter the equation was the children's sense of self, world, and future (CTI-C) which was followed at the second step by a measure of depressive cognitions (ATQ-C). Suggesting that the different disorders were characterized by different self-reported cognitions. Further support for this notion was evident in the correlations between the predictor variables and the canonical discriminant functions where both the children's ratings on the CTI-C and ATQ-C were important contributors to the differentiation of the depressed and anxious children and control children, while the children's ratings on the CTI-C contributed to the differentiation of depressed children and anxious children. In general, children who had a depressive disorder reported more negative cognitions than anxious or control children.

While the cognitive variables were the first to enter the equation and accounted for most of the between group variance, the results indicated that the addition of variables from the behavioral and family domains added to the overall predictive ability of the discriminant functions. Within the behavioral domain, the children's ratings of the degree to which they exhibited impulsive and angry social behaviors differentiated the clinical groups. These social behaviors were especially important predictors for differentiating the depressed and anxious children from the control children. Four variables from the family domain entered the discriminant equation including the children's perception of the messages that they receive about themselves, their world and future from their mothers and fathers, the quality of the relationships they have with other family members, and the parents' style of managing their families. From reviewing the correlations between the predictor variables and the discriminant functions, it appears as though the children's perceptions of the messages they receive about themselves, their world and future from their fathers significantly contributes to the differentiation of depressed children from anxious children.

Clinical Significance

Given the results of existing research, what are the implications for the treatment of depressed youths? It is evident that depression is associated with disturbances in the cognitive, behavioral, and family domains and that a reciprocal relationship exists between the domains. Thus, a disturbance in one domain would affect, and be affected by, each of the other domains. For example, a cognitive disturbance would affect the youngster's mood and the youngster would behave in a manner consistent with the disturbance in thinking. The disturbance in the youngster's behavior would impact the environment and the outcome would feedback to and through the cognitive disturbance. Reactions of significant others in the environment may be misperceived which leads to a confirmation of, or development of, dysfunctional schemata. Once activated, these dysfunctional schemata guide information processing. It has been hypothesized (e.g. Beck, et al., 1979; Cole and Turner, 1993), and research is beginning to appear which supports the notion that the core schemata are formed through early learning experiences and communications within the family (Stark, et al., in press b). In the case of the depressed youngster, negative views of the self, world, and future may develop as a result of negative evaluative statements directed at the child from the parents (Stark, et al., in press b), from interactions that communicate rejection (Puig-Antich, et al., 1985), and an over-reliance on punitive parenting procedures (Poznanski and Zrull, 1970) which once again communicate to the child that he or she is "bad" and the world is an unpleasant place. It is important to note that the child, through genetic predispositions and temperament factors, plays a role in constructing this environment. It is within the family milieu that the child develops crucial interpersonal skills. In the case of the depressive family milieu, the child learns a more impulsive and angry style of interacting and one in which rejection is expected (Stark, et al., 1990). As the child develops, he or she begins to interact with others and these interactions are both shaped by, and shape, existing social skills as well as the youngster's schemata about social situations. The depressed youngster behaves in an impulsive and angry style (Stark, et al., in press a) which leads to rejection. This rejection in turn leads to the development of a sense of self which is comprised of a poorly developed positive self-schema and a more active negative self-schema (Prieto, et al., 1992) and negative world schemata (Kaslow, et al., 1992). In addition, it may lead to withdrawal (Kazdin, et al., 1985) which insulates the youngster from corrective learning experiences. As the youngster matures and faces new stressors, he or she doesn't have the family (Stark, et al., 1990) or peer social support (Blechman, et al., 1986; Jacobsen, et al., 1983; Kennedy, et al., 1989; Peterson, et al., 1985) necessary to help buffer their impact, and the impact is further heightened through negative distortions in information processing (Kendall, et al., 1990) and a possible deficit in coping skills. Affect interacts with the previously mentioned variables in a reciprocal fashion. The youngster may experience dysphoria due to the perception of social or familial rejection, from the conflictual and punitive atmosphere within the family milieu (Forehand, et al., 1988), or from biochemical imbalances. Similarly, the mood disturbance impacts the youngster's information processing and behavior. While this model is speculative, research provides supportive evidence for the reciprocal interplay of three of the major domains of inquiry, and has done so with children (Stark, et al., in press b).

Results of this research have implications for the treatment of children with depressive disorders. It is apparent that the intervention should be a multi-faceted one that includes family intervention, parent training, and interventions directed at the child. The family intervention should include the identification of verbal and behavioral interactions that send maladaptive, schema consistent messages to the depressed child (Stark, et al., 1993 b). In other words, the therapeutic question becomes, what are parents and/or their family members communicating to the child verbally and/or through their interactions that would lead to the development and maintenance of the child's negative view of the self, world, and future and other maladaptive schemata. Once the maladaptive interactions are identified, the therapist works with the family to change them. This may take any of many forms dependent on the therapist's training. From a cognitive-behavioral perspective, it may involve cognitive restructuring procedures to change the beliefs that underlie the participants' behavior, and teaching family members new ways of interacting through education, modelling, rehearsal, coaching, and feedback. Subsequently, a parent would be assigned the homework task of self-monitoring the occurrence of the maladaptive interactions as well as engagement in more adaptive interactions.

When working with the family, it is important to determine whether conflict exists (Forehand, et al., 1988), and if so, its source should be identified and plans should be developed for reducing it. The plans may include marital counselling (Kaslow, et al., 1984). Since a reduced rate of involvement in recreational activities was reported (Stark, et al., 1990), it may prove useful to include the scheduling of pleasant activities into the family therapy. Caution would have to be taken when doing this since it could create more opportunities for family conflict. The reduction in conflict and the engagement in more pleasant activities as a family, could enhance the family's sense of cohesion. Research also suggests that it is important to promote the inclusion of the children in some of the important decisions being made by the family (Stark, et al., 1990). However, a balance needs to be struck between encouraging the children to participate in the decision making process and maintaining a sense of the parents functioning as the executive pair who are in charge (Grossman, et al., 1983).

Results suggest that depression in children is associated with a distortion in self-evaluation rather than a deficiency in information processing (Kendall, et al., 1990). This suggests that an efficacious intervention would be one that teaches depressed children to identify their maladaptive cognitions and modify them or replace them with more adaptive ones. The cognitive restructuring should also be applied to the youngster's social schemata (Stark, et al., in press a). In addition, depressed children could benefit from social skills training (Kazdin, 1989; Matson, 1989) accompanied by coping skills training designed to reduce aversive physical arousal. The content of the social skills training should be directed toward teaching the youngsters to behave in a less angry fashion. It would appear that bossiness, stubbornness, frequent complaining, and expressions of anger and jealousy are potential targets for intervention. Cognitive restructuring interventions should be integrated with the skills training to simultaneously increase engagement in social interactions, reduce negative expectations, negative self-evaluations, and other negative cognitions, and to increase coping self-statements. In addition, since the comorbid depressed-anxious children reported thinking that others were "picking on them," perhaps reflecting the encoding disturbances noted by Prieto, et al., (1992), the children may need to be taught to more accurately monitor, perceive, and evaluate the behaviors and intentions of others. The children noted that they were quick to anger, felt jealous, became angry when someone else was successful, and felt lonely (Stark, et al., in press a), suggesting that cognitive interventions and affective education (Stark, 1990) should be directed toward intervening with the affective nature of the disturbance. Furthermore, these interventions may need to teach children how to monitor their own expression of angry and irritable behavior, as well as encourage the children to engage in more appropriate behavior. Relaxation training could be incorporated into the treatment to help the youngsters cope with and minimize aversive physical arousal.

The results also have broader implications for parent training. Our results (Stark, et al., in press b) argue for the inclusion of a component that teaches parents to be aware of the messages that they are communicating to their children. Basic modules could include teaching parents how to communicate positive and realistic messages to their children about

Table 1. Child, Parent, and Family Disturbance Identified through Research

Child Mood
Dysphoria
Anger
Anhedonia
Excessive worry

Child Behavioral
Social skills disturbances
Inability to obtain reinforcement

Child Cognitive
Maladaptive schemata
Distorted information processing
Depressogenic automatic thoughts
Negative expectations
Negative self-evaluations

Parent Cognitive and Behavioral
Parental Psychopathology
Impulsive Anger
Unrealistic and Perfectionistic Expectations
Dysfunctional Schemata

Family

Behavioral
Low Rates of Positive Reinforcement
Low Rates of Soc. & Rec. Behavior
Abuse and Neglect
Family Communication Deficits
Family Decision Making

Cognitive
Problem Solving Deficits
Conflict Management Deficits
Communication of Negative Messages

Table 2. Comprehensive Treatment Program for Depressed Youths

Child	Parents	Family
	Parent s	**Family Therapy Components**
Intervening with the Mood Disturbance	**Parent Skills Training**	Communiction Training
Affective Education	Positive Behavior Management	Conflict Resolution
Activity Scheduling	Self-esteem Enhancement	Positive Communication
Interventions for Excessive Anxiety	Noncoercive Discipline	Change Schemata-Consistent Interactions
Reducing Excessive Anger	Anger Management	
	Empathic Listening	
Intervening with Maladaptive Behavior	Recreation	
Social Skills Training	Conducting Family Meetings	
Pleasent Events Scheduling		
Acting-Out Behaviors		
Intervening at the Cognitive Level		
Changing Dysfunctional Schemata		
Cognitive restructuring procedures		
What's the evidence.		
Alternative Interpretations.		
What If?		
Behavioral Experiments		
Methods for Altering Faulty Information Processing		
Self-Evaluation Training		
Altering Automatic Thoughts		
Problem Solving Training		

the children themselves, the world, and the future. The training should emphasize teaching the use of positive behavior management skills since a positive approach would send the child positive messages about the self, while a punitive approach communicates to the child that he or she is a "bad person." Furthermore, guilt inducing parental behaviors would lead to a sense of self as worthless, bad, and unlovable. Thus, a common theme throughout the parent training would be to teach the parents to ask themselves, what is the message I am sending to my child about himself or herself through my actions and verbal exchanges.

PROPOSED TREATMENT MODEL

Overview

The treatment model described in the following sections was designed to address the disturbances that research has shown to be associated with depressive disorders during childhood. Consequently, the child is not the sole target of the intervention. The youngster's primary environments and significant others also are targets of intervention through parent training, family therapy, and school consultation. Intervention with the parents, family, and school is necessary to support the individual work being completed with the child, to facilitate the child's use of the coping skills in the extra-therapy environment, and to change the environmental events that may be contributing to the development and maintenance of the disturbances.

The description of the intervention that follows is organized by type of disturbance so as to emphasize the parallelism between the disturbances identified in the research and the interventions developed for them. In other words, for each empirically identified disturbance (Table 1), there is a parallel intervention strategy (Table 2).

The treatment program may have to be modified dependent on the presence, number, and type of co-occurring disorders. Research indicates that depressive disorders occur along with other disorders including anxiety disorders, conduct disorder, and ADHD to mention a few of the more common ones. Some children are experiencing two or more additional disorders. Additional modifications are necessary to address parental psychopathology, a history of abuse, substance abuse, presence of a learning disability, limited intellectual functioning, marital discord, neglect and abandonment, and the presence of features of a developing personality disorder. With all of this said, it also is evident that this presentation may lead the reader to wonder what is the logical order of presentation of the various treatment components and how do they fit together. Consequently, a prototypic outline of the sequence and integration of the treatment components is provided in Table 3.

CHILD

Affective Disturbance

Emphasis during the first few treatment sessions is on helping the youngsters gain a better understanding of their emotional experiences, teaching them the link between thoughts, feelings, and behaviors, and on developing a supportive treatment group. More-over, recognition of emotions and an understanding of the relationship between thoughts, feelings, and behaviors is the cornerstone on which other coping skills are built. To accomplish these as well as additional therapeutic objectives, affective education activities are employed throughout the first eight treatment meetings.

Table 3. Outline of Treatment Program

Session 1

    Introductions

    Establish appropriate expectations

Session 2

    Affective education

        Identify and label emotions

    Establish a within group incentive system

    Self-monitoring pleasant emotions

Session 3

    Affective education

        Identify emotions, link emotions to thoughts and behavior

    Introduction to active coping orientation

    Self-monitoring pleasant emotions

Session 4

    Affective education

        Internal and external cues of emotions, coping with unpleasant emotions, link emotions to

        thoughts and behavior

    Extend coping orientation

    Pleasant events scheduling

    Self-monitoring pleasant emotions

Session 5

    Affective education

        Internal and external cues of emotions, coping with unpleasant emotions, link emotions to

        thoughts and behavior

    Introduction to problem solving

    Self-monitoring pleasant emotions

Session 6

    Affective education

        Internal and external cues of emotions, coping with unpleasant emotions, link emotions to

        thoughts and behavior

    Pleasant events scheduling and self-monitoring pleasant emotions

    Problem solving game

Session 7

Affective education

Internal and external cues of emotions, coping with unpleasant emotions, link emotions to thoughts and behavior

Pleasant events scheduling

Problem solving game

Session 8

Affective education

Internal and external cues of emotions, coping with unpleasant emotions, link emotions to thoughts and behavior

Application of problem solving to mood disturbance

Session 9

Application of problem solving to mood disturbance

Missing solution activity

Session 10

Introduction to relaxation

Exercise and mood

Session 11

Problem solving applied to interpersonal problems

Pleasant events scheduling

Relaxation as a coping strategy

Session 12

Problem solving applied to interpersonal situations

Focus on self-evaluation of solution implementation

Relaxation as a coping strategy

Session 13

Spontaneous use of problem solving

Relaxation and problem solving

Session 14

Introduction to cognitive restructuring

Identification of depressogenic thoughts

Session 15

Practice catching negative thoughts

Cognitive restructuring

Session 16

Improve understanding of cognitive restructuring

Practice catching negative thoughts

Table 3. (continued)

What's the evidence

What to do when a negative thought is true

Session 17

Alternative interpretation

Session 18

Alternative interpretation

Identifying negative expectations

Introduce What if?

Session 19

What if?

Session 20

Review of cognitive restructuring procedures

Introduction to assertiveness training

Generate and rehearse coping statements

Session 21

Positive assertiveness

Generation of coping statements

Session 22

Assertiveness training

Generation of coping statements

Session 23

Identify personal standards

Introduction to self-evaluation training

Identification of areas in need of personal improvement

Session 24

Establish goals and subgoals for self-improvement

Session 25-28

Self-evaluation training/Working toward self-improvement

Session 29 & 30

Termination issues

Programming for generalization

Depressed youths are experiencing either dysphoria, anger, anhedonia, or a mix of mood disturbances. We have designed intervention strategies to help youngsters cope with these disturbances. It is the authors' belief that while some of the intervention strategies specifically target the mood disturbance, ultimately, all of the intervention components have as their goal an improvement in mood. Thus, it is assumed that the mood disturbance will be progressively modified as the youngster begins to cope with the various symptoms of depression; and perceives him of herself, life in general, and the future in a more positive and realistic fashion.

Based on coping skills model of treatment, the goal is to teach the youngsters to use their mood as a cue to engage in various coping activities. The first step to this process involves teaching the youngsters a vocabulary for describing their affective experiences. Depressed youths typically do not have an adequate set of labels for the range of their affective experiences (everything is referred to as "bad" or "sad")," or they mislabel them. In addition, they tend to see themselves as either happy or depressed with nothing in between. Thus, the children and their individual therapist collaboratively assess the continuum of emotions that the child experiences. Emphasis is placed on the fact that (1) the child actually experiences a variety of emotions, and (2) each one is experienced along a continuum of intensity from minimal to extreme.

A series of games including Emotional Vocabulary, Emotional Vocabulary II, Emotion Charades, Emotion Statues, Emotion Pictionary, and Emotion Expression is used in the affective education groups to help the youngsters achieve the aforementioned goals (Stark, 1990). Through participation in these games, the youngsters learn the names of various pleasant and unpleasant emotions and that emotions vary in intensity. In addition, they are better able to recognize when they are experiencing particular emotions and are able to identify them in others. The relationship between emotions, thoughts, and behavior is illustrated through these activities. In addition, strategies for coping with unpleasant emotions are identified and maladaptive thoughts that accompany these emotions are identified.

One of the primary tools for altering dysphoric mood is activity scheduling which is the purposeful scheduling of enjoyable and goal-directed activities into the child's day. Enactment of these activities helps the youngster obtain reinforcement and combat the withdrawal, passivity, and sedentary life style associated with an episode of depression. They also provide the child with a distraction from his of her preoccupation with negative thinking and lead to some cognitive restructuring as the child sees that life can be enjoyable. During individual therapy, the therapist and child literally schedule pleasant activities for the child and solicit parental approval and support for the plan. Within group, the children self-monitor their engagement in pleasant activities, provide each other with encouragement and support for their attempts to become more active, and provide each other with additional ideas about fun things to do. The youngsters contract for an increase in activity level.

It also is important to include in the schedule some mastery activities - activities that have an instrumental value. Completion of the task provides the child with a sense of accomplishment or mastery. For example, completion of a major school project, more homework assignments, a household project, or a hobby kit would lead to a sense of mastery. Within individual therapy, the child and therapist work to combat the child's pessimism and inertia through breaking the project down into manageable steps, creating a schedule for completing the steps, and developing coping statements that can be used when the youngster begins to stall or get stuck in negative thinking. Within the group, this same process is taught through completion of a group project. The sole parameter for choosing an appropriate project is that it should be fun and consist of a number of steps that are completed over an extended period of time.

Excessive anger is a common problem for depressed youths. Teaching children to cope with anger begins with helping them to recognize the sensations that define anger (emotional, cognitive, physical). It is especially important to help the children recognize the initial physical and cognitive cues that they are becoming angry. It is critical to identify early signs or else the child becomes overwhelmed with anger too quickly to be able to manage it. Anger is considered to be a cue that a problem needs to be solved. Either the child has to take action to change the anger provoking situation, or the child has to develop and implement plans for coping with anger. Some of the effective coping strategies are to (a) leave the situation, (b) go and do something enjoyable, (c) use words rather than actions to express anger, (d) do something physically demanding like riding an exercise bike, and (e) expressing anger through drawing or writing. Another useful strategy that is practised during treatment meetings is to leave a provocative situation as soon as anger is evident and to then listen to a progressive muscle relaxation tape as a means of calming down. Once the child is very skilled at using relaxation, he or she is taught to leave the situation and to direct his or her attention to the muscle tension that is associated with the anger and to focus on relaxing it away. We have found that it is necessary to augment the relaxation training with some self-instructional training and cognitive restructuring which is described in the section on interventions for cognitive disturbances. The cognitive interventions are used to change or counter the youngster's inflammatory thinking.

It is very difficult for a child to follow through and enact one of these coping strategies for managing anger. It often is necessary for parents to encourage the child to cope by establishing an incentive program. In some instances it also is possible to make arrangements for a parent to help cue the child that he or she is becoming angry. This is a sensitive endeavour since telling an angry person that they are angry can often escalate the problem. Consequently, a great deal of preplanning and rehearsal are usually necessary. A neutral cueing system typically involving some agreed upon noninflammatory phrase can be used to help the youngster without exacerbating the problem.

Problem Solving Set

As the youngsters appear to be acquiring a better understanding of their emotions, can accurately identify them, recognize their impact on behavior and thinking, and understand that they can take action to moderate the intensity and impact of their emotions, we begin to teach the children to adopt a problem solving set toward life. They are taught that problems and disappointments are a natural part of life and that when a problem is identified, it is best to actively solve it. In addition, they are taught that their manifestations of depression represents problems to be solved. For example, feeling angry is a cue that a problem exists and that the youngster needs to develop a plan for eliminating the stressor and/or for coping with the feelings. Problem solving also has an impact on the disturbance in the child's thinking. It counteracts the rigidity and helps them overcome hopelessness as they see that there may be some options of which they were previously unaware. The children also gain a sense of self-efficacy as they experience some success and sense of mastery over the environment.

The problem solving procedure that we have used is a modified version of the one described by Kendall (e.g. Kendall and Braswell, 1993). Children are taught to break problem solving down into five component steps through education, modelling, coaching, rehearsal, and feedback. Board games are used as an engaging medium for teaching the steps. Games are a fun, concrete method for teaching the process that provides the youngsters with almost immediate feedback in the form of a game-related consequence (e.g. your checker gets jumped) for not following the steps. In addition, the children readily see the advantages to following the process. As they begin to understand each of the five steps and can readily apply them to the games that the group plays, the therapist begins to shift away from game playing within the groups to teaching the youngsters to apply the process to hypothetical problems, to interpersonal problems, and then to problems in daily life.

The first step in the process is problem identification and definition. This may be the most difficult step for children in general to learn. Depressed children often view the existence of a problem as a threat to their self-esteem. If a problem exists, then it means that there is something wrong with them or the problem represents an impending loss. In addition, they feel overwhelmed by problems and as if they cannot solve them, and that even if they did solve an existing problem, it would simply be replaced by another one. Thus, their sense of hopelessness has to be combated over time through concrete evidence in their life experiences that demonstrates that they can in fact overcome problems. Early in treatment when games are being used, each turn or move represents a problem to be defined and solved. Thus, the children get plenty of practice at identifying and defining problems. As treatment progresses, the game format is faded out and children begin to identify their own real life problems and the problems of other group members.

The second step is generation of alternative solutions. Children are taught to brain-storm as many possible solutions as they can without evaluating them. This is difficult for the depressed youngster since he or she can typically come up with more reasons for why a plan won't work rather than why it would work. Even when they can't identify specific reasons for it not working, they base their prediction on how they are feeling (emotional reasoning). When beginning to teach children to generate solutions, they often are very limited in the range and number of possibilities that they can generate. Consequently, they have to be taught additional possibilities. It is important to teach them not to evaluate the alternatives while they are trying to generate them since depressed youths have a tendency to believe that nothing will work. Thus, the youngster will short circuit the process and generate a minimum of possible solutions. Once again, while playing games, the children are taught to consider many possible moves each time their turn comes around. Initially, as they are acquiring the five steps, they are asked to state aloud the possible solutions. This way the therapist and other group members can assist the child in the generation of possible solutions or plans. As treatment progresses and the problems they work on are drawn from real life situations, emphasis is placed on developing solutions that are reasonable, realistic for the context of the adolescent's world, and not just socially acceptable within an adult's world.

The third step involves predicting the likely outcomes for each possible solution. Within the context of the games, this involves predicting the outcome of each possible move. As the group progresses into real-life problems, the therapists often have to help the children recognize potential positive outcomes as well as the limitations and self-defeating conse-quences of other possibilities. Once again it is necessary at this step to combat the youngster's pessimism. The fourth step involves reviewing the possible solutions, choosing the one that is most consistent with the child's goals and enacting the plan. The final step is evaluating the progress the child is making toward solving the problem and the overall outcome of the chosen solution. If the outcome is a desirable one, the child self-reinforces. If the outcome is undesirable, the youngster reconsiders the possible solutions, chooses an alternative one, and enacts it.

Maladaptive Behavior

As mentioned in the discussion of the implications of the research for the treatment of depressed youths, it is necessary to intervene at multiple levels when trying to remediate the disturbance in the depressed youth's interpersonal behavior. In order to accomplish this most effectively, we also treat this disturbance through a combination of group and individual therapy. Group therapy is used both as a means of ongoing assessment and as the primary vehicle for teaching the youngsters social skills. Skills are taught through a combination of education, modelling, rehearsal, coaching and corrective feedback. The children are given weekly homework assignments to try to use their new skills. As social disturbances become evident during the natural exchanges between group members, those disturbances are directly addressed through feedback from the group and by teaching the youngster more adaptive behavior. The cognitive disturbances associated with the maladaptive behavior are dealt with during individual therapy and the new more adaptive ways of thinking are tested out during group. Similarly, individual sessions and the relationship that develops within them, has therapeutic value. The youngster learns how to trust someone and how to deal in a healthy fashion with intimacy. In addition, through the acceptance of the therapist the youngster learns that he or she is likable and worthy.

Another possible behavioral intervention for depression that has support in the adult literature is exercise. Research with both nonclinic (Brown, Ramirez and Taub, 1978; Folkins, 1976; Freemont and Craighead, 1984; Jasnoski and Holmes, 1981; King, Taylor, Haskell and DeBusk, 1989; King, Taylor and Haskell, 1983; McCann and Holmes, 1984; Morgan, Roberts, Brand and Feinerman, 1970; Sime, 1987) and clinical (Doyne, Chambless and Beutler, 1983; Doyne, Ossip-Klein, Bowman, Osborn, McDougall-Wilson and Neimeyer, 1987; Griest, Klein, Eischens, Gurman and Morgan, 1979; Griest, 1987; Martinsen, Hoffart and Solberg, 1989) samples of adults suggests that exercise is an effective intervention for depression. The majority of the exercise programs consisted of some form of aerobic training such as running, jogging, or walking. However, the mechanism for producing the improvement is not clear. Based on the research, it is apparent that the improvement in depressive symptoms is not directly tied to an actual improvement in cardiovascular fitness (Doyne, et al., 1987; Martinsen, et al., 1989). Another possible explanation for the change in level of depression may be due to behavioral and cognitive mechanisms combined with the process of exercise. Participation in a regular exercise program may possibly create a feeling of accomplishment and increased self-efficacy (Bandura, 1977) as noticeable improvements in performance occur.

In the only relevant study with emotionally disturbed children, Shipman (1984) investigated the emotional and behavioral effects of slow long-distance running. The study lasted 18-weeks (6-weeks of training followed by 12-weeks of running) and included a total of 56 children from a residential treatment centre in California between the ages of 6 and 13. After the initial 6-week training period, each group of children was encouraged to run a maximum of 45-minutes, four times per week, for 12 weeks. Participation in the running was found to be significantly associated with a decrease in psychotropic medication, particularly in psychostimulants. The children who ran for longer periods and more frequently evidenced the greatest decline in the need for psychotropic medication. Whether similar reductions in the need for medication would be found for depressed youths remains a question.

Maladaptive Cognitions

As is evident in Table 3, children are taught various strategies for identifying and altering their maladaptive cognitions. With one exception, these treatment components typically appear late in therapy due to the fact that they require the youngster to become more self-focused which actually exacerbates depressive symptoms. In fact, the one exception, altering faulty information processing, is included early in treatment because it is designed to redirect the youngster's attention from negative thoughts and feelings to more pleasant emotions and positive thoughts which appears to produce an elevation in mood and energy. In addition, our goal is to provide the youngsters with a base of potential coping skills that they can use to moderate the severity of symptoms prior to directing them to tune into and try to counter or change maladaptive cognitions. It also appears as though the improvement in mood and symptoms in general that results from the other components of the intervention program, provide the youngster with some personal distance from their maladaptive thoughts and beliefs which seems to open them up for change.

It is apparent that a treatment program for depressed children should address the disturbances in the youngster's schemata, their processing errors, negative self-evaluations, and hopelessness. A number of techniques can be used to directly intervene with disturbances in cognition. Most of the therapeutic work that is designed to change the youngster's maladaptive cognitions is completed during individual sessions. This is not to imply that it is the sole place for using these procedures, as many opportunities arise during group meetings. However, the intensity and intimacy of the individual sessions is better suited for the identification and restructuring of maladaptive thoughts.

Methods for Altering Faulty Information Processing. Depressed children tend to pay attention to the negative things that are occurring in their lives to the exclusion of positive information. This disturbance may stem from a variety of errors in information processing. To counter this, children can be taught to self-monitor (the purposeful and conscious act of observing oneself) positive events and pleasant emotion. This serves as a method for directing the child's attention to more positive things, thus breaking the cycle of negative attention. It helps the children see that there are some positive things going on in their lives. Individualized self-monitoring assignments may be given to the children to fit their specific disturbances. A youngster may be taught to observe certain behaviors, thoughts, feelings, or physical reactions and make a judgment about their occurrence or nonoccurrence. In addition, a youngster may be instructed to monitor what is happening when he or she has a specific thought or emotion.

The first step to teaching children to self-monitor is to collaboratively define the phenomena to be observed and to identify examples and non examples of it. It is useful to begin the training with a behavior that is likely to occur during the session which gives the therapist an opportunity to help the children tune into the occurrence of the behavior, check for accuracy of self-monitoring, model the procedure if necessary, and reward the child for successful and accurate self-monitoring. After identifying and defining the target for self-monitoring which is pleasant emotions early in treatment, the children and therapist devise a method for recording their occurrence or nonoccurrence, how to record, when to record, and how often to record. It is important to devise a system that allows the youngsters to record the occurrence of the target immediately after it occurs. We have created and used an emotions diary. Each page in the diary has a series of cartoon characters that are expressing different pleasant emotions. The youngsters place a check mark next to the ones they experience each day.

Altering Automatic Thoughts. The consciousness of depressed children is dominated by negative automatic thoughts. Especially prevalent are negative self-evaluative thoughts. As these thoughts are identified, the cognitive restructuring procedures discussed below along with cognitive modelling and self-instructional training can be used to directly alter them. These automatic thoughts are commonly the target of the therapist throughout treatment and the youngsters learn how to identify and modify them on their own later in treatment.

The first step for using either procedure is to make the child aware of the tendency to think negatively. This is accomplished through education, thinking aloud while playing games that pull for self-verbalizations (e.g. puzzle building, completing mazes), and helping the child catch them as they occur during the games and other activities during the sessions. It is especially important to watch for signs that the child's mood has changed within the session and then to ask the child to state what he or she was thinking. After catching a negative thought, the youngster is taught to replace it. One method for accomplishing this is for the therapist to model more adaptive thoughts.

Cognitive modelling involves the therapist verbalizing his or her thoughts, or verbalizing more adaptive thoughts that the child might use to replace existing thoughts or ones that he or she might have the next time a particular situation arises. Typically the procedure involves modelling more adaptive thoughts and asking the child to put them into his or her own words and then rehearsing them. In addition to using cognitive modelling when specific thoughts are being targeted, the therapist thinks aloud whenever he or she confronts a problem or some other situation that enables him or her to model adaptive thoughts for the child. This is done throughout treatment as a means of planting seeds of more adaptive thinking.

When a depressed child is having an especially difficult time replacing thoughts, self-instructional training can be used. Self-instructional training (Meichenbaum, 1977) is used to help a child internalize any set of self-statements that guide the child's thinking and/or behavior. In our work with depressed children, we have used Kendall's (e.g., 1977) adaptation of Meichenbaum's procedure. Any content of thoughts can be taught. It is especially useful with children who are experiencing a deficit in their verbal mediational skills. Such as a child who simply blows up and exerts no control over his or her emotions.

Changing Dysfunctional Schemata. One of the ultimate goals of the treatment program is changing the dysfunctional schemata that are hypothesized to give rise to the errors in information processing, depressogenic automatic thoughts, dysfunctional emotions, and behaviors associated with depressive disorders in children. Cognitive restructuring procedures are designed to modify the client's thinking and the premises, assumptions, and attitudes underlying the client's thoughts (Meichenbaum, 1977). The program includes a number of the cognitive restructuring procedures developed by Beck and colleagues (Beck, et al., 1979) including (1) What's the evidence?, (2) What's another way to look at it?, (3) What if?, and (4) behavioral experiments. Children are taught to be "Thought Detectives" who identify maladaptive thoughts and (a) evaluate the evidence for the thought, (b) consider alternative interpretations, and/or (c) think about what really would happen if the undesirable event occurred. These procedures are used throughout treatment by the therapist, although the goal is for the children to learn how to independently restructure their negative thoughts. This is accomplished through therapist modelling and the techniques are taught to the youngsters (see Table 3).

Behavioral Experiments. Perhaps the most efficient way to change a child's thinking is to strategically alter behaviors that serve as the base of evidence for the child's thoughts. The alternation in behavior and the resultant change in outcomes provide the child with immediate, direct, and concrete contradictory evidence for an existing maladaptive schema or supportive evidence for a new more adaptive schema. This process of assigning personal experiments requires creativity as the therapist has to be able to first identify a maladaptive thought or schema, bring it to the child's recognition, work with the child to establish the necessary evidence to support or refute the thought or schema, and then devise a behavioral assignment that directly tests the validity of it. Furthermore, steps have to be taken to ensure that the experiment is actually carried out as planned. In some instances, role playing ahead of time, imaginably walking through the assignment, or writing a contract may be used to promote compliance. After the experiment has been completed, the therapist works with the child to process the results. This is an important step since the child may distort the results without the therapist's objective input.

Negative Self-Evaluations. The last portion of treatment is focused on changing the depressed youngster's negative self-evaluations. This occurs last because all of the other self-control and coping skills are brought to bare on the process of working toward and recognizing self-improvement and changing the negative sense of self. Depressed children evaluate their performances, possessions, and personal qualities more negatively than nondepressed youths and their self-evaluations tend to be negatively distorted (Kendall, et al., 1990). In other words, they tend to be unrealistically and unreasonably negative in their self-evaluation. Children can be taught to evaluate themselves more reasonably and positively when it is realistic to do so. During this process they learn to recognize their positive attributes, outcomes, and possessions. The first step of the procedure is to identify the existence and nature of the disturbance. This can be accomplished through the use of the My Standards Questionnaire-Revised (Stark, 1990). This measure allows the therapist to determine whether the child is setting unrealistically stringent standards for his of her performance. Consequently, when the child evaluates his or her performance relative to these standards, the outcome is inadequacy. When this is the case, cognitive restructuring procedures are used to help the child accept more reasonable standards. When the child sets realistic standards, but evaluates him or herself negatively, cognitive restructuring and self-monitoring are used. The cognitive restructuring procedures of "What's the evidence" and cognitive modelling may be used. Self-monitoring would be used as a means of solidifying the new self-evaluation as the child is instructed to self-monitor the evidence that supports it. Over the course of treatment, the therapist and child review the evidence that supports the new self-evaluation.

In some instances, the child can benefit from change. In such instances, the goal of self-evaluation training becomes helping the child translate personal standards into realistic goals, and then, to develop and carry out a plan for attaining the goals. Following the translation process, the child prioritizes the areas where he or she is working toward self-improvement. Initially, a plan is formulated for producing improvement in an area where success is probable. The long-term goal is broken down into subgoals and problem-solving is used to develop a plan that will lead to subgoal and eventually goal attainment. Prior to enacting the plan, the children try to identify possible impediments to carrying out the plan. Once again, problem-solving is used to develop contingency plans for overcoming the impediments. Once the plan, including the contingency plans, has been developed, the children self-monitor progress toward change. Alterations in the plan are made along the way.

Parents

Parents are seen as a central link between the child's acquisition of skills during therapy sessions and their application to the natural environment. Thus, the parents begin the parent training component at the same time as the child begins therapy. The parent training program is designed to foster a more positive family environment through teaching the parents how to use positive behavior management techniques, reducing conflict, increasing the child's role in the family decision-making process, and by teaching the parents methods for improving their child's self-esteem.

One of the central components of the parent training program is teaching them to use primarily positive behavior management procedures. To accomplish this objective, procedures have been borrowed from Barkley (1987). Initially, the parents are taught to recognize and attend to positive affect and behavior through a series of role play activities. When they can clearly recognize positive behavior as it occurs, can appropriately comment on it, and understand the notion of extinguishing undesirable behavior through non attention, the parents are assigned the task of spending 15-20 minutes each day playing with their child. They are instructed to make it an enjoyable activity in which they strive to pay particular attention to their child's positive actions. These positive behaviors are socially reinforced and recorded in a diary by the parent throughout the week.

During the next few meetings, parents are taught how to use reinforcement techniques and about the impact reinforcement has on their child's self-esteem. Once again, role-play activities are used to facilitate acquisition of these skills. Parents collaboratively work with the therapist to identify targets for change and to develop plans to use reinforcement procedures to produce change.

In addition to reinforcement techniques, parents are taught the value of praise. Specifically, praise helps children feel good, boosts self-esteem, and can increase the occurrence of desirable bahaviors. Thus, parents are instructed to praise their child a minimum of four to six times per day. Moreover, they are taught to be concrete, genuine, and specific when giving praise. They also are cautioned against using hyperbole and left-handed compliments with their child. During this time, as parents are increasing the use of praise, they are also asked to note how often they criticize their depressed child. The goal of this activity is to eventually reduce the number of criticisms by one each day until they are eliminated.

Parents are then taught how to avoid getting caught in a coercive system. Parents are taught how to give clear and effective directives, the time-out procedure, and the use of natural consequences. Following the training, parents are given an additional homework assignment to monitor their effectiveness in implementing the new disciplinary procedures and to record any problematic situations for consideration at the next meeting.

Observations of some families with depressed children have revealed an especially hostile and angry environment in which parents frequently express their anger in a destructive manner. Such personal verbal attacks on the child shatter self-esteem. Although this tendency to lash out at the child is reduced as a result of the skills taught previously, additional steps are taken to teach the parents to control their own anger. In particular, parents receive instruction in the identification of the triggers of their anger and their underlying thoughts. They are taught to use their anger as a cue to leave the situation, cool off, and then take action. Adaptive coping statements and relaxation techniques are used to combat their angry outbursts. The parents are then asked to apply these skills and to gauge their impact on the family as additional homework.

Some of the difficulties in the relationship between depressed youths and their parents stem from the parent's inability to listen empathically. Through education, parents can learn how to express empathy. A four step model is used to accomplish this. The first step, active listening, includes avoiding interruptions during the child's communication and providing the child with nonverbal cues that convey undivided attention. Secondly, reflection techniques are taught to parents. These techniques serve the dual purpose of forcing parents to listen to their child and ensuring the child that he or she has been heard correctly. Since some parents tend to editorialize during reflection, avoidance of such remarks is stressed during role-plays. The third step in the model consists of helping parents to gain an understanding of their child's feelings. The culmination of the training model involves assisting parents in the use of their new skills when interacting with their child. Again, homework is assigned to encourage skill acquisition.

Our previously cited research indicates that families of depressed children often fail to engage in recreational activities. Thus, it is important to teach these families to have fun. Parents are asked to identify various low-cost no-cost activities in which the family can participate. Problem-solving is then used to facilitate the scheduling of such activities during the week. In addition to engaging in pleasant activities, parents are instructed to self-monitor the impact of these events on the family.

Family

Research has associated disturbances in family functioning with depressive disorders in childhood. The therapeutic question becomes, what are the family interaction patterns, verbal and nonverbal communications, and family rules that both lead to and maintain the child's skills deficits and cognitive disturbances? Common procedures for altering maladaptive family interactions include education, modelling, rehearsal, communication training, coaching, and feedback. Problem-solving and negotiation skills also are used to reduce family conflict.

CONCLUSIONS

The treatment model described in the previous sections was designed to address the cognitive, behavioral, and familial disturbances commonly associated with depressive disorders during childhood. Components of the treatment program have demonstrated utility in previous studies, but the entire package has yet to be evaluated. Support for the cognitive components is evident in the studies conducted by Butler and colleagues (1980) and in the second of our own studies. However, in both cases, the cognitive therapy component was not as well developed or as central to the overall treatment program as it is in the proposed treatment model. Results of a pair of case studies and two control-group treatment outcome studies suggest that social skills training (Frame, Matson, Sonis, Fialkov and Kazdin, 1982; Petti, Bornstein, Delamater and Conners, 1980), especially when it is combined with social problem-solving training (Butler, Miezitis, Friedman and Cole, 1980; Stark, Reynolds and Kaslow, 1987), may have beneficial effects on depressed children. Relaxation training also appears to be an effective intervention (Reynolds and Coats, 1986). Support for the inclusion of parents in the treatment program also is evident, although the degree to which it increases the potency of the intervention over solely a child component is not apparent (Lewinsohn, Clarke, Hops, Andrews and Williams, 1990). With a few exceptions, most of the existing research has been conducted with subclinical populations within schools. Thus, the effectiveness of psychosocial treatments for clinic populations is unknown. However, given the ever changing nature of psychiatric hospitals, it is likely that the primary location for the treatment of severe psychological disorders in the future is going to be the schools. Thus, these school-based models may have greater relevance than once thought. A glaring void in the literature is a comparison of the effectiveness of psychosocial, pharmacological, and a combined intervention. Based on clinical experience, some children seem to need the emotional foothold that an antidepressant gives them in order to be able to benefit from the psychosocial interventions. This is especially true for the youngsters who are experiencing anhedonia as their primary mood disturbance. Many additional basic issues remain to be addressed. It is hoped that the treatment model described in this chapter will serve as a catalyst for some of this needed research.

REFERENCES

Abramson, L.Y., Metalsky, G.I. and Alloy, L.B. (1989). Hopelessness depression: A theory-based subtype of depression. *Psychological Review, 96*, 358-372.

Abramson, L.Y., Seligman, M.E.P. and Teasdale, J. (1978). Learned helplessness in humans: Critique and reformulation. *Journal of Abnormal Psychology, 87*, 49-74.

Akiskal, H.S. and McKinney, W.T. (1975). Overview of recent research in depression: Integration of ten conceptual models into a comprehensive clinical frame. *Archives of General Psychiatry, 32*, 285-305.

Ambrose, B. and Rholes, W. (1993). Automatic cognitions and the symptoms of depression and anxiety in children and adolescents: An explanation of the content-specificity hypothesis. *Cognitive Therapy and Research, 17*, 153-171.

Arieti, S. and Bemporad, J.R. (1980). The psychological organization of depression. *American Journal of Psychiatry, 137*, 1360-1365.

Asarnow, J.R. and Bates, S. (1988). Depression in child psychiatric inpatients: Cognitive and attributional patterns. *Journal of Abnormal Child Psychology, 16*, 601-615.

Asarnow, J.R., Carlson, G.A. and Guthrie, D. (1987). Coping strategies, self-perceptions, hopelessness, and perceived family environments in depressed and suicidal children. *Journal of Consulting and Clinical Psychology, 55*, 361-366.

Bandura, A. (1977), *A social learning theory*. Englewood Cliffs, N.J.: Prentice-Hall.

Barkley, R.A. (1987). *Defiant children: A clinician's manual for parent training*. New York: Guilford Press.

Baron, R.M. and Kenny, D.A. (1986). The moderator-mediator variable distinction in social psychological research: Conceptual, strategic, and statistical considerations. *Journal of Personality and Social psychology, 51*, 1173-1182.

Beck, A.T. (1967). *Depression: Clinical, experimental and theoretical aspects*. New York: Hoeber.

Beck, A.T. (1976), *Cognitive therapy and the emotional disorders*. New York: International Universities Press.

Beck, A.T., Rush, A.J., Shaw, B.F. and Emery, G. (1979). *Cognitive therapy of depression*. New York: Guilford Press.

Bedrosian, R.C. (1989). Treating depression and suicidal wishes within the family context. In: N. Epstein, S.E. Schlesinger and W. Dryden (Eds.). *Cognitive-behavioral therapy with families* (pp. 292-324). New York: Brunner/Mazel.

Bell-Dolan, D.J., Reaven, N.M. and Peterson, L. (1993). Depression and social functioning: A multidimensional study of the linkages. *Journal of Clinical Child Psychology, 22*, 306-315.

Benfield, C.Y., Palmer, D.J., Pfefferbaum, B. and Stowe, M.L. (1988). A comparison of depressed and nondepressed disturbed children on measures of attributional style, hopelessness, life stress and temperament. *Journal of Abnormal Child Psychology, 16*, 397-410.

Blechman, E.A., McEnroe, M.J., Carella, E.T. and Audette, D.P. (1986). Childhood competence and depression. *Journal of Abnormal Psychology, 95*, 223-227.

Brown, R.S., Ramirez, D.E. and Taub, J.M. (1978). The prescription of exercise for depression. *Physician and sports Medicine, 6*, 34-45.

Burbach, D.J. and Borduin, C.M. (1986). Parent-child relations and the etiology of depression: A review of methods and findings. *Clinical Psychology Review, 6*, 133-153.

Butler, L., Miezitis, S., Friedman, R. and Cole, E. (1980). The effect of two school-based intervention programs on depressive symptoms in preadolescents. *American Educational Research Journal, 17*, 111-119.

Clarkin, J.F., Haas, G.L., Glick, I.D. (1988). *Affective disorders and the family: Assessment and treatment*. New York: The Guilford Press.

Cole, D. and Turner, J., Jr. (1993). Models of cognitive mediation and moderation in child depression. *Journal of Abnormal Psychology, 102*, 271-281.

Coyne, J.C. (1976). Toward an interactional description of depression. *Psychiatry, 39*, 28-40.

Dixon, J.F. and Ahrens, A.H. (1992). Stress and attributional style as predictors of self-reported depression in children. *Cognitive Therapy and Research, 16*, 623-634.

Doyne, E.J., Chambless, D.L. and Beutler, L.E. (1983). Aerobic exercise as a treatment for depression in women. *Behavior Therapy, 14*, 434-440.

Doyne, E.J., Ossip-Klein, D.J., Bowman, E.D., Osborn, K.M., McDougall-Wilson, I.B. and Neimeyer, R.A. (1987). Running versus weight lifting in the treatment of depression. *Journal of Consulting and Clinical Psychology, 55*, 748-754.

Faust, J., Baum, C.G. and Forehand, R. (1985). An examination of the association between social relationships and depression in early adolescence. *Journal of Applied Developmental Psychology, 6*, 291-297.

Folkins, C.H. (1976). Effects of physical training and mood. *Journal of Clinical Psychology, 32*, 385-388.

Forehand, R., Brody, G., Slotkin, J., Fauber, R., McCombs, A. and Long, N. (1988). Young adolescent and maternal depression: Assessment, interrelations, and predictors. *Journal of Consulting and Clinical Psychology, 56*, 422-426.

Frame, C., Matson, J.L., Sonis, W.A., Fialkov, M.J. and Kazdin, A.E. (1982). Behavioral treatment of depression in a prepubertal child. *Journal of Behavior Therapy and Experimental Psychiatry, 3*, 239-243.

Freemont, J. and Craighead, L.W. (1987). Aerobic exercise and cognitive therapy in the treatment of dysphoric moods. *Cognitive Therapy and Research, 11*(2), 241-251.

Garber, J. (1992). Cognitive models of depression: A developmental perspective. *Psychological Inquiry, 3*, 235-240.

Garber, J., Weiss, B. and Shanley, N. (1993). Cognitions, depressive symptoms, and development in adolescents. *Journal of Abnormal Psychology, 102*, 47-57.

Gotlib, I.H., Lewinsohn, P.M., Seeley, J.R., Rohde, P. and Redner, J.E. (1993). Negative cognitions and attributional style in depressed adolescents: An examination of stability and specificity. *Journal of Abnormal Psychology, 102*, 607-615.

Griest, J.H. (1987). Exercise intervention with depressed outpatients. In: W.P. Morgan and S.E. Goldston (Eds.). *Exercise and Mental Health* (pp. 111-115). Washington, DC: Hemisphere Publishing Corporation.

Griest, J.H., Klein, M.H., Eischens, R.R., Faris, J., Gurman, A.S. and Morgan, W.P. (1979). Running as treatment for depression. *Comprehensive Psychiatry*, *20*, 41-54.

Grossman, J.A., Poznanski, E.O., and Banegas, M.E. (1983). Lunch: Time to study family interactions. *Journal of Psychosocial Nursing and Mental Health Services*, *21*, 19-22.

Haley, B.M.T., Fine, S.L., Marriage, K., Moretti, M.M. and Freeman, R.J. (1985). Cognitive bias and depression in psychiatrically disturbed children and adolescents. *Journal of Consulting and Clinical Psychology*, *53*, 535-537.

Hammen, C. (1991). *Depression runs in families: The social context of risk and resilience in children of depressed mothers*. New York: Springer-Verlag.

Hammen, C., Adrian, C. and Hiroto, D. (1988). A longitudinal test of the attributional vulnerability model in children at risk for depression. *British Journal of Clinical Psychology*, *27*, 37-46.

Hammen, C. and Zupan, B.A. (1984). Self-Schemes, depression, and the processing of personal information in children. *Journal of Experimental Child Psychology*, *37*, 598-608.

Jacobsen, R.H., Lahey, B.B. and Strauss, C. (1983). Correlates of depressed mood in normal children. *Journal of Abnormal Child Psychology*, *11*, 29-40.

Jaenicke, C., Hammen, C., Zupan, B., Hiroto, D., Gordon, D., Adrian, C. and Burge, D. (1987). Cognitive vulnerability in children at risk for depression. *Journal of Abnormal Child Psychology*, *15*, 559-572.

Kashani, J.H., Ray, J.S. and Carlson, G.A. (1984). Depression and depressive-like states in preschool-age children in a child development unit. *American Journal of Psychiatry*, *141*, 1397-1402.

Kaslow, N.J., Rehm, L.P. and Siegel, A.W. (1984). Social-cognitive and cognitive correlaties of depression in children. *Journal of Abnormal Child Psychology*, *12*, 605-620.

Kaslow, N.J., Stark, K.D., Printz, B., Livingston, R. and Tsai, Y. (1992). Cognitive Triad Inventory for Children: Development and relationship to depression and anxiety. *Journal of Clinical Child Psychology*, *21*, 339-347.

Kazdin, A.E. (1989). Childhood depression. in: E.J. Mash and R.A. Barkley (Eds.), *Treatment of childhood disorders* (pp. 135-166) New York: The Guilford Press.

Kazdin, A.E., Esveldt-Dawson, K., Sherick, R.B. and Colbus, D. (1985). Assessment of overt behavior and childhood depression among psychiatrically disturbed children. *Journal of Consulting and Clinical Psychology*, *53*, 201-210.

Kazdin, A.E., Rodgers, A. and Colbus, D. (1986). The Hopelessness Scale for Children: Psychometric characteristics and concurrent validity. *Journal of Consulting and Clinical Psychology*, *54*, 241-245.

Kendall, P.C. (1977). On the efficacious use of verbal self-instructional procedures with children. *Cognitive Therapy and Research*, *1*, 331-341.

Kendall, P.C. and Braswell, L. (1993). *Cognitive - behavioral therapy for impulsive children*. New York: Guilford Press.

Kendall, P.C., Stark, K.D. and Adam, T. (1990). Cognitive deficit or cognitive distortion in childhood depression. *Journal of Abnormal Child Psychology*, *18*, 255-270.

Kenney, E., Spence, S.H. and Hensley, R. (1989). An examination of the relationship between childhood depression and social competence amongst primary school children. *Journal of Child Psychology and Psychiatry*, *30*, 561-573.

King, A.C., Taylor, C.B., Haskell, W.L. and Debusk, R.F. (1989). Influence of regular aerobic exercise on psychological health: A randomized, controlled trial of healthy middle-aged adults. *Health Psychology*, *8*, 305-324.

King, A.C., Taylor, C.B. and Haskell, W.L. (1983). Effects of differing intensities and formats of 12 months of exercise training on psychological outcomes in order adults. *Health Psychology*, *12*, 292-300.

Kovacs, M. (1981). Rating scales to assess depression in school aged children. *Acta Paedopsychiatrica*, *46*, 305-315.

Lewinsohn, P.M., Clark, G.N., Hops, H. and Andrews, J. (1990). Cognitive-behavioral treatment for depressed adolescents. *Behavior Therapy*, *21* 385-401.

Martinsen, E.W., Hoffart, A. and Solberg, O. (1989). Comparing aerobic with nonaerobic forms of exercise in the treatment of clinical depression: A randomized trial. *Comprehensive Psychiatry*, *30*, 324-331.

Matson, J.L. (1989). *Treating depression in children and adolescents*. New York: Pergamon Press.

Matson, J.L. and Ollendick, T.H. (1988). *Enhancing children's social skills: Assessment and Training*. New York: Pergamon Press.

Matson, J.L., Rotatori, A.F. and Helsel, W. J. (1983). Development of a rating scale to measure social skills in children: The Matson Evaluation of Social Skills with Youngsters (MESSY). *Behavioral Research and Therapy*, *41*, 335-340.

McCann, I.L. and Holmes, D.S. (1984). Influence of aerobic exercise on depression. *Journal of Personality and Social Psychology*, *46*, 1142-1147.

Meichenbaum, D. (1977). *Cognitive-Behavior modification*. New York: Plenum Press.

Moilanen, D.L. (1993). Depressive experiences of nonreferred adolescents and young adults a cognitive-developmental perspective. *Journal of Adolescent Research*, *8*, 311-325.

Morgan, W.P., Roberts, J.A., Brand, R.F. and Feinerman, A.D. (1970). Psychological effect of chronic physical activity. *Medicine and Science in Sport*, *2*, 213-217.

Mullins, L.L., Peterson, L., Wonderlich, S.A. and Reaven, N.M. (1986). The influence of depressive symptomatology in children on the social responses and perceptions of adults. *Journal of Clinical Child Psychology*, *15*, 233-240.

Nolen-Hoeksema, S., Girgus, J.S. and Seligman, M.E.P. (1986). Learned helplessness in children: A longitudinal study of depression, achievement, and explanatory style. *Journal of Personality and Social Psychology*, *51*, 435-442.

Peterson, L., Mullins, L.L. and Ridley-Johnson, R. (1985). Childhood depression: Peer reactions to depression and life styles. *Journal of Abnormal Child Psychology*, *13*, 597-609.

Petti, T.A., Bornstein, M., Delamater, A. and Conner, C.K. (1980). Evaluation and multimodality treatment of a depressed prepubertal girl. *Journal of the American Academy of Child Psychiatry*, *19*, 690-702.

Poznanski, E.O. and Zrull, J. (1970). Childhood depression: Clinical characteristics of overtly depressed children. *Archives of General Psychiatry*, *23*, 8-15.

Pieto, S.L., Cole, D.A. and Tageson, C.W. (1992). Depressive self-schemes in clinic and nonclinic children. *Cognitive Therapy and Research*, *16*, 521-534.

Puig-Antich, J., Lukens, E., Davies, M., Goetz, D., Brennan-Quatrock, J. and Todak, G. (1985). Psychosocial functioning in prepubertal major depressive disorders; I. Interpersonal relationships during the depressive episode. *Archives of General Psychiatry*, *42*, 500-507.

Reynolds, W.M., Anderson, G. and Bartell, N. (1985). Measuring depression in children: a multimethod assessment investigation. *Journal of Abnormal Child Psychology*, *13*, 513-526.

Reynolds, W.M. and Coates, K.I. (1986). A comparison of cognitive-behavioral therapy and relaxation training for the treatment of depression in adolescents. *Journal of Consulting and Clinical Psychology*, *54*, 653-660.

Rholes, W., Blackwell, J., Jordan, C. and Walters, C. (1980). A developmental study of learned helplessness. *Developmental Psychology*, *16*, 616-624.

Sacco, W.P. and Graves, D.J. (1984). Childhood depression, interpersonal problem-solving, and self-ratings of performance. *Journal of Clinical Child Psychology*, *13*, 10-15.

Schwartz, M., Friedman, R., Lindsay, P. and Narrol, H. (1982). The relationships between conceptual tempo and depression in children. *Journal of Consulting and Clinical Psychology*, *50*, 488-490.

Seligman, M.E.P., Peterson, C. Kaslow, N.J., Tanenbaum, R.L., Alloy, L.B. and Abramson, L.Y. (1984). Attributional style and depressive symptoms among children. *Journal of Abnormal Psychology*, *93*, 235-238.

Sime, W.E. (1987). Exercise in the prevention and treatment of depression. In: W.P. Morgan and S.E. Goldston (Eds.), *Exercise and Mental Health* (pp. 145-152).

Stark, K.D. (1990). *The treatment of depression during childhood: A school-based program*. New York: Guilford Press.

Stark, K.D. and Brookman, C. (1982). Childhood depression: Theory and family-school intervention. In: M.J. Fine and C. Carlson (Eds.), *Family-school intervention: A systems perspective* (pp. 247-271). Massachusetts: Allyn & Bacon.

Stark, K.D., Humphrey, L.L., Crook, K. and Lewis, K. (1990). Perceived family environments of depressed and anxious children: Child's and maternal figure's perspectives. *Journal of Abnormal Child Psychology*, *18*, 527-547.

Stark, K., Humphrey, L., Laurent, J., Livingston, R. and Christopher, J. (1993). Cognitive, behavioral, and family factors in the differentiation of depressive and anxiety disorders during childhood. *Journal of Consulting and Clinical Psychology*, *61*, 878-886.

Stark, K.D., Linn, J.D., MacGuire, M. and Kaslow, N.J. (in press a). The social functioning of depressed and anxious children: Social skills, social knowledge, automatic thoughts, and physical arousal. *Journal of Clinical Child Psychology*.

Stark, K.D., Schmidt, K., Joiner, T.E. and Lux, M.G. (in press b). Depressive cognitive triad: Relationship to severity of depressive symptoms in children, parents' cognitive triad, and perceived parental messages about the child him or herself, the world, and the future. *Journal of Abnormal Child Psychology*.

Stark, K.D., Reynolds, W.M. and Kaslow, N.J. (1987). A comparison of the relative efficacy of self-control therapy and a behavioral problem-solving therapy for depression in children. *Journal of Abnormal Child Psychology*, *15*, 91-113.

Strauss, C.C., Forehand, R., Frame, C. and Smith, K. (1984). Characteristics of children with extreme scores on the Children's Depression Inventory. *Journal of Clinical Child Psychology, 16*, 235-239.

Tems, C., Stewart, S., Skinner, J. Jr., Hughes, C. and Emslie, G. (1993). Cognitive distortions in depressed children and adolescents: Are they state dependent or trait like? *Journal of Clinical Child Psychology, 22*(3), 316-326.

Young, J. (1991). *Cognitive therapy for personality disorders: A schema-focused approach*. Sarasota, Florida: Professional Resource Exchange, Inc.

Zupan, B.A., Hammen, C. and Jeanicke, C. (1987). The effects of current mood and prior depressive history on self-schematic processing in children. *Journal of Experimental Child Psychology, 43*, 149-158.

11

COGNITIVE BEHAVIORAL THERAPY OF AGGRESSIVE CHILDREN
Effects of Schemas

John E. Lochman and L. Lenhart

Duke University Medical Center
Department of Psychology
PO Box 2917
Durham, North Carolina 27710

INTRODUCTION

Children who are identified as excessively aggressive by peers and teachers display a range of behaviors including verbal provocations and threats, physical fights, poorly controlled anger, low frustration tolerance, bullying, and disruptive behavior. Aggressive children typically have various subsets of these behavioral symptoms, and research and clinical efforts have focused on identifying meaningful subtypes of aggressive children. However, a common characteristic of all aggressive children is that they have intense, negative effects on the people who interact with them. Peers are victimized, teachers are disrupted from their teaching mission, and parents are frustrated with being unable to control these children's coercive, provocative behavior. Because of these flagrant effects on others, aggressive children are referred for mental health services at higher rates than are children with most other forms of psychopathology.

In addition to these immediate effects of children's aggressive behavior, we are concerned as clinicians and researchers about these children's future adjustment. Children who display high rates of aggressive behavior in the elementary school years are on a developmental trajectory that can lead to serious criminal and contra-normative behavior in adolescence and adulthood (Loeber, 1990). Reviews of longitudinal research decades ago (e.g. Olweus, 1979) had documented the troubling stability of aggressive behaviors over long periods of time. Substantial stability in children's aggressive and disruptive behavior has been noted even as children transition from kindergarten to first grade, with a true positive prediction rate of 70% for these high risk children (Lochman and the Conduct Problems Prevention Research Group, in press). In general, the research suggests that an aggressive pattern of behavior settles into a stable form at a relatively early age.

This stable pattern of aggressive behavior throughout the elementary school years serves as a compelling risk marker for other later forms of behavior problems as well.

Behavioral Approaches for Children and Adolescents, Edited by
H. P. J. G. van Bilsen et al., Plenum Press, New York, 1995

Children with Childhood Onset Conduct Disorder in the DSM-IV taxonomic system display symptoms such as initiating physical fights, using weapons, being physically cruel to people or animals, destroying property and stealing from others. When this pattern of adolescent conduct problems has a childhood onset, and is preceded by physical aggression and disturbed peer relationships in childhood, the course of the conduct disorder is expected to be more persistent and to more likely develop into adult Antisocial Personality Disorder than would be the case for adolescent-onset conduct problems without the aggressive childhood history (American Psychiatric Association, 1994). As aggressive children move into the middle school years (grades six to eight), they have high rates of school failure and other externalizing problems according to parent, teacher and self reports (Coie, Lochman, Terry and Hyman, 1992). In the latter study, children who were both aggressive and rejected by their peers in third grade were three times more likely (62%) than nonaggressive and nonrejected children (18%) to have significant adjustment problems in middle school, while children who were aggressive only (10%) or rejected-only (34%) had twice the risks rates of the nonaggressive, nonrejected children. Similarly, boys identified as aggressive by peers' sociometric ratings in elementary school had significant risk for self-reported substance use and crimes against persons and for externalizing behavior problems reported by peers, teachers and independent observers at the time of entry into high school (Lochman and Wayland, 1994). These findings suggest that children who are identified as aggressive in elementary school express continuing problematic behaviors in adolescence, and that these problem behaviors occur in multiple behavioral domains and in several social contexts.

A variety of explanations have been advanced to account for the stability and malignant progression of aggressive behaviors during childhood and adolescence, The children's cross-situational consistency in behavior has been linked to biologically-based temperament patterns (e.g., Loeber, 1990) which may be genetically linked to parents' personality style (Szczepanski, 1994). The aggressive child also recreates his own hostile environment in interactions with peers, teachers, and parents. The child's aggressive behavior pulls for counteraggressive behavior from others, and the child's significant others develop persistent expectations for aggression in the child. Because of the aggressive child's reputation, other people often behave in controlling and aversive ways early in interactions with the aggressive child. the role of parents with the aggressive child is particularly complex. The parents often play a formative role in developing the child's aggressive behavior through their authoritarian and inconsistent parenting practices, and the parents and children then reciprocally maintain their aversive patterns through their coercive, hostile interchanges (Patterson, 1986). This set of biological, behavioral, and interpersonal factors promote and maintain the aggressive child's established ways of perceiving and thinking about their social environment, and the child's subsequent stable and consistent aggressive behavior (Lochman, White and Wayland, 1991). In the next sections, we will examine a social cognitive model for children's aggressive behavior, and a cognitive behavioral intervention approach that is consistent with this model.

SOCIAL COGNITIVE MODELS

Cognitive behavioral intervention is based on the premise that cognitions or thoughts influence the behavior that an individual displays in various situations, and thus aims to alter both an individual's general response (behavioral) patterns and the cognition that accompany or precede the behaviors. Cognitive-behavioral intervention with aggressive children is thus designed to have an impact on social behavior and related cognitive processes. This form of intervention is based on a social-cognitive theoretical model, which describes social behavior as a function of perceptions of the social environment and ideas regarding how best to resolve perceived social conflicts.

Anger Arousal Model

An early form (the Anger Control Program) of our current cognitive behavior intervention program was based on an anger arousal model (Lochman, Nelson and Sims, 1981) which was primarily derived from Novaco's (1978) work with aggressive adults. In this conceptualization of anger arousal, which stressed sequential cognitive processing, the child responded to problems such as interpersonal conflicts or frustrations with environmental obstacle (i.e., difficult schoolwork). However, it was not the stimulus event itself that provoked the child's response, but rather the child's cognitive processing of and about that event. This first stage of cognitive processing was similar to Lazarus (Smith and Lazarus, 1990) primary appraisal stage, and consisted of labelling, attributions, and perceptions of the problem event. The second state of processing, similar to Lazarus (Smith and Lazarus, 1990) secondary appraisal, consisted of the child's cognitive plan for his/her response to the perceived threat or provocation. This level of cognitive processing was accompanied by anger-related physiological arousal. The Anger Arousal model indicated that the child's cognitive processing of the problem event and of his/her planned response led to the child's actual behavioral response (ranging from aggression to assertion, passive acceptance or withdrawal) and to the positive or negative consequences that the child experienced due to the event.

This Anger Arousal model served as the basis for the social cognitive model in our revised Anger Coping Program (Lochman, White and Wayland, 1991). This social cognitive model stressed the reciprocal, interactive relationships between the initial cognitive appraisal of the problem situation, the cognitive appraisal of the problem solutions, and the child's physiological arousal, and the behavioral response. The Anger Coping Program introduced the role that affect labelling, cognitive operations, and schematic propositions can have on the child's social-cognitive processes. The schematic aspects of this model will be discussed in more detail in a subsequent section. In this model, there is greater emphasis on the recursive nature of the different elements in the model with all processing steps/components having some influence in all other elements.

Furthermore, the reciprocal nature of interpersonal interactions is made more explicit with the depiction of the consequences of one's behavior operating as the stimulus for the next behavioral response; thus, there is greater emphasis on the ongoing nature of interpersonal interaction. The level of physiological arousal will depend on the individual's biological predisposition to become aroused, and will vary depending on the interpretation of the event. The level of arousal will further influence the social problem solving, operating either to intensify the fight or flight response, or interfering with the generation of solutions. This model helps to explain the chronic nature of aggressive children's difficulties, as there is emphasis on the ongoing and reciprocal nature of interactions which suggests that there will be a cyclical element to aggressive children's difficulties and it may be difficult for them to extricate themselves from the aggressive behavior pattern.

Social Information Processing Model

The social information processing model developed by Dodge (1993; Dodge, Pettit, McClaskey and Brown, 1986) explicitly expands on substeps in the child's cognitive processing of social problems and serves as an important heuristic for research with aggressive children. In this model, there are five sequential steps involved in the processing of social information, which include encoding relevant social cues, interpreting these cues, generating possible solutions, evaluating these solutions, and enacting the chosen response. The first two steps involve cognitive processing of the problem event, and the next two steps involve cognitive processing about responses. Aggressive children have been found to have difficulties at each of these stages.

Aggressive children have cognitive distortions when (1) encoding incoming social information, and (2) interpreting social events and others' intentions; cognitive deficiencies in (3) generating alternative adaptive solutions for perceived problems and (4) evaluating the consequences for different solutions; and behavioral deficiencies enacting (5) the solution believed to be most appropriate.

Considerable research has indicated that aggressive children do have the deficiencies hypothesized above. In terms of the initial state, or the encoding of information, aggressive children have been found to recall fewer relevant cues about events (Lochman and Dodge, 1994), to base interpretations of events on fewer cues (Dodge and Newman, 1981; Dodge, et al, 1986), to selectively attend to hostile rather than neutral cues (Gouze, 1987; Milich and Dodge, 1984), and to recall the most recent cues in a sequence, with selective inattention to earlier presented cues (Milich and Dodge, 1984). McKinnon, Lamb, Belsky, and Baum (1990) have suggested that these biases at the encoding phase, which involves selective attention to particular cues in the environment, are a direct result of prior social interactions and in fact are a logical outcome of the aggressive child's early relationships which are affectively toned. In this model, the child learns to pay attention to interaction patterns and social cues that are affectively similar to cues they have previously experienced; if a child has experienced primarily negative or aggressive interactions with the parent, he/she will more likely attend to, and process, aggressively toned cues.

As the next stage, or the interpretation stage, aggressive children have been shown to have a hostile attributional bias, as they tend to excessively infer that others are acting towards them in a provocative and hostile manner. (Dodge, et al, 1986; Nasby, Hayden and DePaulo, 1979). Both aggressive girls (Feldman and Dodge, 1987) and aggressive boys (Guerra and Slaby, 1989; Lochman and Dodge, 1994; Sancilio, Plumert, and Hartup, 1989; Waas, 1988) have been found to have this attributional biases. Furthermore, this attributional bias has been displayed during live dyadic interactions (Lochman, 1987; Steinberg and Dodge, 1983) as well as with the use of hypothetical vignettes. Lochman (1987) found that aggressive boys have underperceptions of their own aggressive behavior, as well as distorted overperceptions of their dyadic partner's aggression. As a result, aggressive boys develop attributions that their peers have relative responsibility for conflict rather than assuming responsibility themselves. These attributional biases tend to be more prominent in reactively aggressive children than in proactively aggressive children (Dodge and Coie, 1987), which offers support for the need for a sub-classification of aggressive children, as the particular social-cognitive deficits may be different in different aggressive children. A recent study examined this attributional bias in rejected children and found that knowledge of the antagonists' affect influenced non-rejected children's interpretation of the behavior, while rejected children do not alter their interpretations based on this additional information (Keane and Parrish, 1992); this suggest that rejected children are more inflexible at the interpretation phase, and may not take into account relevant information.

The third information processing stage involves a generative process whereby potential solutions for coping with a perceived problem are recalled from memory. At this stage, aggressive children demonstrate deficiencies in both the quality and the quantity of their problem solving solutions (Lochman, Meyer, Rabiner, and White, 1991). These differences are most pronounced for the quality of the solutions offered, with aggressive children offering fewer verbal assertion solutions (Asarnow and Callan, 1985; Deluty, 1981; Joffe, Dobson, Fine, Marriage, and Haley, 1990; Lochman and Lampron, 1986), fewer compromise solutions (Lochman and Dodge, 1994), more direct action solutions (Lochman and Lampron, 1986), a greater number of help-seeking or adult intervention responses (Asher and Renshaw, 1981; Dodge, Murphy, and Buschbaum, 1984; Lochman, Lampron and Rabiner, 1989; Rabiner, Lenhart, and Lochman, 1990), and more physically aggressive responses (Richard and Dodge, 1982; Slaby and Guerra; 1988, Waas 1988; Waas and French, 1989) to hypothetical vignettes describing interpersonal conflicts. There has been some evidence that this qualitative difference is most apparent for the second or back-up solutions to the conflict offered by aggressive children (Evans and Short, 1991; Richard and Dodge, 1982), although other studies have found aggressive children's aggressive solutions to be more evident in the initial solutions (Lochman and Lampron, 1986). In terms of the quantity of solutions offered by aggressive children, there is little evidence that they offer in general a fewer number of responses (Fischler and Kendall, 1988; Rubin, Bream, and Rose-Krasnor, 1991), although boys who display the highest level of aggression generate fewer solutions overall than moderately aggressive and nonaggressive boys (Lochman and Dodge, 1994; Lochman, Lampron, Burch and Curry, 1985). These results suggest that the type and frequency of the aggressive behavior may be related to the level of deficiency in the quantity of solutions generated.

The fourth processing step involves the evaluation of solutions that have been generated, and choosing the solution that would produce the desired outcome. This stage, thus, involves a two-step process: first, identifying the consequences for each of the solutions generated and second, evaluating each solution and consequence in terms of the individual's desired outcome.

Aggressive children are more likely to believe that aggressive behavior will lead to tangible rewards and will have a positive outcome (Hart, Ladd and Burleson, 1990; Perry, Perry, and Rasmussen, 1986), will reduce others' aversive behaviors (Lochman and Dodge, 1994; Perry, et al 1986), will result in a more positive image, and will not cause suffering in others (Slaby and Guerra, 1988). In general, aggressive children evaluate aggressive behavior as less negative (Deluty, 1983) and more positive (Crick and Ladd, 1990) than children without aggressive behavior difficulties. Perry, Perry, and Weiss (1989) demonstrated that the hypothesized target of aggression (male vs. female), and the stimulus for aggression (provoked vs. unprovoked) can influence the outcome evaluation for aggressive behaviors, as there is the expectation that unprovoked aggression and aggression directed towards females will receive more disapproval than provoked aggression or aggression directed towards a male. Children's beliefs about the utility of aggression and about their ability to successfully enact an aggressive response can operate to increase the likelihood of aggression being displayed, as children who hold these beliefs will be more likely to also believe that this type of behavior will help them to achieve the desired goals which then influences response evaluation.

The final processing stage enumerated by Dodge, et al (1986) involves behavioral enactment, or displaying the response that was chosen in the above steps. Aggressive children have been found to be less adept at enacting positive or prosocial interpersonal behaviors (Dodge, et al, 1986), which may be an important element in the evaluation phase, as aggressive children's belief that they will be more adept at enacting aggressive behaviors may be reality based, rather than a distortion; this interpretation would suggest that improving the ability to enact positive behaviors (i.e., through social skills training) may influence aggressive children's belief about their ability to engage in these more prosocial behaviors and thus function to change the response evaluation.

A more recent modification of the original model was proposed by Crick and Dodge (1994), with this model also emphasizing the reciprocal nature of interpersonal interactions and the reciprocal nature of the different social-cognitive elements within the model. They indicated that this revised model describes more of the on-line processing that actually occurs when individuals are engaged in social interactions, and their model also contains an explicit reference to the idea that the consequences of one's behavior will feed back into the system and function as the stimulus for the subsequent interaction. Additionally, a sixth step was included in the information processing model; which involves a clarification of goals that the individual wishes to attain; this stage in the process involves selecting the desired goal from different possible goals (i.e., to avoid punishment, to get even with another individual, to affiliate), or determining which goal predominates during the particular interaction. The goal that the individual chooses to pursue will then affect the responses generated for resolving the conflict, which occurs in the next processing stage. Within this model, the data base can be accessed at any of the processing stages, and can be influenced by stored knowledge related to similar situations; furthermore, each stage will provide information to the data base, which will then have an impact on future interactions.

The research reviewed above has provided a fundamental basis for understanding the social cognitive functioning of aggressive children, which has had an impact on the goals and structure of intervention programs. However, results of empirical research are based on the mean or model child, and individual differences are often overlooked, which can have adverse effects on the practical application of these studies. Treatment outcome depends on appropriately identifying the specific areas of deficit and targeting these areas. The implication is that individual differences in various social cognitive skills will influence the treatment goals. Studies have begun to examine how certain social cognitive dysfunctions are more predominate in particular subgroups of aggressive children, such as reactive versus proactive aggressive children (Dodge and Coie, 1987, Dodge, Lochman, Harnish, Bates and Pettit, under review) and aggressive-rejected versus nonaggressive-rejected children (French, 1988; Lochman, Coie, Underwood, and Terry, 1993; Rabiner et al, 1990), have unique social-cognitive dysfunctions and unique responses to cognitive-behavioral interventions.

Role of Schemas

Recent revisions of social-cognitive models have more explicitly introduced the role that children's cognitive schemas have on their information processing (Crick and Dodge, 1994; Lochman, Wayland and White, 1993; Lochman, White and Wayland 1991). Schemas account for how organisms actively construct their perceptions and experiences, rather than merely being passive receivers and processors of social information (Ingram and Kendall, 1986). Schemas have been defined n somewhat different ways by various theoreticians and researchers, but they are commonly regarded as consistent, core beliefs and patterns of thinking. These underlying cognitive structures form the basis for individuals' specific perceptions of current events (De Rubeis and Beck, 1988). Similar to Adler's concept of "style of life" (Freeman and Leaf, 1989) schemas are cognitive blueprints or master plans which construe, organize and transform peoples' interpretations and predictions about events in their lives (Kelly, 1955; Mischel, 1990). The Adleian "style of life" included (1) apperceptive schemas which expressed individuals' beliefs and expectations about their world and themselves, and which led them to understand the meaning of events around them, and (2) guiding ideals which were goals that individuals' behaviors moved towards. These goal can be linked to individuals' self-schemas or implicit theories about their abilities and dispositions (Erdley, Dumas-Hines, Lomis, Cain, Olshekshy and Dweck, 1990). Thus schemas are part of individuals' motivation for behaving in certain ways, in the teleological framework of Adlerian theory, as well as representing ideas and knowledge accessed in memory.

Schemas have certain basic attributes. First, a distinction can be made between <u>active</u> schemas which are often conscious and govern everyday behavior, and <u>dormant</u> schemas, which are typically out of individuals' awareness and emerge only when the individuals are faced with specific events or stressors. The dormant schemas are in a state of "chronic accessibility" (Higgins, King and Maren, 1982; Mischel, 1990) or state of potential activation, ready to be primed by minimal cues. Thus, individuals' beliefs and expectations which emerge when they are intensely stressed or aroused may not be at all apparent when they are calm and nonaroused. Second, existing schemas can be either *compelling* or *noncompelling* (Freeman and Leaf, 1989).

Noncompelling schemas are not strongly held by a person, and can be given up easily. In contrast, compelling schemas are strongly entrenched in the person's way of thinking. They promote more filtering and potential distortions of the person's perceptions of self and others (Fiske and Taylor, 1984; Wyer, Lambert, Budesheim and Greenfield, in press). The compelling schemas lead to more rapid judgements about the presence of these schema-related traits in self and others, and they often operate outside of conscious awareness (Erdley, 1990). Third, schemas can be more or less *permeable*. Permeable schemas permit a person to alter their interpretation of events through successive approximations, a process identified as "constructive alternativism" by Kelly, 1955. A person with relatively permeable schemas can readily adapt their schemas to the specific situations and conditions he or she encounters, thereby adding new elements and complexity to the schema.

Schemas are typically more permeable and situational as individuals develop and have experiences in a number of situations (Mischel, 1990; Rotter, Chance and Phares, 1972). Relatively nonpermeable schemas are preemptive, and promote rigid black-white thinking (Kelly, 1955).

The process of altering schemas is essentially conservative (Lochman and Dodge, under review), as preexisting beliefs are accepted over new ones, and self-centered, because one's own personal preexisting beliefs are held more strongly than new information provided by others (Fiske and Taylor, 1984). Nonpermeable schemas are self-maintaining because they lead the individual to seek and recall information that is consistent with their conceptions of others and self. Fourth, schemas permit individuals to *predict* the outcomes of events (Adler, 1964). Schemas allow people to efficiently operate in their social worlds by providing expectations for how others will react and how they will be able to meet their own goals and needs (Lochman and Dodge, under review).

Schemas Within the Social Cognitive Model. Schemas have been proposed to have a significant impact on the information processing steps within the Social Cognition model underlying cognitive-behavioral interventions with aggressive children (Lochman, White and Wayland, 1991). Ingram and Kendall (1986; Kendall, 1991) have organized individuals' cognitive processing of events into four categories in their Cognitive Taxonomic System. Cognitive products refer to the actual cognitions that individuals have in the present when dealing with events (e.g., attributions, decisions, beliefs, thoughts, recognition of stimuli), and cognitive operations represent the procedures which process information (e.g., attention, encoding, retrieval). Cognitive operations operation on the immediate stimuli and on schemas to produce cognitive products. Schemas have two forms within the Cognitive Taxonomic System: cognitive structures and cognitive propositions. Cognitive structures are the architecture of the cognitions in memory, representing the structure in which information is organized and stored, These functional psychological mechanisms store information in both short and long term memory, placing information in interconnecting categories and nodes. Cognitive propositions are the content within the cognitive structures, and is the information that is actually stored. Cognitive propositions include information both in semantic memory (general knowledge that has been acquired and learned) and in episodic memory (personal information gleaned through one's experiences in the world).

Within the Social-Cognitive Model, social-cognitive products include elements within the social information processing steps such as encoded cues, attributions, problem solutions, goals and anticipated consequences which individuals experience during moment-to-moment processing.

Schematic propositions are those beliefs, ideas, and expectations which can have direct and indirect effects on the social-cognitive products. Schematic propositions include information stored in memory about individuals' beliefs, general social goals, generalized expectations, and their understanding of their competence and self-worth. A subsequent section will examine examples of how schematic propositions impact social-cognitive products.

Evolution of Children's Schemas. Children's schemas within the Social Cognitive Model evolve from their experiences with early caregivers, and can be substantially affected by subsequent interactions with significant others, such as teachers and peers, (Lochman, White and Wayland, 1991). The ways in which parents and other key social figures act with and around the child will shape the evolving schemas about others and self. Aggressive children's parents often have parenting styles that are highly aversive, controlling, inconsistent and lacking in warmth and mutual problem-solving (e.g., Lochman, 1990; McMahon and Wells, 1989; Patterson, 1986). Parents of aggressive children often have highly conflicted and aggressive behavior between the parents as well, and this marital conflict contribute to sons' reactive, aggressive behavior (Lochman and Craven, 199). Parents' cognitive processing has been formed to parallel their behavior. Mothers of aggressive boys have been found to display their own attributional biases, as they have attributed causes of misdeeds more to children's dispositions rather than to the parents' reactions, in contrast to mothers of nonaggressive boys (Dix and Lochman, 1990). Mothers of aggressive boys have displayed similar hostile attributional biases in their responses to adult authority figures (e.g., bosses, police offers) in hypothetical vignettes as well (Reinhold, 1990). Children's schemas about their interpersonal world and their emotional regulation develop through the models that parents provide of ways to perceive and respond to conflicts with spouses, children, and others.

An interesting aspect of Crick and Dodge's (1994) model is the incorporation of concepts from attachment theory, in particular the relevance of the relationship with parently figures for understanding behavior in subsequent social interaction. Crick and Dodge (1994) refer to "cognitive heuristics" , which are referred to as schema or working models. Cognitive heuristics are defined as cognitive structures that contain information related to past social experiences (i.e., information stored in the data base), and rules regarding how to interpret the cues present in social situations. It is suggested that these heuristics develop as a result of interpersonal experiences and memories of these interactions, which then influence the processing of incoming social cues and thus affect the behavior exhibited in social situations.

Attachment and Object Relations Perspectives on Schema Development. Attachment and object relations theoretical viewpoints both focus on the early parent-child relationship as relevant for understanding current behavior. The premise within these theories is that early interactions affect current behavior in an indirect manner through the development of expectations of how others will respond to the self, a similar process to that described above.

Bowlby (1988) has been one of the leading proponents of attachment theory; he has suggested that infants and children engage in behavior that maintains proximity to the mother, which serves the biological function of safety and self-preservation. Thus, attachment behavior is considered to be innate and to have a biological basis. Later revisions of attachment theory suggested that all children form attachments during childhood but the quality of the attachment will differ depending on the type and sensitivity of caregiving the child receives. Ainsworth, Blehar, Waters, and Wall (1978) developed a procedure for assessing the quality of the attachment relationship between a child and parent (referred to as the "strange situation"), and delineated different types of attachment patterns (secure, anxious, avoidant, disorganized, attached) based on this assessment strategy. The quality of attachment is proposed to have an impact on the development of interpersonal behavior, with considerable research supporting the hypothesis that the early attachment relationship is related to later functioning and interpersonal adjustment (Matas, Arend, and Sroufe, 1978; Waters, 1978; Lieberman, 1977; Kroger, 1989; Dozier, 1989; Jenkins and Fisher, 1989). As noted above, one of the possible mechanisms for this influence is the development of expectations for how others will respond to the self, based on the response of the attachment figure of the self, which will then lead to the child behaving in accordance with these expectations; the expectations will influence both the perceptions of others in social inter-actions and of the self, and ultimately the behavior believed to be most appropriate. Baldwin (1992) discussed the concept of relational schema, which was defined as the cognitive structure that contains representations of the patterns of relating that the individual has experienced; these schema contain expectations for how the self will be perceived by others and how others will respond or react to the self.

Recently, great interest has been directed at the relationship between parenting styles and child behavioral styles. Although limited, there has been research examining the relationship between caregiving styles and children's behavior, offering some validation for the hypothesis that the parental relationship can be an important predictor of behavior in children. The parent-child relationship can affect a child's sense of self-efficacy or ability to achieve certain goals, with the parental response to the child impacting the child's beliefs about himself. Self-efficacy is related to social-cognitive functioning, as one's sense of efficacy will influence the expectations one has for how well particular behaviors may be enacted and therefore will influence which behaviors one attempts to enact (Bandura, 1989). Empirical evidence for the relationship between expectations and behavior was shown by Allen, Leadbeater, and Aber (1990), who noted that male adolescents with the lowest sense of efficacy exhibited the highest levels of problem behaviors. These researchers hypothe-sized that adolescents' expectations and belief systems may mediate the relationship between early negative interactions with the parents and later interpersonal difficulties. A somewhat different version of this idea is that the child's cognitive model of the attachment relationship, developed from parent-child interactions, mediates the connection between problematic parenting styles and negative behavior patterns in children (Allen, Aber, and Leadbeater, 1990). Relatedly, Perry, Perry, and Kennedy (1992) indicated that children with inconsistent and insensitive caregiving develop insecure attachments, and subsequently expect that others will respond to them in an unpredictable or unfair manner; they proposed that children's cognitive representations of social experiences will mediate aggressive behavior through the expectations that are developed as a result of these experiences. The opposite effect has also been proposed, with the idea that parents who exhibit warm and loving behaviors will provide a positive social experience for children, which would lead to the development of a positive orientation towards others and towards social interactions (Putallaz and Sheppard, 1992). Thus, it appears that the trend is to focus on the parent-child relationship as having an indirect impact on a child's interpersonal relationships through the formation of expectations regard-ing how others will respond to the self. Object relations theory, which developed out of psychoanalytic theory, also operated on the assumption that the parent-child relationship will have an impact on subsequent interpersonal relationships by forming expectations for how others will respond to the self. The early mother-child relationship is proposed to underlie the development of the child's sense of self, as the child will internalize the relationship with the object (mother), and this internalized view of the other will affect the child's approach to the individuals encountered during later interactions (Greenberg and Mitchell, 1983). The internal view of self and other will become activated during ongoing interactions, in the same way that schema are activated, and the internal representations will influence the interpretation of others in the environment, and thus will influence the behavior exhibited in interactions. Although there has been less research examining object relations theory, there is evidence that the object representations level (internalized view of others) is related to parental nuturance, peer ratings of competence, the capacity for emotional investment in relationships, and understanding social causality (Avery and Ryan, 1988, Westen, Klepser, Ruffins, Silverman, Lifton, and Boekamp, 1991).

Westen (1991) suggested that incorporating concepts from social-cognitive theory with object relations theory would allow for a fuller understanding of interpersonal behavior, as both theories focus on the cognitive and affective components of interpersonal relations. Both theoretical approaches have some emphasis on how expectations for the self and others affect the interpretations of others and of interpersonal interactions. The expectations for how others will respond to the self is one of the primary foci of object relations theory, with these expectations developing during early childhood as a result of interactions with the primary caretaker(s). Within social cognitive research, expectations are a part of the model that describes interpersonal behavior, with the expectations proposed to affect the interpretation of self and others and therefore to impact the behaviors chosen in different situations. As alluded to earlier, there are similarities in the conceptual framework of different theories, and an integration of these theories may allow for a fuller understanding of social behavior.

Direct Effects of Schemas on Social Information Processing. Schemas can influence the sequential steps information processing in different ways. Early in the information processing sequence, when the individual is orienting to the situation, perceiving and interpreting new social cues, schemas can have a clear direct effect by narrowing the child's attention to certain aspects of the social cue array (e.g., Lochman, Nelson and Sims, 1981). A child who believes that it is essential to be in control of others and who expects that others try to dominate him, often in aversive ways, will attend particularly to verbal and nonverbal signals about someone else's control efforts, but can easily miss accompanying signs of the other person's friendliness, or attempts to negotiate. For example the distorted perceptions of aggressive boys in live dyadic interaction tasks involving conflict are significantly predicted by their lower eye contact in comparison to nonaggressive boys (Lochman, Wayland, and Sczcepanski, under review).

This disengagement in eye contact may be partially a social skill difficulty for these boys, but also may be partially due to the boys strong schema about interpersonal aggression leading the aggressive boys to rely on their prior expectations for the interaction rather than to actively orient to visual cues about their partners' behavior. The impermeable and compelling nature of these schematic expectations will be explored in the following section. This child's schema about control and aggression will also heavily influence the second stage of processing, as the child interprets the malevolent meaning and intentions in others' behavior.

Schemas can also play a significant role in the fourth stage of information processing, as the child anticipates consequences for different problem solutions available to him or her, and as the child decides which strategy will be enacted. Social goals (or outcome values) and outcome expectations are schemas which, from a Social Learning Theory view (Mischel, 1990; Rotter, Chance and Phares, 1972), combine to produce children's potential for behaving in specific ways. When the child places a higher value on certain goals or reinforcements, then the child will engage in behaviors that he expects will have a high probability of meeting his goal. Aggressive adolescent boys have been found to place higher value on social goals for dominance and for revenge, and lower value on social goals for affiliation, than do nonaggressive boys (Lochman, Wayland, and White, 1993). In this study, there was a clear relation between social goal choice and problem-solving, indicating a direct effect of cognitive schemas on information processing.

Aggressive and nonaggressive adolescents did not differ in their endorsement of which behavioral solutions could be used to attain each of the four social goals examined in this study. Differences in problem-solving between these two groups of adolescents emerged only when the boys' solutions to gain their main social goal were analyzed. In this analysis, aggressive boys proposed using fewer bargaining solutions and more aggressive and verbal assertion solutions, in comparison to nonaggressive boys. Children's schemas about social goals and outcome expectations affect their response decisions in the fourth stage of information-processing.

Indirect Effects of Schemas on Information Processing. Schemas can also have indirect or mediated effects on information processing through the influence of schemas on children's expectations for their own behavior and for other's behavior in specific situations, through the associated affect and arousal when schemas are activated, and through schemas influence on the style and speed of processing. Schemas about attributes of self and of others such as aggressiveness or dominance, produce expectations about the anticipated presence or absence of these attributes as individuals prepare to interact with people in specific situations. Lochman and Dodge (under review) asked aggressive and nonaggressive boys to rate how much they expected they and a peer would be aggressive during a brief verbal conflict with a peer. After they made their expectation ratings, an aggressive boy and a nonaggressive boy had a four-minute dyadic interaction in which they were instructed to stick up for their opinions and to try to win a verbal disagreement with their peer partner. After the interaction the boys rated how aggressive they actually perceived themselves and their partner to be during the prior interaction.

Videotapes of the interactions were subsequently rated by research assistants on the same dimensions of aggression to provide an objective observation of the actual behavior used by the dyadic partners. Results indicated that aggressive boys' perceptions of their own aggressive behavior was primarily affected by their prior expectations, while nonaggressive boys relied more on their actual behavior to form their perceptions. These results indicate that the schemas of aggressive boys about their aggressive behavior are strong and compelling, leading the aggressive boys to display cognitive rigidity between their expectations and perceptions. The aggressive boys' perceptions of their behavior, driven by their schemas, were relatively impermeable to actual behavior, and instead were heavily governed by the boys' preconceptions.

Schemas are complex blends of cognition and associated emotion, and as schemas are activated during interactions they can contribute to the intense levels of affect and arousal that a person can experience in response to a provocative event. Thus, while provocative events produce some emotional and physiological arousal in most children, the intense reactive anger and rage of some individuals can be due to the activation of their schemas about the general hostility of others, and of their schemas that others are responsible for initiating unjust and unfair conflicts. Emotions have been hypothesized to be the glue between attributions and behavior (Weiner, 1990) and the adaptational systems which motivate individuals to solve their perceived problems (Smith and Lazarus, 1990). For example, when a child attributes blame for a conflict to another person, the child experiences anger, but when the child has perceived self-responsibility for the problem, the child experiences guilt (Weiner, 1990). These attribution-emotion linkages can then produce quite different decisions about behavioral responses (e.g., aggression vs. apology, help-seeking, nonconfrontation, or compromise). Schemas about accountability and responsibility, with their implications for who receives blame or credit for events, are closely linked to the experience of anger. Accountability appraisals generate "hot" emotional reactions when a provocative person is perceived to act intentionally, unjustly, and in a controllable manner (Smith and Lazarus, year 1990). The arousal and emotional reactions in early stages of interactions then serve to flood the information-processing system (Lochman, 1984), and to maintain the hostile attributions and aggressive response style overtime during an interaction. This makes it more difficult for the aggressive individual to avoid escalating cycles of aggression and violence. Aggressive children and adolescents are further hampered by schemas and appraisal styles which make them relatively unaware of emotional states associated with vulnerability (e.g., fear, sadness), leading them to over-label their arousal during frustration or conflict as anger (Lochman and Dodge, 1984).

Aggressive children have been found to have an impulsive cognitive style (Camp, 1977), meaning they spend less time deliberately and carefully evaluating perceptions and response decisions during interpersonal events. Instead they rely on reflexive and automatic information-processing (Lochman, Nelson and Sims, 1981). Schemas can influence aggressive children's overuse of automatic processing in several ways. Aggressive children can form a belief that it is important to respond quickly to provocative events rather than to carefully evaluate their potential solutions to the problems. This belief can form because of real dangers they previously faced within their family or neighbourhood setting, but when the belief is strong, compelling, and impermeable, the children may not easily recognize that contextual differences (e.g., when at school, or with less threatening peers) make the belief less necessary in certain situations. In addition, because of the arousal and emotion activated by schemas about provocation or threat, aggressive children will tend to use rapid, automatic processing. Prior research (Lochman, Lampron and Rabiner, 1989; Rabiner, Lenhart and Lochman, 1990) has found that aggressive children's social problem-solving style becomes less competent when they use automatic processing rather than deliberate processing. When using automatic processing, aggressive boys generate more action-oriented solutions, more help-seeking solutions, and fewer verbal assertion solutions. Thus, children's schemas can have additional indirect effects on their appraisals of self and others and on their problem-solving by eliciting excessive automatic processing, which short-circuits the children's more competent, deliberate processing.

INTERVENTION ISSUES

Cognitive-behavioral intervention with aggressive children is based on the Social Cognitive Model that has been discussed. The model provides a template (or a schema for intervention) for identifying relevant intervention goals with aggressive children in general, which is necessary in the development of programmatic interventions. In addition, the model can be used during clinical assessment to identify the particular areas of cognitive distortions and cognitive deficiencies for specific aggressive children. In this section we will provide overviews of two of our related, school-based intervention program for aggressive children.

The Anger Coping Program

The Anger coping Program is a structured 18-session group intervention for aggressive children, based largely on an earlier 12 session Anger Control Program (Lochman, Nelson and Sims, 1981).

Both programs have been used in school settings for prevention and early intervention purposes, and for intervention research, so that comparable control conditions can be obtained. Both programs can also be used in outpatient mental health clinics, either as an adjunct to other treatments or as part of specialty programs for children with Oppositional Defiant Disorder or Conduct Disorder. An extended outline of the Anger Coping Program group sessions (Lochman, Lampron, Gemmer and Harris, 1987) and detailed summaries of the program (Lochman, Dunn and Klimes-Dougan, 1993; Lochman and Lenhart, 1993;

Lochman, White and Wayland, 1991) can be found elsewhere. In this section we will overview the structure and the primary intervention goals.

The Anger Coping Program is implemented usually as a group intervention to promote group problem-solving, peer modelling of competent solutions to social conflicts, peer reinforcement for working on behavioral change, and role-playing of alternative strategies for handling anger-arousing situations with peers and adults. As with any group, and especially with groups of aggressive, disruptive children, group leaders need to be prepared to work with negative peer pressure and peer modelling of negative solutions to conflicts. However, since these children's problems are social in nature, the advantages of group work generally outweigh the disadvantages. Groups are usually composed of four to six children, and two co-leaders conduct the group. When the groups are implemented in a school setting, we attempt to have a school counsellor or other school staff be the group co-leader. This enhances the school's acceptance of the program, and permits more active consultation with teachers and other school personnel. The program has been used most with boys in the fourth to sixth grades, but the program has been clinically used with girls, and with boys in the fourth to sixth grades, but the program has been clinically used with girls, and with younger children (down to second grade) and young adolescents (usually up to 15 or 16 years of age). Groups usually meet once a week, although twice weekly groups have sometimes been used (e.g., Lochman, Nelson and Sim, 1981). The groups are "closed" because of the structured nature of the groups, and children are rarely added to the groups after the third or fourth session.

The goals for group sessions include: (1) introduction and establishment of the group rules and reinforcement systems (Session 1), (2) self-instruction training (Sessions 2 and 3), (3) perspective-taking (Sessions 4 and 5), (4) awareness of physiological arousal (Session 6), (5) goal-setting (Session 7), and (6) social problem-solving (Sessions 8 to 18). In the first session, we overtly discuss that our aim in the group sessions is to develop other ways of handling anger. Group members assist in establishing group rules (e.g., no hitting, one person talks at a time, keep hands and feet to self, no swearing), and a strike system is introduced to give feedback about children's violations of group rules. This response cost system consists of children receiving up to three strikes for breaking group rules during a session, and if a child receives all three strikes, he loses his rule point for that day. Children can also receive one positive participation point in each session, and up to two or three points for meeting their weekly goal (see Session 7, below).

Group leaders create a chart to record the number of points earned by each group member, the number of points children spend on small reinforcers (pencils, erasers, pads, small cars, sports trading cards), and the total number of points accumulating across all group members for a large group reinforcement (e.g., pizza party). Thus, the operant system includes both short-term and long-term reinforcements.

Self-instruction training focuses on assisting children to use anger-management tactics, especially coping self-instruction, when they are in anger arousing situations. The self-instructions serve to disrupt children's reflexive aggressive responses, and to facilitate more adaptive problem-solving.

Structured tasks during these sessions include having each group member use self-instructions to keep other group members from distracting him or her as he or she tries to remember a series of cards and to build domino towers. After identifying how successful anger management helps children perform better on their noninterpersonal tasks, we use several versions of Goodwin and Mahoney's 1975 Verbal Taunting Task, in which children practice one at a time to use self-instructions when they are being directly teased by other group members.

Perspective-taking sessions focus on understanding how others can have a range of intentions in a situation, and on attribution-retraining, so that children can see that others can engage in ambiguously provocative behavior for accidental or non-hostile reasons Activities in these two sessions include discussing the number of different possible social problems that can exist in drawings of ambiguous social situations, and discussing the intentions and feeling of characters in brief role-play of these situations. We also use a task in which group members write down six to eight different reasons why a pictured character appears to be acting in a certain manner and then have group members try to guess the intention of peers who take turns role-playing the incident using the different motives or intentions.

To enhance children's awareness of their physiological state when they begin to become angry, we discuss a brief video in which a boy describes how his body feels when he is angry. Increased physiological awareness (rapid breathing, muscle tightness, etc.) can then serve as a cue to use self-instructions and to begin problem-solving about how to handle the difficult situation they are in.

In our more recent applications of this program, we have moved the goal setting session up to one of the early weeks to begin addressing children's out-of-group behavior at the beginning of our work with them. We typically meet with teachers before the session, and identify four or five behavioral goals that each child could work on to reduce his disruptive, aggressive, and inattentive behavior at school. Group leaders shape children's identification of a goal that they wish to work on, so that the goal is compatible with teacher expectations. Children write the goal (e.g., not argue with the teacher, not call someone names, remain in seat) on a goal form, and then ask the teacher daily to indicate whether or not they met their goal. The children return the goal sheets to the group session the next week, and receive points if they met their goal. This form of behavioral goal-setting has augmented intervention effects (Lochman, Burch, Curry and Lampron, 1984) by increasing the generalization of intervention effects out of the group into the children's real interpersonal world.

The largest part of the program focuses on social problem-solving, which also includes work on the earlier sections on self-instruction and perspective-taking as well. Children practice brainstorming multiple possible solutions to problem situations, and then how to evaluate the long-term and short-term consequences of each solution. A brief video illustrates the problem-solving process, and then group members plan and make their own problem-solving videotape about a problem situation that is common to them. The last half-dozen sessions are less structured, and include the opportunity for more role-playing and discussion of real-life social problems that the children are encountering.

The Coping Power Program

We are currently implementing a major revision of the Anger Coping Program as part of a grant-funded preventive intervention research study. This new program, the Coping Power Program, also includes a school-based group intervention. However, the group program lasts longer, including approximately 33 structured sessions over a 15 month intervention period, and will address additional substantive areas, including emotion awareness, relaxation training, social skill enhancement, positive social and personal goals, and dealing with peer pressure. Additional elements of the program include twice-monthly individual sessions increase generalization of the program to the children's actual social problem situations, and periodic consultation with teachers. In addition, half of the intervention children have parent groups offered to their parents. These parent groups last for 12 to 16 sessions and focus on increasing parents' social reinforcement and positive attention, appropriate discipline strategies, and their own anger management. These parent also receive periodic home visits to promote generalization. In this preventive research study, the effects of the two intervention conditions (child program only, child plus parent program) will be compared to a randomly assigned high risk control condition and to a non-risk control condition. This study identified children as being at risk in the years prior to their transition to middle school. Risk status is based on teacher and parent ratings of boys' aggressive and disruptive behavior. Proximal outcome indicators will be the boys' level of parent, teacher, peer, and observer-rated aggressive and disruptive behavior at the end of the program.

Distal prevention outcome indicators, assessed as the boys move through middle school into high school, will measure boys subsequent drug and alcohol use rates, their delinquent behavior, and their rates of Conduct Disorder. It is hypothesized that the inclusion of behavioral parent training will substantially increase the short and long term positive outcome for boys who participate in the Coping Power Program, by affecting the parents' discipline and monitoring practices, and by enhancing parents' modelling and development of boys' schemas and beliefs related to conflict management.

Schema-Related Intervention Issues

Expectations and Attribution. The Anger Coping and Coping Power Program are directed not only at children's information-processing, but also at their enduring interpersonal schemas.

The interventions address children's attribution styles and schematic expectations for others' intentionally aggressive behavior. By repeatedly reinforcing ideas that some seemingly provocative and frustrating events are not due to purposefully hostile or mean intentions by others, the perspective-taking aspects of the intervention promote more permeable, situational-based schemas and attributions. Because the base schemas are strong and compelling, it is anticipated that these changes will take place slowly, and only with repeated discussion and role-playing. As children become more proficient in accurately interpreting others' nonhostile intention in specific social situations, their general expectations about others' hostility can begin to change.

Delay When Aroused and Angry. Because individuals' expectations and beliefs about conflict are usually highly emotionally charged, an important intervention goal is to assist children in delaying their first responses when conflict-related schemas are activated. Through the use of self instructions and relaxation strategies, children are encouraged to inhibit initial aggressive responses. As arousal and high levels of anger dissipate, the child can successfully use more socially competent problem-solving strategies. In the Coping Power Program, we introduce an anger thermometer to children so they can concretely process variations in the degree of anger they experience, and discuss how they can problem solve better when their anger is lower.

Accurate Affect Labelling. Aggressive children's self schemas lead them to mislabel their arousal and vulnerable affective states as anger, which promotes outer-directed aggressive behavior. Intervention thus focuses on identifying and discussing instances when these other affective states, such as fear and sadness and their variants, are experienced. The modelling of the group leaders discussing their own range of feelings is important in this process. It is also useful for group leaders to take advantage of moments when children talk about their emotional reactions spontaneously, and to reinforce the legitimacy of these feelings.

Social Goals. For social problem-solving training to have an effect in children's lives, their social goals must be considered. In early stages of intervention, aggressive children should be reinforced for considering other, less noxious strategies for accomplishing their existing primary goals. Because these goals often revolve around dominance and revenge, initially children should be assisted to find other ways to feel they are in control, that they "win" situations, and that they "save face." These strategies will often involve seeking retribution from authority figures, forceful verbal assertion, use of nonverbal behaviors that save face (e.g., use of eye contact, walking away slowly), and frustration of peers who try to control them through taunting by not responding.

Over time, we also focus on how aggressive children often have multiple equally-valued social goals, creating a "muddy" social goal structure (Lochman, Wayland and White, 1993). Many Aggressive boys continue to value affiliation goals, as well as dominance and revenge motives.

Ultimately, problem solving training can focus on how to use verbal strategies such as bargaining, assertion or compromise to meet desired goals and yet maintain positive relationships with peers.

As children become more socially competent, affiliation goals can assume increasing value and children can have higher expectations about attaining these outcomes.

Processing Style. During group sessions, we primarily are working with children's deliberate processing style. They generate multiple solutions to solve social problems, then consider and rate the consequences of the various solutions, and then select the "winning" solution for them. Although this deliberate style does not replicate what usually occurs in these children's social interactions, when they believe they must respond quickly, the children's deliberate processing in groups can increase the salience of the more competent options (Lochman, Lampron and Rabiner, 1989). Then, when children are in a position where they will be using automatic processing, they will quickly retrieve the most salient solution from their "memory bin" of solutions, and enact that solution. Ideas become more salient in memory bins through repeated frequent activation of the idea, which can occur during group discussions and role-playing. At times within the group sessions, we are also working directly with children's automatic processing. During the verbal taunting task, for example, children can experience some level of irritation or low levels of anger. Role-playing in these situations mimics how children can begin to retrieve more competent strategies from memory even when they are experiencing some level of arousal or anger.

Enhance Permeability of Schemas. Old schematic patterns of thinking are well-entrenched, and alterations in these schemas require addressing the range of situational affective and interpersonal cues which comprise the schema.

Thus, intervention focuses on the emotion and cognition linkages, and how patterns of thinking are, or could be, different in varying contexts and settings. In addition, intervention can impact the strong, compelling nature of schemas by: (1) working with parents as well as children, because parents have substantial roles in erecting and maintaining children's schema, (2) providing intervention over a sufficiently long period, (Lochman, 1985) and at critical periods of developmental transition, such as when school changes occur (Conduct Problems Prevention Research Group, 1992), and (3) use of operant goal-setting procedures to reinforce children's behavioral change. Children have to maintain these behavioral changes over a relatively long period of time before they can begin to elicit more positive, supportive behavior from peers and adults, which in turn can produce changes in children's schematic expectation of others.

Therapeutic Relationship. One of the most powerful nonspecific aspects of intervention involves the child's relationship with the intervention staff. In the context of a warm, supportive relationship with a group leader, who exerts firm, clear limits when needed, the child is exposed not just to an operant reinforcer and punisher, but to a unique and powerful socializing agent. Children's enduring schemas, or ways of thinking about interpersonal relationships, can be substantially altered by an intervener who models and talks about his or her perceptions of social situations in the group, and about his emotional, cognitive, and behavioral responses to the situation. Through this relationship, the child can try on new ways of thinking about other people's goals, intentions and feelings.

ANGER COPING INTERVENTION OUTCOMES

The effects of the Anger Coping Program have been reviewed in greater detail elsewhere (Lochman, Dunn, and Klimes-Dougan, 1993, Lochman and Lenhart, 1993; Lochman, White and Wayland, 1991). In this section, we will overview evidence for the short-term and long-term effects of the program, and indications of program and child characteristics which predict positive outcomes.

In an initial uncontrolled study, 12 aggressive second and third grade children displayed significant reductions in teachers' daily ratings of children's aggressive behavior, and tended to have reductions in teacher checklist ratings of acting-out behavior at the end of a twelve session Anger Control program. These improvements in children's aggressive behavior were accompanied by increases in teachers' daily ratings of children's on-task behavior (Lochman, Nelson and Sims, 1980). In a subsequent controlled study, 76 aggressive boys were randomly assigned to anger coping (AC), goal setting (GS), anger coping plus goal setting (AC+GS) or untreated control (UC) cells (Lochman, Burch, Curry and Lampron, 1984). The boys were in the fourth through the sixth grades, and participated in a 12-week Anger Coping program. The two Anger Coping conditions (AC;AC+GS) produced significant reductions in parents' ratings of boys aggression, reductions in independent observers' time-sampled ratings of boys' disruptive classroom behavior and tended to produce improvement in children's self esteem. Treatment effects tended to be strongest in the AC+GS condition, indicating the utility of a goal-setting component in promoting stronger generalization of effects. Secondary analyses of this data indicated that Anger Coping boys who had the greatest reductions in parent-rated aggression were boys who initially had the poorest social problem-solving skills (Lochman, Lampron, Burch and Curry, 1985). This was a particularly important predictor of treatment effectiveness because boys with the poorest social problem-solving skills in the untreated control (UC) condition were likely to have increasingly higher levels of aggressive behavior by the end of the school year.

The Anger Coping Program effects have been found to be augmented by the use of an 18 session version of the group program, in comparison to a 12 session version (Lochman, 1985). With the longer program, aggressive boys displayed greater improvement in on-task behavior and greater reduction in passive off-task behavior, illustrating the need for longer intervention periods for children with chronic acting-out behavior problems. In contrast, treatment effects were not augmented by the inclusion of a self-instruction training component focusing on academic tasks (Lochman and Curry, 1986), or by a structured five-session teacher consultation component (Lochman, Lampron, Gemmer, Harris and Wynkoff, 1989). In the latter two studies, boys in the Anger Coping condition did display reductions in parent-rated child aggression (Lochman and Curry, 1986), teacher-rated child aggression (Lochman et al, 1989), improvements in self esteem and perceived social competence (Lochman and Curry, 1986, Lochman et al, 1989), and reductions in off-task classroom behavior (Lochman and Curry, 1986, Lochman et al, 1989).

A three-year followup study of the Anger Coping Program has indicated that 31 boys (AC) who had participated in Anger Coping groups in elementary school had lower substance use rates, higher self esteem and more competent problem-solving skills than did 52 boys

(UA) in an untreated aggressive cell (Lochman, 1992). The AC boys' positive outcomes in this study, when they were at an average age of 15 years old, were within the range of 62 nonaggressive boys.

However, the AC boys did not have significantly lower rates of delinquent behavior than did the UC boys, and only a subset of AC boys who had received a six session booster intervention in the following school year were able to maintain reductions in observed off-task classroom behavior.

Overall these results indicate that this form of cognitive-behavioral intervention can have positive short term effects with aggressive children, in a similar manner to other recent cognitive-behavioral and social skill programs (e.g., Bierman, Miller and Staub, 1987; Feindler, Ecton, Kingsley and Dubey, 1986; Graham, Hadley and Williams, 1992; Kazdin, Bass, Siegel and Thomas, 1989; Lochman, Coie, Underwood and Terry, 1993; Ollendick and Hersen, 1979; Vitaro and Tremblay, 1994). In addition, the program's effects on problem-solving skills and self esteem appear to be maintained at a three-year followup, and the program has important prevention effects in reducing these boys risk of substance use during middle adolescence. However, boys' aggressive and acting-out behavior tended to revert to untreated aggressive boys' levels. These results indicate the promise of cognitive-behavioral intervention with aggressive children, but also clearly indicate the need for interventions that also focus on the parents' behavior and that span a sufficient period of time to promote maintenance and internalization of the cognitive and behavior charges (e.g., Conduct Problem Prevention Research Group, 1992).

ACKNOWLEDGEMENTS

This chapter was completed with the support of grant DA-08453 from the National Institute of Drug Abuse.

REFERENCES

Adler, A. (1964). *Social Interest: A challenge to mankind.* New York: Capricorn

Ainsworth, M., Blehar, M., Waters, E., and Wall, S. (1978). *Patterns of Attachment.* Hillsdale, NJ: Lawrence Erlbaum.

Allen, J.P., Leadbeater, B.J., and Aber, J.L. (1990). The relationship of adolescents' expectations and values to delinquency, hard drug use, and unprotected sexual intercourse. *Development and Psychopathology, 2,* 85-98.

Allen, J.P., Aber, J.L., and Leadbeater, B.J. (1990). Adolescent problem behaviors: The influence of attachment and autonomy. *Psychiatric Clinics of North America, 13,* 455-467.

Asarnow, J.R., and Callan, J.W. (1985). Boys with peer adjustment problems: Social cognitive processes. *Journal of Consulting and Clinical Psychology, 53,* 80-87.

Asher, S.R., and Renshaw, P.D. (1981). Children without friends: Social knowledge and social skills training. In: S.R. Asher and J.M. Gottman (Eds.), The development of children's friendships (pp. 273-296). New York: Cambridge University Press.

Avery, R.R., and Ryan, R.M. (1988). Object relations and ego development: Comparison and correlates in middle childhood. *Journal of Personality, 56,* 547-569.

Baldwin, M.W. (1992). Relational schemas and the processing of social information. *Psychological Bulletin, 112,* 461-484.

Bandura, A. (1989). Regulation of cognitive processes through perceived self-efficacy. *Developmental Psychology, 25,* 729-735.

Bierman, K.L., Miller, C.L. and Staub, S.D. (1987). Improving the social behavior and peer acceptance of rejected boys: Effects of social skills training with instructions and prohibitions. *Journal of Consulting and Clinical Psychology, 55,* 194-200.

Bowlby, J. (1988). *A secure base: Parent-child attachment and healthy human development.* New York: Basic Books.

Camp, B.W. (1977). Verbal mediation in young aggressive boys. *Journal of Abnormal Psychology, 86,* 145-153.

Coie, J.D., Lochman, J.E., Terry, R., and Hyman, C. (1992). Predicting early adolescent disorder from childhood aggression and peer rejection. *Journal of Consulting and Clinical Psychology, 60,* 783-792.

Conduct Problems Prevention Research Group (In alphabetical order: K. Bierman, J. Coie, K. Dodge, M. Greenberg, J. Lochman, and R. McMahon) (1992). A developmental and clinical model for the prevention of conduct disorder: The FAST Track Program. *Development and Psychopathology, 4,* 509-527.

Crick, N.R., and Dodge, K.A. (1994). A review and reformulation of social-information processing mechanisms in children's social adjustment. *Psychological Bulletin, 115,* 74-101.

Crick, N.R., and Ladd, G.W. (1990). Children's perceptions of the outcomes of aggressive strategies: Do the ends justify the means? *Developmental Psychology, 29,* 244-254.

Deluty, R.H. (1981). Alternative-thinking ability of aggressive, assertive, and submissive children. *Cognitive Therapy and Research, 5,* 309-312.

Deluty, R.H. (1983). Children's evaluation of aggressive, assertive, and submissive responses. *Journal of Consulting and Clinical Psychology, 51,* 124-129.

DeRubeis, R.J. and Beck, A.T. (1988). Cognitive therapy. In: K.S. Dobson (Ed.), *Handbook of cognitive-behavioral therapies.* (Pp. 85-135). New York: Guilford.

Dix, T., and Lochman, J.E. (1990). Social cognition and negative reactions to children: A comparison of mothers of aggressive and nonaggressive boys. *Journal of Social and Clinical Psychology, 9,* 418-438.

Dodge, K.A. (1993). The future of research on the treatment of conduct disorder. *Development and Psychopathology, 5,* 311-319.

Dodge, K.A., and Coie, J.D. (1987). Social information processing factors in reactive and proactive aggression in children's peer groups. *Journal of Personality and Social Psychology, 53,* 1146-1158.

Dodge, K.A., Murphy, R.R., and Buchsbaum, K. (1984). The assessment of intention-cue detection skills in children: Implications for developmental psychopathology. *Child Development, 55,* 163-173.

Dodge, K.A., and Newman, J.P. (1981). Biased decision making processes in aggressive boys. *Journal of Abnormal Psychology, 90,* 375-379.

Dodge, K.A., Petit, G.S., McClaskey, C.L., and Brown, M.M. (1986). Social competence in children. *Monographs of the Society for Research in Child Development, 51.*

Dozier, M. (1989). Working models of attachment for individuals with serious psychiatric disorders. Paper presented at the biennial meeting of the Society for Research in Child Development. Kansas City, Missouri: April, 1989.

Erdley, C.A. (1990). An analysis of children' attributions and goals in social situations: Implications of children's friendship outcomes. Unpublished paper, University of Illinois.

Erdley, C.A., Dumas-Hines, F., Lomis, C.C., Cain, K.M., Olshekshy, L.M. and Dweck, C.S., (1991). Children's implicit theories and social goals as mediators of responses to social failure. Manuscript submitted for publication, University of Illinois.

Evans, S.W., and Short, E.J. (1991). A qualitative and serial analysis of social problem-solving in aggressive boys. *Journal of Abnormal Child Psychology, 19,* 331-340.

Feindler, E.L., Ecton, R.B., Kingsley, D., and Dubey, D.R. (1986). Group anger-control training for institutionalized psychiatric male adolescents. *Behavior Therapy, 17,* 109-123.

Feldman, E., and Dodge, K.A. (1987). Social information processing and sociometric status: Sex age, and situational effects. *Journal of Abnormal Child Psychology, 15,* 211-227.

Fischler, G.L., and Kendall, P.C. (1988). Social cognitive problem solving and childhood adjustment: Qualitative and topological analyses. *Cognitive Therapy and Research, 12,* 133-153.

Fiske, S.T., and Taylor, S.E. (1984). *Social Cognition.* Reading, MA: Addison-Wesley.

Freeman, A. and Leak, R.C. (1989). Cognitive therapy applied to personality disorders. In: A. Freeman, K.M. Simm, L.E. Beutler, and H. Arkowitz (Eds.), *Comprehensive Handbook of Cognitive Therapy* (pp. 403-433). New York: Plenum.

French, D.C. (1988). Heterogeneity of peer rejected boys: Aggressive and nonaggressive subtypes. *Child Development, 59,* 976-985.

Godwin, S.F. and Mahoney, J.J. (1975). Modification of aggression through modelling: An experimental probe. *Journal of Behavior Therapy and Experimental Psychiatry, 6,* 200-202.

Gouze, K.R. (1987). Attention and social problem solving as correlates of aggression in preschool males. *Journal of Abnormal Child Psychology, 15,* 181-197.

Graham, S., Hudley, C., and Williams, E. (1992). Attributional and emotional determinants of aggression among African-American and Latino young adolescents. *Developmental Psychology, 28,* 731-740.

Greenberg, J.R., and Mitchell, A. (1983). *Object relations in psychoanalytic theory*. Cambridge, Mass: Harvard University Press.

Guerra, N.G., and Slaby, R.G. (1989). Evaluative factors in social problem solving by aggressive boys. *Journal of Abnormal Child Psychology, 17*, 277-289.

Hart, C.H., Ladd, G.W., and Burleson, B.R. (1990). chilaren's expectations of the outcomes of social strategies: Relations with sociometric status and maternal disciplinary style. *Child Development, 61*, 127-137.

Higgins, E.T., King, G.A., and Marvin, G.H. (1982). Individual construct accessibility and subjective impressions and recall. *Journal of Personality and Social Psychology, 43*, 35-47.

Ingram, R.E., and Kendall, P.C. (1986). Cognitive clinical psychology: Implications of an informational processing perspective. In: R.E. Ingram (Ed.), *Information processing approaches to clinical psychology*. New York: Academic, pp. 3-21.

Jenkins, V.Y., and Fisher, D.A. (1989). Patterns of adolescent attachment and coping. Paper presented at the biennial meeting of the Society for Research in Child Development. Kansas City, Missouri: April 1989.

Joffe, R.D., Dobson, K.S., Fine, S., Marriage, K., and Haley, G. (1990). Social problem-solving in depressed, conduct-disordered, and normal adolescents. *Journal of Abnormal Child Psychology, 18*, 565-575.

Kazdin, A.E., Bass, D., Siegel, T., and Thomas, C. (1989). Cognitive-behavioral therapy and relationship therapy in the treatment of children referred for antisocial behavior. *Journal of Consulting and Clinical Psychology, 57*, 522-535.

Keane, S.P., and Parrish, A.E. (1992). The role of affective information in the determination of intent. *Developmental Psychology, 28*, 159-162.

Kelly, G.A., (1955). *The psychology of personal constructs*. New York: Norton.

Kendall, P.C. (1991). Guiding theory for therapy with children and adolescents. In: P.C. Kendall (Ed.) *Child and adolescent therapy: Cognitive-behavioral procedures* (pp. 3-22). New York: Guilford.

Kroger, J. (1989). Ego structuralization in late adolescence as seen through early memories and ego identity status. Paper presented at the biennial meeting of the Society for Research in Child Development. Kansas City, Missouri: April 1989.

Lieberman, A.F. (1977). preschoolers' competence with a peer: Relations with attachment and peer experience. *Child Development, 48*, 1277-1287.

Lochman, J.E. (1984). Psychological characteristics and assessment of aggressive adolescents. In: C.R. Keith (Ed.), *The aggressive adolescent: Clinical perspectives*. New York: Free Press, pp. 17-62.

Lochman, J.E. (1985). Effects of different treatment lengths in cognitive behavioral interventions with aggressive boys. *Child Psychiatry and Human Development, 16*, 45-56.

Lochman, J.E. (1987). Self and peer perceptions and attributional biases of aggressive and nonaggressive boys in dyadic interactions. *Journal of Consulting and Clinical Psychology, 55*, 404-414.

Lochman, J.E. (1990). Modification of childhood aggression. In: M. Hersen, R. Eisler, and P.M. Miller (Eds.), *Progress in behavior modification* (Vol 25). Newbury Park, CA: Sage.

Lochman, J.E. (1992). Cognitive-behavioral interventions with aggressive boys: Three year follow-up and preventive effects. *Journal of Consulting and Clinical Psychology, 60*, 426-432.

Lochman, J.E., Burch, P.R., Curry, J.F. and Lampron, L.B. (1984). Treatment and generalization effects of cognitive-behavioral and goal-setting interventions with aggressive boys, *Journal of Consulting and Clinical Psychology, 52*, 915-916.

Lochman, J.E. and the Conduct Problems Prevention Research Group (in alphabetical order: K. Bierman, J. Coie, K. Dodge, M. Greenberg, J. Lochman, R. McMahon), (in press). Screening of child behavior problems for prevention programs at school entry. *Journal of Consulting and Clinical Psychology*.

Lochman, J.E. and Craven, S.V. (March 1993). Family conflict associated with reactive and proactive aggression at two age levels. Paper presented at the biennial meeting of the Society for Research in Child Development, New Orleans.

Lochman, J.E., and Curry, J.F. (1986). Effects of social problem solving training and self-instruction training with aggressive boys. *Journal of Clinical Child Psychology, 15*, 159-164.

Lochman, J.E., and Dodge, K.A. (under review). Distorted perceptions in dyadic interactions of aggressive and non-aggressive boys: Effects of prior expectations and boys' age.

Lochman, J.E., and Dodge, K.A. (1994). Social cognitive processes of severely violent, moderately aggressive, and nonaggressive boys. *Journal of Consulting and Clinical Psychology, 62*, 366-374.

Lochman, J.E., Dunn, S.E., and Klimes-Dugan, B. (1993). An intervention and consultation model from a social cognitive perspective: A description of the Anger Coping Program. *School Psychology Review, 22*, 458-471.

Lochman, J.E., and Lampron, L.B. (1986). Situational social problem-solving skills and self-esteem of aggressive and nonaggressive boys. *Journal of Abnormal Child Psychology, 14*, 605-617.

Lochman, J.E., Lampron, L.B., Burch, P.R., and Curry, J.F. (1985). Client characteristics associated with behavior change for treated and untreated boys. *Journal of Abnormal Child Psychology, 13,* 527-538.

Lochman, J.E., Lampron, L.B., Gemmer, T.V., and Harris, R. (1987). Anger coping interventions for aggressive children: Guide to implementation in school settings. In: P.A. Keller and S.R. Heyman (Eds.), *Innovations in clinical practice: A source book* (Vol. 6, pp. 339-356). Sarasota, FL: Professional Resource Exchange.

Lochman, J.E., Lampron, L.B., Gemmer, T.V., Harris, R., and Wyckoff, G.M. (1989). Teacher consultation and cognitive behavioral interventions with aggressive boys. *Psychology in the Schools, 26,* 230-136.

Lochman, J.E., Lampron, L.B., and Rabiner, D.L. (1989). Format and salience effects in the social problem-solving of aggressive and nonaggressive boys. *Journal of Clinical Child Psychology, 18,* 230-236.

Lochman, J.E., and Lenhart, L.A. (1993). Anger coping intervention for aggressive children: Conceptual models and outcome effects. *Clinical Psychology Review, 13,* 785-805.

Lochman, J.E., Meyer, B.L., Rabiner, D.L., and White, K.J. (1991). Parameters influencing social problem solving of aggressive children. In: R. Prinz (Ed.), *Advances in behavioral assessment of children and families* (Vol. 5, pp. 31-63). Greenwich, CT: JAI Press.

Lochman, J.E., Nelson, W.M., and Sims, J.P. (1981). A cognitive behavioral program for use with aggressive children. *Journal of Clinical Child Psychology, 13,* 146-148.

Lochman, J.E. and Wayland, K.K. (1992). Aggression, social acceptance, and race as predictors of negative outcomes. *Journal of the American Academy of Child and Adolescent Psychiatry, 33,* 1026-1035.

Lochman, J.E., Wayland, K.K. and Sczepanski, R. (under review). The relationship between attributional bias and behavior of aggressive and nonaggressive boys in dyadic interaction. Manuscript under review, Duke University.

Lochman, J.E., Wayland, K.K., and White, K.J. (1993). Social goals: Relationship to adolescent adjustment and to social problem solving. *Journal of Abnormal Child Psychology, 21,* 135-151.

Lochman, J.E., White, K.J., and Wayland, K.K., (1991). Cognitive-behavioral assessment and treatment with aggressive children. In: P.C. Kendall (Ed.), *Child and Adolescent Therapy* (pp. 25-65).

Loeber, R. (1990). Development and risk factors of juvenile antisocial behavior and delinquency. Clinical Psychology Review, *10,* 1-41.

Mackinnon, C.E., Lamb, M.E., Belsky, J., and Baum, C. (1990). An affective-cognitive model of mother-child aggression. *Development and Psychopathology, 2,* 1-13.

Matas, L., Arend, R.A., and Sroufe, L.A. (1978). Continuity of adaptation in the second year: The relationship between quality of attachment and later competence. *Child Development, 49,* 547-556.

McMahon, R.J., and Wells, K.C. (1989). Conduct disorders. In: E.J. Mash and R.A. Barkley (Eds.), *Treatment of childhood disorders*. New York: Guilford Press, pp. 73-134.

Milich, R., and Dodge, K.A. (1984). Social information processing in child psychiatric populations. *Journal of Abnormal Child Psychology, 12,* 471-490.

Mischel, W. (1990). Personality disposition revisited and revised: A view after three decades. In: L. Pervin (Ed.)., *Handbook of Personality: Theory and research* (pp. 111-134). New York: Guilford.

Nasby, W., Hayden, B., and DePaulo, B.M. (1979). Attributional bias among aggressive boys to interpret ambiguous social stimuli as displays of hostility. *Journal of Abnormal Psychology, 89,* 459-468.

Novaco, R.W. (1978). Anger and coping with stress: Cognitive behavioral interventions. In: J.P. Foreyet and D.P. Rathjen (Eds.) *Cognitive behavioral therapy: Research and application*. New York: Plenum.

Ollendick, T.H., and Hersen, M. (1979). Social skills training for juvenile delinquents. *Behavior Research and Therapy, 17,* 547-554.

Olweus, D. (1979). Stability of aggressive behavior patterns in males: A review. *Psychological Bulletin, 86,* 852-875.

Patterson, G.R. (1986). Performance models for antisocial boys. *American Psychologist, 41,* 432-444.

Perry, D.G., Perry, L.C., and Kennedy, E. (1992). Conflict and the development of antisocial behavior. In: C.U. Shantz, and W.W. Hartup (Eds.), *Conflict in child and adolescent development* (pp. 301-329). Cambridge: Cambridge University Press.

Perry, D.G., Perry, L.C., and Rasmussen, P. (1986). Cognitive social learning mediators of aggression. *Child Development, 57,* 700-711.

Perry, D.G., Perry, L.C., and Weiss, R.J. (1989). Sex differences in the consequences that children anticipate for aggression. *Developmental Psychology, 25,* 312-319.

Putallaz, M., and Sheppard, B.H. (1992). Conflict management and social competence. In: C.U. Shantz and W.W. Hartup (Eds.), *Conflict in child and adolescent development* (pp. 330-355). Cambridge: Cambridge University Press.

Rabiner, D.L., Lenhart, L., and Lochman, J.E. (1990). Automatic vs. reflective problem solving in relation to children's sociometric status. *Developmental Psychology, 71,* 535-543.

Reinhold, D.P. (1990). Attributions and affect in the parent-child context of childhood aggression. Unpublished doctoral dissertation, Duke University.

Richard, B.A., and Dodge, K.A. (1982). Social maladjustment and problem-solving in school-aged children. *Journal of Consulting and Clinical Psychology, 50,* 226-233.

Rotter, J.B., Chance, J.E., and Phares, E.J. (1972). *Applications of a social learning theory of personality.* New York: Holt, Rinehart, and Winston.

Rubin, K.H., Bream, L.A., and Rose-Krasnor, L. (1991). Social problem solving and aggression in childhood. In: D.J. Pepler and K.H. Rubin (Eds.), *The development and treatment of childhood aggression* (pp. 219-248). Hillsdale, NJ: Erlbaum.

Sancilio, M., Plumert, J.M., and Hartup, W.W. (1989). Friendship and aggressiveness as determinants of conflict outcomes in middle childhood. *Developmental Psychology, 25,* 812-819.

Slaby, R.G., and Guerra, N.G. (1988). Cognitive mediators of aggression in adolescent offenders: 1. Assessment. *Developmental Psychology, 24,* 580-588.

Smith, C.A. and Lazarus, R.W. (1990). Emotion and adaptation. In: L. Previn (Ed.), Handbook of personality: *Theory and research* (pp. 609-637). New York: Guilford.

Steinberg, M.D., and Dodge, K.A. (1983). Attributional bias in aggressive adolescent boys and girls. *Journal of Social and Clinical Psychology, 1,* 312-321.

Sczcepanski, R. (1994). The association between marital disturbance, problematic parenting practices, and child aggression: The role of emotion-linked personality traits. Unpublished major area paper. Duke University.

Vitaro, F., and Tremblay, R.E. (1994). Impact of a prevention program on aggressive children's friendships and social adjustment. *Journal of Abnormal Child Psychology, 22,* 457-475.

Waas, G.A. (1988). Social attributional biases of peer-rejected and aggressive children. *Child Development, 59,* 969-975.

Waas, G.A., and French, D.C. (1989). Children's social problem solving: Comparison of the open middle interview and children's assertive behavior scale. *Behavioral Assessment, 11,* 219-230.

Weiner, B. (1990). Attribution in personality psychology. In: L. Pervin, (Eds.). *Handbook of personality: Theory and research* (pp. 609-637). New York: Guilford.

Westen, D. (1991). Social cognition and object relations. *Psychological Bulletin,* 109, 429-455.

Westen, D., Klepser, J., Ruffins, S., Silverman, M., Lifton, N., and Boekamp, J. (1991). Object relations childhood and adolescence: The development of working representations. *Journal of Consulting and Clinical Psychology, 59,* 400-409.

Wyer, R.S., Jr., Lambert, J.A., Budesheim, T.L. and Greenfield, D.H. (in press). Theory and research on person impression information: A look to the future. In: L. Martin and A. Tesser (Eds.), *The construction of social judgement.* Hillsdale, N.J.: Erlbaum.

12

MOTIVATION AS A PRECONDITION AND BRIDGE BETWEEN UNMOTIVATED CLIENT AND OVERMOTIVATED THERAPIST

Henck P. J. G. van Bilsen

Pedologisch Instituut
PO Box 8639
3009 AP Rotterdam
The Netherlands

INTRODUCTION

Providing therapy for children, young people and parents is a complex matter, made even more complex when the child, young person or parent feels unmotivated towards receiving help.

Therapies and treatments often assume motivation and a willingness to change by clients, irrespective of the type of therapy provided - be it within out-patient or residential care or within the education system. However, therapists are often confronted with clients who are less motivated than they feel they should be if they are going to make full use of the help provided.

Motivation and Assumptions of the Therapist

A person is regarded as unmotivated when he/she disagrees with the therapist's views, does not admit to having any problems and does not follow the recommended line of treatment. A widespread response to this among therapists is that they should then suffer the consequences. In other words, if clients will not take advice, they are sometimes left to their lot until they come to their senses. Here demotivation is seen as a characteristic of the individual, as a subconscious resolving of inner conflicts, or as one step in a series that influence the client system. This assumption leads to a passive attitude among therapists (Van Bilsen, 1985).

Another assumption relates to overestimating therapy and treatment: that change is always the better choice; that change with the help of a therapist is the best choice and following a therapist's advice to the letter is the best choice of all. Studies have shown, however, that most psychosocial problems can be resolved by people themselves, ie without professional help (Schippers, Van Ernst and Van Bilsen, 1989; Schippers, 1980). If people

Behavioral Approaches for Children and Adolescents, Edited by
H. P. J. G. van Bilsen et al., Plenum Press, New York, 1995

want help than apparently they prefer informal to professional help (Knibbe and Garretsen, 1985).

Motivation is regarded as an all-or-nothing phenomenon. This means it is considered futile to work with clients who have not yet reached this point (Bartels, 1988). Motivation techniques in therapy are often based on this underlying assumption. Traditional ones include:

- convincing by reasoning and/or exercising power;
- allowing clients "to stew in their own juice" until they realise the awfulness of the situation;
- moralistically confronting the client with "evidence" of the need to change.

In recent studies on motivation other lines of thinking have come to the fore.

Stages of Change

In their book *The Transtheoretical Approach: crossing traditional boundaries of therapy*, Prochaska and DiClemente (1984) present a practical approach towards changing processes. They discovered that among many types of problems related to stress, family or addiction there is a set pattern in a client developing a willingness to change. They describe this as occurring according to a "revolving door" model comprising six stages: precontemplation, contemplation, decision-taking, change, consolidation and relapse (see fig 1).

The term "revolving door" refers to the fact that going through these six stages is no "one-off" occurrence. Clients may go through these stages several times before permanent change is effected.

In the first *precontemplation* stage, the individual experiences no problems, while on the other hand other people indicate that something is wrong. If the person does indicate that something is bothering him/her, than it is usually the others that need to change. Barriers to developing an awareness of having problems at this stage include:

- a low self-esteem. When a person already has a not all too good impression of themselves, self-esteem can quickly drop below a critical threshold if problems must also be recognised;
- insufficient acknowledgement of the problems. Personally recognising the problem is essential, not in the sense of having a fundamental insight but acknow-

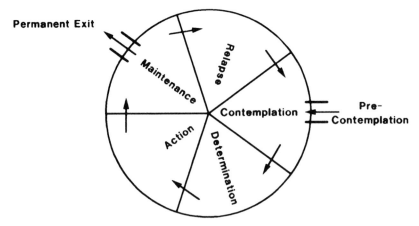

Figure 1. Stages of change (according to Prochaska and DiClemente, 1984).

ledging the fact that certain behaviour - or absence of it - creates problems. If parents are to be motivated to allow their daughter to take part in social skills training they first need to know it is unacceptable for a child not to have friends;

- insufficient concern for the problem. Knowledge on its own is not enough. Parents may well know that being without friends has certain negative consequences; showing concern for this is the next step. This concern is essential in creating motivation for change and for receiving help. After all, without experiencing suffering there is no motivation.

In the *contemplation* stage the idea begins to dawn that there might be a problem that makes change necessary. However, fear both of losing the pleasurable aspects of the present situation and being incapable of making the necessary changes can create barriers for actually tackling change (Bandura, 1977 and 1982).

If the situation now exists whereby the person is sufficiently aware of the problems and shows enough concern, as well as having the right amount of self-regard and confidence in their own ability to change, than a *decision* to change can be taken (Janis and Mann, 1977; Kanfer and Grimm, 1978). Prochaska and DiClemente (1984) see a decision to change behaviour as only possibly when the client has sufficient:

- awareness of any problems;
- concern about these problems;
- self-esteem to make the effort;
- confidence in their ability to make their effort produce results.

After the decision to change has been taken, the person concerned makes an *active effort* to tackle the causes and maintaining factors of the problem behaviour. This decision to change need not imply that the client wants to bring about change with a therapist. It is possible that the individual decides to use their own strength to tackle the changes deemed necessary. It is also possible a person decides not to change. Sometimes the outlook is so bleak that the client no longer believes in his/her possibilities or own self-worth and decides to make no attempt to change.

In the *consolidation* stage the individual attempts to sustain the goals achieved. Whether the changes have been reached with or without therapy, it is necessary to consolidate the new situation. Specific methods are needed to sustain change. Beginning a process of change is sometimes straightforward, but showing perseverance during the process - especially at difficult moments - is often trying.

If a person fails to sustain the changes brought about and the problem behaviour returns, than there has been a *relapse*. The revolving door than opens again by the first preview stage. This stage will be passed through quickly again or more slowly, depending on the reaction of the person and of the environment towards a regression.

In order to influence the motivation process, techniques have been developed based on this revolving model of change. Motivation is not seen as trying to convince a client, but largely to guide the process of wise decision making. This means a client taking decisions after all problem-related factors have been examined. Motivation is thus more of a facilitating process - the therapist helps the client to look at all the facts.

Studies have shown that motivation is not something only the client determines. Moreover, motivation is not an all or nothing phenomenon, but a process that passes through various stages.

Problem awareness, concern, self-regard and competence are factors which are determined by a person's interaction with the environment. During the process of diagnosing and providing help, the therapist is an extremely important link. The willingness of a client to talk about problems and discuss possible ways of changing behaviour is dependent on the therapist's approach: there are ways of increasing the willingness to change and ways of reducing it (Kanfer and Grimm, 1978; Endler, 1981; Endler and Magnusson, 1976).

Essential Starting Points for the Therapist

- Complete and unconditional acceptance.

It is important to give a client the feeling that he/she is accepted as a person, with all the strengths and weaknesses that that implies. According to Carl Rogers (1975) we can assume that people are not motivated to change those aspects of behaviour which the therapist does not accept. This means that the therapist should reserve his/her own moral judgement on what is "right" or "wrong."

- Objectives.

It is the therapist's task to create a situation with the client that is best described as cognitive dissonance. On the one hand the client needs to be sufficiently satisfied with his/her behaviour while on the other being aware that certain aspects of it are unacceptable. At the same time he/she needs to show concerned about this. This can lead to changes in behaviour if the client sees himself/herself as being sufficiently competent to bring this about (Garfield, 1978).

- Self-motivation.

It is essential to activate self-motivation in the client. Studies have shown that the more people feel they have taken decisions for themselves, the more they will stand by them (Miller, 1983).

Techniques

Within the structure of the aforementioned starting points there are a number of techniques aimed at increasing the willingness to change:

- Maintaining contact.

An important means of promoting the willingness to change is to keep in touch with clients (obviously according to the basic principles just described). Studies have shown that simply remaining in contact with clients has a motivating effect. As part of the social skills training program of the Pedological Institute Rotterdam (Van Bilsen, Jonkers, Schuurman and Swager, 1991) contact is maintained with parents who reject help through telephone calls, letters and detailed reports on their child's progress within the social skills group.

- Freedom of choice.

There is the archetypical image of the traditional therapist taking his/her diagnostic thermometer and reading the results. After these have been noted and discussed in a multidisciplinary team, the therapist concludes that a specific treatment is called for and announces this to the client. Literature on decision-taking procedures and effectiveness studies of treatment show, however, that this approach has a demotivating effect (Prochaska and DiClemente, 1984). On the other hand, drawing one's own conclusions based on objective information and being able to choose from possible alternative treatments has a powerful motivating effect.

To illustrate this point there is the case study of Peter. Based on his diagnostic data, a functional analysis was made of Peter's problems. From this it emerged that his angry outbursts were related to dysfunctional family patterns. This resulted in Peter lacking social skills and being unable to deal with negative emotions. In keeping with the motivational interviewing technique model the following holistic assessment was presented to his parents in a non-threatening and non-accusing manner. "Peter has angry outbursts some 12 times a week. As a family this must make you very sad. You would wish to find a way no doubt of preventing these terrible scenes." If parents indicate they would like to change the situation, possible effective interventions are then mentioned and information given on them. Parents are then invited to make a choice: family therapy, social skills training or play therapy.

- Information.

It is also the therapist's task to give an overview of the client's situation and provide objective information on the seriousness of the problems. This information is necessary so that the client is aware of the possibilities and can express any concern. At the same time the therapist should supply information on different treatment methods. In this way the client can make a choice based on objective information and own individual preference.

Interview Techniques

The aforementioned gives a broad overview of the therapist's role. Keeping in touch, negotiating goals, providing information etc require several specific interview techniques:

- Selective active listening.

Actively listening means paying attention to what is being said by summing this up to the client, reflecting, posing open and clear questions and giving non-verbal signals. The selective element occurs by not always giving the same degree of attention to everything the client says. Motivation signals (= self-motivation statements = signals from the earlier-mentioned objectives: self-regard, competence, concern and knowledge) are rewarded more than unmotivated ones. The more often self-motivated statements are rewarded, the more frequently they are used. The more frequently they are expressed, the more a client will begin to believe in them.

- Structure

The therapist brings some form of structure to the client's story by helping him/her to present it in concrete and specific terms. This results in presenting the client with an overview of the history of his/her problems.

- Restructuring

Restructuring or positive labelling is a technique whereby something positive is made from something negative. For instance, if Karen's mother thinks that being over-protective towards her daughter is a bad thing, then the therapist's view that she is being well aware of the dangers a young person has to be wary of in today's society, can give her a more positive view of her child-rearing skills.

- Provocation

With provocation or paradoxical intention, the therapist takes on an unmotivated stance in an attempt to seduce the client into taking up a motivated position.

Stages of the Motivation Process in Daily Practice

The client has to take a number of steps towards change. In order to achieve this, the therapist must complete a number of tasks - his/her action run through all the stages of motivation.

The therapist's role in the first *eliciting* phase is to elicit self-motivated statements. The therapist attempts to get the client at least to the point where he/she is motivated enough to make a new appointment. The more the therapy has a compulsory aspect to it, however, the longer this phase will last. This phase ends with the client's acquiesence that the therapist may go deeper into the problems. In this phase the interview technique of actively listening, clarifying and restructuring are mainly applied. Contact can be maintained with clients who decide not to have any more therapy by informative letters or from talks so that the therapist can learn from those who do not make use of therapy.

In the second, *information* phase the diagnostic interventions are carried out. However as a starting point it is essential to convey to the client that it is not his or her shortcomings that are being traced, but rather the untapped use of one's full potential. In order to emphasise a client's responsibility and range of choices available, the traditional "doctor's prescription" approach should be dropped. Instead, the therapist provides no cut and dried conclusions. At the end of this phase, the therapist presents the client with an overview of the - as yet - untapped possibilities. In a neutral, non-judgemental manner the therapist reviews all the aspects related to the client's problem. It is then the latter's role to draw any conclusions about this. At the same time all the basic principles of therapy are used alongside the earlier-mentioned interview techniques: ie provocation, freedom of choice, information, feedback and clarification. Sometimes it's useful to set down the information in a report and let the client read this. This phase ends with the client deciding whether or not to change.

In the third, *negotiating* phase, client and therapist discuss the goals of change and the way these can best be implemented. The therapist uses a negotiation model rather than a prescribed model in which possible options are presented and the client decides which are best suited to his/her needs.

Concluding Remark

'Motivation as a precondition' was the title of this petition and this viewpoint is only partly endorsed here. Motivation to change is a precondition for change but it is no precondition for starting therapy. In fact in those situations where clients are still not prepared to change, it is important to come into contact with therapy to activate motivation. The model described here can be useful in this.

REFERENCES

Bandura. A. (1977). Self-efficacy: Toward a unifying theory of behavior change. *Psychological Review. 84,* 191-215.

Bandura. A. (1982). Self-efficacy mechanism in human agency. *Psychologist, 37,* 122-147.

Bartels. A. (1988). Sociale vaardigheidstherapie voor jeugdige delinquenten en jongeren met ernstige gedragsproblemen. In: J.W.G. Orlemans, *Handboek gedragstherapie* - aflevering 20. Deventer: Van Loghum Slaterus.

Bilsen, H.P.J.G. van (1985). Valkuilen voor de therapeut. *Tijdschrift voor Psychotherapie, 11,* 192-195.

Bilsen, H.P.J.G. van (1988). *Even bijpraten met het Pedologisch Instituut.* Rotterdam: Pedologisch Instituut. Interne notitie. (Paedological Institute. Internal memorandum.

Bilsen, H.P.J.G. van, Jonkers, J., Schuurman, C.M.A. en Swager, H.D., (1991). Geïntegreerde behandeling van sociale vaardigheidstekorten bij kinderen uit het speciaal onderwijs. *Kind en Adolescent, 12,* 78-86.

Dollard, J. and Miller, N. (1950). *Personal and psychotherapy.* New York: McGraw-Hill.

Endler, N.S. (1981). Situational aspects of interactional psychology. In: D. Magnusson (Ed.), *Toward a psychology of situations: An interactional perspective.* Hillsdale: N.J. Erlbaum.

Endler, N., and Magnusson, D. (Eds.) (1976). *Interactional psychology and personality.* New York: John Wiley and Sons.

Garfield, S. (1978). Research on client variables in psychotherapy. In: S. Garfield and A. Bergin (Eds.). *Handbook of psychotherapy and behavior change*. New York: John Wiley and Sons.

Janis, I.L. and Mann, L. (1977). *Decision making. A psychological analysis of conflict, choice and commitment*. New York: Free Press.

Kanfer, F., and Grimm, L. (1978). Freedom of choice and behavioral change. *Journal of Consulting and Clinical Psychology, 45*, 873-878.

Knibbe, R.A. and Garretsen, H.F.L. (1985). Kennis van en opvattingen over hulpverlening aan probleemdrinkers. *Tijdschrift voor alcohol, drugs en andere psychotrope stoffen, 2*, 55-60.

Miller, W. (1983). Motivational interviewing with problem drinkers. *Behavioral Psychotherapy, 11*, 147-172.

Prochaska, J.O. and DiClemente, C.C. (1984). *The Transtheoretical Approach: Crossing Traditional Boundaries of Therapy*. Homewood, Illinois: Dow-Jones-Irwin.

Prochaska, J.O. (1979). *Systems of psychotherapy: A transtheoretical analysis*. Homewood, Illinois: Dorsey Press.

Rogers, C. (1975). The necessary and sufficient conditions of therapeutic personality change. *Journal of Consulting Psychology, 21*, 95-113.

Schippers, G.M., van Emst, A.J. and van Bilsen, H.P.J.G. (1989). Motiveringstechnieken. *Tijdschrift voor Directieve therapie, 8*, 135-148.

Schippers, G.M., (1980). Het "Rand Report:" Alcoholhulpverlening gespiegels. *Tijdschrift voor alcohol, drugs en andere psychotrope stoffen, 6*, 85-93.

INDEX

(ABA) 59
Academic performance 49
Acute conditions 25
A family system approach 71
Aggression 9
Aggresive children 165
Alcohol Related Birth Defects 35
Alleviation of tasks 89
Anger Arousal Model 166
Anger Coping Program 177
Antisocial youth 85
Anxiety disorders 11
Applied Behavioural Analysis 59
Attention-deficit Hyperactivity Disorder (ADHD) 4
Automatic Thoughts 149

Behaviour analysis 23
Behaviour modification 49
Behavioural Experiments 150
Behavioural problems 61
Brain Injury 28

Changing Dysfunctional Schemata 150
Children at-risk 25
Chronic Pain 8
Classroom 49
Classroom management 61
Coaches 91
Coaching 91
Cognitive content 5
Cognitive deficiency 6
Cognitive distortion 6
Cognitive process 5
Cognitive products 5
Cognitive structure 5
Community Based Service Provision 35
Competence 86
Competency-based treatment 85
Connectionist theory 1
Consultant 3
Consumer Empowerment 35
Contemplation 192
Contingencies 8

Contingent 61
Coping 4
Coping model 7
Coping Power Program 179
Coping skills 2
Coping template 4
Corrective feedback 49
Curriculum intervention 111
Cystic fibrosis 25

Depression 9, 131
Depressive Cognitive Style 135
Developmental 3
Developmental disorders 25
Diagnostician 3
Didactic 3
Disadvantaged pupils 50

Educator 4
Elimination disorders 25
Etiology 3

Family 13, 153
Faulty Information Processing 149
Feedback 61
Feeding disorders 25
Fellow pupils as fellow teachers 61
Fetal Alcohol Syndrome 35
Fetal Exposure 34
Flooding 1
Functional analysis 87

General cognitive behavioral strategies 7
Group therapy 112

Health-risk behaviours 25
HIV infection/AIDS 25
Hybrid 1

Implementation 52
Information-processing 1, 2
In-vivo exposure 7
Instruction 89

Instruction and attainment 60
Intermittent 61
Introduction of new tasks 89

Juvenile delinquency 85

Learned Helplessness/Hopelessness Model 134
Learning language and social skills 60
Learning problems 99
Liaison psychiatry 25
LOM pupils 100
LOM school 100

Mastery learning 49
Mastery model 7
Mediational 1
Medications 10
Modelling 89
Motivation 103, 119

Negative responses 25
Negative Self-Evaluations 151

Pain-related disorders 25
Parental guidance 113
Parents 71
Pediatrics 24
Physical disabilities 25
Pin-pointing 61
Positive feedback 88
Posture 3
Practising 89
Pre-school children 60
Precontemplation 192
Problem Solving Set 146
Programmed instruction 49
Protective factors 90
Psychosomatic medicine 25

Reform 52
Reforms 51

Reinforcement 49, 61
Reinforcements 8
Relapse 192
Relaxation training 8
Response cost 61
Response systems 100
Revolving door 192
Rheumatic disease 25
Role playing 7

Schemas 170
School 13
Self-instruction 61
Shaping 61
Sickle cell disease 25
Skill-building approach 2
Skill training 88
Sleep disorders 25
Social Cognitive Models 166
Social Information Processing Model 167
Social learning 2
Social milieu 13
Social skills 109
Social/interpersonal world 2
Stages of change 192
STOP THINK DO 118
Stress reduction 89
Systematic desensitization 1

Teacher guidance 114
Teacher training 61
Teaching Family Model 85
Teaching-approach 85
Technology of change 68
Think Aloud program 75
Time-on-task 61
Token 61
Traumatic brain injury (TBI) 28

ZMOK pupils 100
ZMOK school 100